DERIVATIVES WORKBOOK

CFA Institute is the premier association for investment professionals around the world, with over 170,000 members in more than 160 countries. Since 1963 the organization has developed and administered the renowned Chartered Financial Analyst® Program. With a rich history of leading the investment profession, CFA Institute has set the highest standards in ethics, education, and professional excellence within the global investment community, and is the foremost authority on investment profession conduct and practice. Each book in the CFA Institute Investment Series is geared toward industry practitioners along with graduate-level finance students and covers the most important topics in the industry. The authors of these cutting-edge books are themselves industry professionals and academics and bring their wealth of knowledge and expertise to this series.

DERIVATIVES WORKBOOK

WILEY

Published by John Wiley & Sons, Inc., Hoboken, New Jersey.
Published simultaneously in Canada.

For general information on our other products and services or for technical support, please contact our Customer Care Department within the United States at (800) 762-2974, outside the United States at (317) 572-3993 or fax (317) 572-4002.

Wiley publishes in a variety of print and electronic formats and by print-on-demand. Some material included with standard print versions of this book may not be included in e-books or in print-on-demand. If this book refers to media such as a CD or DVD that is not included in the version you purchased, you may download this material at http://booksupport.wiley.com. For more information about Wiley products, visit www.wiley.com.

ISBN 9781119853275 (Paperback)
ISBN 9781119853282 (ePDF)
ISBN 9781119853299 (ePub)

Printed in the United States of America

SKY10097911_020525

CONTENTS

DERIVATIVES WORKBOOK

PART I

LEARNING OBJECTIVES, SUMMARY OVERVIEW, AND PROBLEMS

CHAPTER 1

DERIVATIVE MARKETS AND INSTRUMENTS

LEARNING OUTCOMES

The candidate should be able to:

- define a derivative and distinguish between exchange-traded and over-the-counter derivatives;
- contrast forward commitments with contingent claims;
- define forward contracts, futures contracts, options (calls and puts), swaps, and credit derivatives and compare their basic characteristics;
- determine the value at expiration and profit from a long or a short position in a call or put option;
- describe purposes of, and controversies related to, derivative markets;
- explain arbitrage and the role it plays in determining prices and promoting market efficiency.

SUMMARY OVERVIEW

This first reading on derivatives introduces you to the basic characteristics of derivatives, including the following points:

- A derivative is a financial instrument that derives its performance from the performance of an underlying asset.
- The underlying asset, called the underlying, trades in the cash or spot markets and its price is called the cash or spot price.
- Derivatives consist of two general classes: forward commitments and contingent claims.
- Derivatives can be created as standardized instruments on derivatives exchanges or as customized instruments in the over-the-counter market.
- Exchange-traded derivatives are standardized, highly regulated, and transparent transactions that are guaranteed against default through the clearinghouse of the derivatives exchange.

- Over-the-counter derivatives are customized, flexible, and more private and less regulated than exchange-traded derivatives, but are subject to a greater risk of default.
- A forward contract is an over-the-counter derivative contract in which two parties agree that one party, the buyer, will purchase an underlying asset from the other party, the seller, at a later date and at a fixed price they agree upon when the contract is signed.
- A futures contract is similar to a forward contract but is a standardized derivative contract created and traded on a futures exchange. In the contract, two parties agree that one party, the buyer, will purchase an underlying asset from the other party, the seller, at a later date and at a price agreed on by the two parties when the contract is initiated. In addition, there is a daily settling of gains and losses and a credit guarantee by the futures exchange through its clearinghouse.
- A swap is an over-the-counter derivative contract in which two parties agree to exchange a series of cash flows whereby one party pays a variable series that will be determined by an underlying asset or rate and the other party pays either a variable series determined by a different underlying asset or rate or a fixed series.
- An option is a derivative contract in which one party, the buyer, pays a sum of money to the other party, the seller or writer, and receives the right to either buy or sell an underlying asset at a fixed price either on a specific expiration date or at any time prior to the expiration date.
- A call is an option that provides the right to buy the underlying.
- A put is an option that provides the right to sell the underlying.
- Credit derivatives are a class of derivative contracts between two parties, the credit protection buyer and the credit protection seller, in which the latter provides protection to the former against a specific credit loss.
- A credit default swap is the most widely used credit derivative. It is a derivative contract between two parties, a credit protection buyer and a credit protection seller, in which the buyer makes a series of payments to the seller and receives a promise of compensation for credit losses resulting from the default of a third party.
- An asset-backed security is a derivative contract in which a portfolio of debt instruments is assembled and claims are issued on the portfolio in the form of tranches, which have different priorities of claims on the payments made by the debt securities such that prepayments or credit losses are allocated to the most-junior tranches first and the most-senior tranches last.
- Derivatives can be combined with other derivatives or underlying assets to form hybrids.
- Derivatives are issued on equities, fixed-income securities, interest rates, currencies, commodities, credit, and a variety of such diverse underlyings as weather, electricity, and disaster claims.
- Derivatives facilitate the transfer of risk, enable the creation of strategies and payoffs not otherwise possible with spot assets, provide information about the spot market, offer lower transaction costs, reduce the amount of capital required, are easier than the underlyings to go short, and improve the efficiency of spot markets.
- Derivatives are sometimes criticized for being a form of legalized gambling and for leading to destabilizing speculation, although these points can generally be refuted.
- Derivatives are typically priced by forming a hedge involving the underlying asset and a derivative such that the combination must pay the risk-free rate and do so for only one derivative price.
- Derivatives pricing relies heavily on the principle of storage, meaning the ability to hold or store the underlying asset. Storage can incur costs but can also generate cash, such as dividends and interest.

- Arbitrage is the condition that two equivalent assets or derivatives or combinations of assets and derivatives sell for different prices, leading to an opportunity to buy at the low price and sell at the high price, thereby earning a risk-free profit without committing any capital.
- The combined actions of arbitrageurs bring about a convergence of prices. Hence, arbitrage leads to the law of one price: Transactions that produce equivalent results must sell for equivalent prices.

PROBLEMS

1. A derivative is *best* described as a financial instrument that derives its performance by:
   A. passing through the returns of the underlying.
   B. replicating the performance of the underlying.
   C. transforming the performance of the underlying.
2. Derivatives are similar to insurance in that both:
   A. have an indefinite life span.
   B. allow for the transfer of risk from one party to another.
   C. allow for the transformation of the underlying risk itself.
3. A beneficial opportunity created by the derivatives market is the ability to:
   A. adjust risk exposures to desired levels.
   B. generate returns proportional to movements in the underlying.
   C. simultaneously take long positions in multiple highly liquid fixed-income securities.
4. Compared with exchange-traded derivatives, over-the-counter derivatives would *most likely* be described as:
   A. standardized.
   B. less transparent.
   C. more transparent.
5. Exchange-traded derivatives are:
   A. largely unregulated.
   B. traded through an informal network.
   C. guaranteed by a clearinghouse against default.
6. The clearing and settlement process of an exchange-traded derivatives market:
   A. provides a credit guarantee.
   B. provides transparency and flexibility.
   C. takes longer than that of most securities exchanges.
7. Which of the following statements *best* portrays the full implementation of post-financial-crisis regulations in the OTC derivatives market?
   A. Transactions are no longer private.
   B. Most transactions need to be reported to regulators.
   C. All transactions must be cleared through central clearing agencies.
8. A characteristic of forward commitments is that they:
   A. provide linear payoffs.
   B. do not depend on the outcome or payoff of an underlying asset.
   C. provide one party the right to engage in future transactions on terms agreed on in advance.

9. In contrast to contingent claims, forward contracts:
   A. have their prices chosen by the participants.
   B. could end in default by either party.
   C. can be exercised by physical or cash delivery.
10. Which of the following statements *best* describes the payoff from a forward contract?
    A. The buyer has more to gain going long than the seller has to lose going short.
    B. The buyer profits if the price of the underlying at expiration exceeds the forward price.
    C. The gains from owning the underlying versus owning the forward contract are equivalent.
11. Which of the following statements regarding the settlement of forward contracts is correct?
    A. Contract settlement by cash has different economic effects from those of a settlement by delivery.
    B. Non-deliverable forwards and contracts for differences have distinct settlement procedures.
    C. At cash settlement, when the long party acquires the asset in the market, it effectively pays the forward price.
12. A futures contract is *best* described as a contract that is:
    A. standardized.
    B. subject to credit risk.
    C. marked to market throughout the trading day.
13. Which of the following statements explains a characteristic of futures price limits? Price limits:
    A. help the clearinghouse manage its credit exposure.
    B. can typically be expanded intra-day by willing traders.
    C. establish a band around the final trade of the previous day.
14. Which of the following statements describes an aspect of margin accounts for futures?
    A. The maintenance margin is always less than the initial margin.
    B. The initial margin required is typically at least 10% of the futures price.
    C. A margin call requires a deposit sufficient to raise the account balance to the maintenance margin.
15. Which of the following factors is shared by forwards and futures contracts?
    A. Timing of profits
    B. Flexible settlement arrangements
    C. Nearly equivalent profits by expiration
16. Which of the following derivatives is classified as a contingent claim?
    A. Futures contracts
    B. Interest rate swaps
    C. Credit default swaps
17. In contrast to contingent claims, forward commitments provide the:
    A. right to buy or sell the underlying asset in the future.
    B. obligation to buy or sell the underlying asset in the future.
    C. promise to provide credit protection in the event of default.
18. Which of the following derivatives provide payoffs that are non-linearly related to the payoffs of the underlying?
    A. Options
    B. Forwards
    C. Interest-rate swaps

19. An interest rate swap is a derivative contract in which:
    A. two parties agree to exchange a series of cash flows.
    B. the credit seller provides protection to the credit buyer.
    C. the buyer has the right to purchase the underlying from the seller.
20. Forward commitments subject to default are:
    A. forwards and futures.
    B. futures and interest rate swaps.
    C. interest rate swaps and forwards.
21. A swap is:
    A. more like a forward than a futures contract.
    B. subject to simultaneous default by both parties.
    C. based on an exchange of two series of fixed cash flows.
22. A plain vanilla interest rate swap is also known as:
    A. a basis swap.
    B. a fixed-for-floating swap.
    C. an overnight indexed swap.
23. The notional principal of a swap is:
    A. not exchanged in the case of an interest rate swap.
    B. a fixed amount whenever it is matched with a loan.
    C. equal to the amount owed by one swap party to the other.
24. Which of the following derivatives is *least likely* to have a value of zero at initiation of the contract?
    A. Futures
    B. Options
    C. Forwards
25. The buyer of an option has a contingent claim in the sense that the option creates:
    A. a right.
    B. an obligation.
    C. a linear payoff with respect to gains and losses of the underlying.
26. Which of the following options grants the holder the right to purchase the underlying prior to expiration?
    A. American-style put option
    B. European-style call option
    C. American-style call option
27. A credit derivative is a derivative contract in which the:
    A. clearinghouse provides a credit guarantee to both the buyer and the seller.
    B. seller provides protection to the buyer against the credit risk of a third party.
    C. the buyer and seller provide a performance bond at initiation of the contract.
28. The junior and senior tranches of an asset-backed security:
    A. have equivalent expected returns.
    B. have claims on separate underlying portfolios.
    C. may be differentially impacted by prepayments or credit losses.
29. In a declining interest rate environment, compared with a CMO's Class A tranche, its Class C tranche will be repaid:
    A. earlier.
    B. at the same pace.
    C. later.

30. For a given CDO, which of the following tranches is *most likely* to have the highest expected return?
    A. Equity
    B. Senior
    C. Mezzanine
31. Which of the following derivatives allows an investor to pay the return on a stock index and receive a fixed rate?
    A. Equity swap
    B. Stock warrant
    C. Index futures contract
32. Which of the following is *most likely* the underlying of a plain vanilla interest rate swap?
    A. 180-day Libor
    B. 10-year US Treasury bond
    C. Bloomberg Barclay's US Aggregate Bond Index
33. Currency swaps are:
    A. rarely used.
    B. commonly used to manage interest rate risk.
    C. executed by two parties making a series of interest rate payments in the same currency.
34. Which of the following statements regarding commodity derivatives is correct?
    A. The primary commodity derivatives are futures.
    B. Commodities are subject to a set of well-defined risk factors.
    C. Commodity traders and financial traders today are distinct groups within the financial world.
35. Compared with the underlying spot market, derivative markets are *more likely* to have:
    A. greater liquidity.
    B. higher transaction costs.
    C. higher capital requirements.
36. Which of the following characteristics is *least likely* to be a benefit associated with using derivatives?
    A. More effective management of risk
    B. Payoffs similar to those associated with the underlying
    C. Greater opportunities to go short compared with the spot market
37. Which of the following statements *best* represents information discovery in the futures market?
    A. The futures price is predictive.
    B. Information flows more slowly into the futures market than into the spot market.
    C. The futures market reveals the price that the holder of the asset can take to avoid uncertainty.
38. The derivative markets tend to:
    A. transfer liquidity from the broader financial markets.
    B. not reflect fundamental value after it is restored in the underlying market.
    C. offer a less costly way to exploit mispricing in comparison to other free and competitive financial markets.
39. Which of the following statements *most likely* contributes to the view that derivatives have some role in causing financial crashes?
    A. Derivatives are the primary means by which leverage and related excessive risk is brought into financial markets.
    B. Growth in the number of investors willing to speculate in derivatives markets leads to excessive speculative trading.

    C. Restrictions on derivatives, such as enhanced collateral requirements and credit mitigation measures, in the years leading up to crashes introduce market rigidity.

40. In contrast to gambling, derivatives speculation:
    A. has a positive public image.
    B. is a form of financial risk taking.
    C. benefits the financial markets and thus society.

41. Derivatives may contribute to financial contagion because of the:
    A. centrally cleared nature of OTC derivatives.
    B. associated significant costs and high capital requirements.
    C. reliance by derivatives speculators on large amounts of leverage.

42. The complex nature of derivatives has led to:
    A. reliable financial models of derivatives markets.
    B. widespread trust in applying scientific principles to derivatives.
    C. financial industry employment of mathematicians and physicists.

43. Which of the following is *most likely* to be a destabilizing consequence of speculation using derivatives?
    A. Increased defaults by speculators and creditors
    B. Market price swings resulting from arbitrage activities
    C. The creation of trading strategies that result in asymmetric performance

44. The law of one price is *best* described as:
    A. the true fundamental value of an asset.
    B. earning a risk-free profit without committing any capital.
    C. two assets that will produce the same cash flows in the future must sell for equivalent prices.

45. Arbitrage opportunities exist when:
    A. two identical assets or derivatives sell for different prices.
    B. combinations of the underlying asset and a derivative earn the risk-free rate.
    C. arbitrageurs simultaneously buy takeover targets and sell takeover acquirers.

For questions 46–49, consider a call option selling for \$4 in which the exercise price is \$50

46. Determine the value at expiration and the profit for a *buyer* if the price of the underlying at expiration is \$55.
    A. \$5
    B. \$1
    C. −\$1

47. Determine the value at expiration and the profit for a *buyer* if the price of the underlying at expiration is \$48.
    A. −\$4
    B. \$0
    C. \$2

48. Determine the value at expiration and the profit for a *seller* if the price of the underling at expiration is \$49.
    A. \$4
    B. \$0
    C. −\$1

49. Determine the value at expiration and the profit for a *seller* if the price of the underling at expiration is $52.
    A. −$2
    B. $5
    C. $2

For questions 50–52, consider the following scenario

Suppose you believe that the price of a particular underlying, currently selling at $99, is going to increase substantially in the next six months. You decide to purchase a call option expiring in six months on this underlying. The call option has an exercise price of $105 and sells for $7.

50. Determine the profit if the price of the underlying six months from now is $99.
    A. $6
    B. $0
    C. −$7
51. Determine the profit if the price of the underlying six months from now is $112.
    A. $7
    B. $0
    C. −$3
52. Determine the profit if the price of the underlying six months from now is $115.
    A. $0
    B. $3
    C. −$3

For questions 53–55, consider the following scenario

Suppose you believe that the price of a particular underlying, currently selling at $99, is going to decrease substantially in the next six months. You decide to purchase a put option expiring in six months on this underlying. The put option has an exercise price of $95 and sells for $5.

53. Determine the profit for you if the price of the underlying six months from now is $100.
    A. $0
    B. $5
    C. −$5
54. Determine the profit for you if the price of the underlying six months from now is $95.
    A. $0
    B. $5
    C. −$5
55. Determine the profit for you if the price of the underlying six months from now is $85.
    A. $10
    B. $5
    C. $0

CHAPTER 2

BASICS OF DERIVATIVE PRICING AND VALUATION

LEARNING OUTCOMES

The candidate should be able to:

- explain how the concepts of arbitrage, replication, and risk neutrality are used in pricing derivatives;
- explain the difference between value and price of forward and futures contracts;
- calculate a forward price of an asset with zero, positive, or negative net cost of carry;
- explain how the value and price of a forward contract are determined at expiration, during the life of the contract, and at initiation;
- describe monetary and nonmonetary benefits and costs associated with holding the underlying asset and explain how they affect the value and price of a forward contract;
- define a forward rate agreement and describe its uses;
- explain why forward and futures prices differ;
- explain how swap contracts are similar to but different from a series of forward contracts;
- explain the difference between value and price of swaps;
- explain the exercise value, time value, and moneyness of an option;
- identify the factors that determine the value of an option and explain how each factor affects the value of an option;
- explain put–call parity for European options;
- explain put–call–forward parity for European options;
- explain how the value of an option is determined using a one-period binomial model;
- explain under which circumstances the values of European and American options differ.

SUMMARY OVERVIEW

This reading on derivative pricing provides a foundation for understanding how derivatives are valued and traded. Key points include the following:

- The price of the underlying asset is equal to the expected future price discounted at the risk-free rate, plus a risk premium, plus the present value of any benefits, minus the present value of any costs associated with holding the asset.
- An arbitrage opportunity occurs when two identical assets or combinations of assets sell at different prices, leading to the possibility of buying the cheaper asset and selling the more expensive asset to produce a risk-free return without investing any capital.
- In well-functioning markets, arbitrage opportunities are quickly exploited, and the resulting increased buying of underpriced assets and increased selling of overpriced assets returns prices to equivalence.
- Derivatives are priced by creating a risk-free combination of the underlying and a derivative, leading to a unique derivative price that eliminates any possibility of arbitrage.
- Derivative pricing through arbitrage precludes any need for determining risk premiums or the risk aversion of the party trading the option and is referred to as risk-neutral pricing.
- The value of a forward contract at expiration is the value of the asset minus the forward price.
- The value of a forward contract prior to expiration is the value of the asset minus the present value of the forward price.
- The forward price, established when the contract is initiated, is the price agreed to by the two parties that produces a zero value at the start.
- Costs incurred and benefits received by holding the underlying affect the forward price by raising and lowering it, respectively.
- Futures prices can differ from forward prices because of the effect of interest rates on the interim cash flows from the daily settlement.
- Swaps can be priced as an implicit series of off-market forward contracts, whereby each contract is priced the same, resulting in some contracts being positively valued and some negatively valued but with their combined value equaling zero.
- At expiration, a European call or put is worth its exercise value, which for calls is the greater of zero or the underlying price minus the exercise price and for puts is the greater of zero and the exercise price minus the underlying price.
- European calls and puts are affected by the value of the underlying, the exercise price, the risk-free rate, the time to expiration, the volatility of the underlying, and any costs incurred or benefits received while holding the underlying.
- Option values experience time value decay, which is the loss in value due to the passage of time and the approach of expiration, plus the moneyness and the volatility.
- The minimum value of a European call is the maximum of zero and the underlying price minus the present value of the exercise price.
- The minimum value of a European put is the maximum of zero and the present value of the exercise price minus the price of the underlying.
- European put and call prices are related through put–call parity, which specifies that the put price plus the price of the underlying equals the call price plus the present value of the exercise price.

- European put and call prices are related through put–call–forward parity, which shows that the put price plus the value of a risk-free bond with face value equal to the forward price equals the call price plus the value of a risk-free bond with face value equal to the exercise price.
- The values of European options can be obtained using the binomial model, which specifies two possible prices of the asset one period later and enables the construction of a risk-free hedge consisting of the option and the underlying.
- American call prices can differ from European call prices only if there are cash flows on the underlying, such as dividends or interest; these cash flows are the only reason for early exercise of a call.
- American put prices can differ from European put prices, because the right to exercise early always has value for a put, which is because of a lower limit on the value of the underlying.

PROBLEMS

1. For a risk-averse investor, the price of a risky asset, assuming no additional costs and benefits of holding the asset, is:
   A. unrelated to the risk-free rate.
   B. directly related to its level of risk.
   C. inversely related to its level of risk.
2. An arbitrage opportunity is *least likely* to be exploited when:
   A. one position is illiquid.
   B. the price differential between assets is large.
   C. the investor can execute a transaction in large volumes.
3. An arbitrageur will *most likely* execute a trade when:
   A. transaction costs are low.
   B. costs of short-selling are high.
   C. prices are consistent with the law of one price.
4. An arbitrage transaction generates a net inflow of funds:
   A. throughout the holding period.
   B. at the end of the holding period.
   C. at the start of the holding period.
5. Which of the following combinations replicates a long derivative position?
   A. A short derivative and a long asset
   B. A long asset and a short risk-free bond
   C. A short derivative and a short risk-free bond
6. Most derivatives are priced by:
   A. assuming that the market offers arbitrage opportunities.
   B. discounting the expected payoff of the derivative at the risk-free rate.
   C. applying a risk premium to the expected payoff of the derivative and its risk.
7. The price of a forward contract:
   A. is the amount paid at initiation.
   B. is the amount paid at expiration.
   C. fluctuates over the term of the contract.

8. Assume an asset pays no dividends or interest, and also assume that the asset does not yield any non-financial benefits or incur any carrying cost. At initiation, the price of a forward contract on that asset is:
   A. lower than the value of the contract.
   B. equal to the value of the contract.
   C. greater than the value of the contract.

9. With respect to a forward contract, as market conditions change:
   A. only the price fluctuates.
   B. only the value fluctuates.
   C. both the price and the value fluctuate.

10. The value of a forward contract at expiration is:
    A. positive to the long party if the spot price is higher than the forward price.
    B. negative to the short party if the forward price is higher than the spot price.
    C. positive to the short party if the spot price is higher than the forward price.

11. At the initiation of a forward contract on an asset that neither receives benefits nor incurs carrying costs during the term of the contract, the forward price is equal to the:
    A. spot price.
    B. future value of the spot price.
    C. present value of the spot price.

12. Stocks BWQ and ZER are each currently priced at $100 per share. Over the next year, stock BWQ is expected to generate significant benefits whereas stock ZER is not expected to generate any benefits. There are no carrying costs associated with holding either stock over the next year. Compared with ZER, the one-year forward price of BWQ is *most likely*:
    A. lower.
    B. the same.
    C. higher.

13. If the net cost of carry of an asset is positive, then the price of a forward contract on that asset is *most likely*:
    A. lower than if the net cost of carry was zero.
    B. the same as if the net cost of carry was zero.
    C. higher than if the net cost of carry was zero.

14. If the present value of storage costs exceeds the present value of its convenience yield, then the commodity's forward price is *most likely*:
    A. less than the spot price compounded at the risk-free rate.
    B. the same as the spot price compounded at the risk-free rate.
    C. higher than the spot price compounded at the risk-free rate.

15. Which of the following factors *most likely* explains why the spot price of a commodity in short supply can be greater than its forward price?
    A. Opportunity cost
    B. Lack of dividends
    C. Convenience yield

16. When interest rates are constant, futures prices are *most likely*:
    A. less than forward prices.
    B. equal to forward prices.
    C. greater than forward prices.

17. In contrast to a forward contract, a futures contract:
    A. trades over-the-counter.
    B. is initiated at a zero value.
    C. is marked-to-market daily.
18. To the holder of a long position, it is more desirable to own a forward contract than a futures contract when interest rates and futures prices are:
    A. negatively correlated.
    B. uncorrelated.
    C. positively correlated.
19. The value of a swap typically:
    A. is non-zero at initiation.
    B. is obtained through replication.
    C. does not fluctuate over the life of the contract.
20. The price of a swap typically:
    A. is zero at initiation.
    B. fluctuates over the life of the contract.
    C. is obtained through a process of replication.
21. The value of a swap is equal to the present value of the:
    A. fixed payments from the swap.
    B. net cash flow payments from the swap.
    C. underlying at the end of the contract.
22. If no cash is initially exchanged, a swap is comparable to a series of forward contracts when:
    A. the swap payments are variable.
    B. the combined value of all the forward contracts is zero.
    C. all the forward contracts have the same agreed-on price.
23. For a swap in which a series of fixed payments is exchanged for a series of floating payments, the parties to the transaction:
    A. designate the value of the underlying at contract initiation.
    B. value the underlying solely on the basis of its market value at the end of the swap.
    C. value the underlying sequentially at the time of each payment to determine the floating payment.
24. A European call option and a European put option are written on the same underlying, and both options have the same expiration date and exercise price. At expiration, it is possible that both options will have:
    A. negative values.
    B. the same value.
    C. positive values.
25. At expiration, a European put option will be valuable if the exercise price is:
    A. less than the underlying price.
    B. equal to the underlying price.
    C. greater than the underlying price.
26. The value of a European call option at expiration is the greater of zero or the:
    A. value of the underlying.
    B. value of the underlying minus the exercise price.
    C. exercise price minus the value of the underlying.

27. For a European call option with two months until expiration, if the spot price is below the exercise price, the call option will *most likely* have:
    A. zero time value.
    B. positive time value.
    C. positive exercise value.

28. When the price of the underlying is below the exercise price, a put option is:
    A. in-the-money.
    B. at-the-money.
    C. out-of-the-money.

29. If the risk-free rate increases, the value of an in-the-money European put option will *most likely*:
    A. decrease.
    B. remain the same.
    C. increase.

30. The value of a European call option is inversely related to the:
    A. exercise price.
    B. time to expiration.
    C. volatility of the underlying.

31. The table below shows three European call options on the same underlying:

	Time to Expiration	Exercise Price
Option 1	3 months	$100
Option 2	6 months	$100
Option 3	6 months	$105

The option with the highest value is *most likely*:
    A. Option 1.
    B. Option 2.
    C. Option 3.

32. The value of a European put option can be either directly or inversely related to the:
    A. exercise price.
    B. time to expiration.
    C. volatility of the underlying.

33. Prior to expiration, the lowest value of a European put option is the greater of zero or the:
    A. exercise price minus the value of the underlying.
    B. present value of the exercise price minus the value of the underlying.
    C. value of the underlying minus the present value of the exercise price.

34. A European put option on a dividend-paying stock is *most likely* to increase if there is an increase in:
    A. carrying costs.
    B. the risk-free rate.
    C. dividend payments.

35. Based on put–call parity, a trader who combines a long asset, a long put, and a short call will create a synthetic:
    A. long bond.
    B. fiduciary call.
    C. protective put.

36. Which of the following transactions is the equivalent of a synthetic long call position?
    A. Long asset, long put, short call
    B. Long asset, long put, short bond
    C. Short asset, long call, long bond
37. Which of the following is *least likely* to be required by the binomial option pricing model?
    A. Spot price
    B. Two possible prices one period later
    C. Actual probabilities of the up and down moves
38. To determine the price of an option today, the binomial model requires:
    A. selling one put and buying one offsetting call.
    B. buying one unit of the underlying and selling one matching call.
    C. using the risk-free rate to determine the required number of units of the underlying.
39. Assume a call option's strike price is initially equal to the price of its underlying asset. Based on the binomial model, if the volatility of the underlying decreases, the lower of the two potential payoff values of the hedge portfolio:
    A. decreases.
    B. remains the same.
    C. increases.
40. Based on the binomial model, an increase in the actual probability of an upward move in the underlying will result in the option price:
    A. decreasing.
    B. remaining the same.
    C. increasing.
41. If a call option is priced higher than the binomial model predicts, investors can earn a return in excess of the risk-free rate by:
    A. investing at the risk-free rate, selling a call, and selling the underlying.
    B. borrowing at the risk-free rate, buying a call, and buying the underlying.
    C. borrowing at the risk-free rate, selling a call, and buying the underlying.
42. An at-the-money American call option on a stock that pays no dividends has three months remaining until expiration. The market value of the option will *most likely* be:
    A. less than its exercise value.
    B. equal to its exercise value.
    C. greater than its exercise value.
43. At expiration, American call options are worth:
    A. less than European call options.
    B. the same as European call options.
    C. more than European call options.
44. Which of the following circumstances will *most likely* affect the value of an American call option relative to a European call option?
    A. Dividends are declared
    B. Expiration date occurs
    C. The risk-free rate changes
45. Combining a protective put with a forward contract generates equivalent outcomes at expiration to those of a:
    A. fiduciary call.
    B. long call combined with a short asset.
    C. forward contract combined with a risk-free bond.

46. Holding an asset and buying a put on that asset is equivalent to:
    A. initiating a fiduciary call.
    B. buying a risk-free zero-coupon bond and selling a call option.
    C. selling a risk-free zero-coupon bond and buying a call option.

47. If an underlying asset's price is less than a related option's strike price at expiration, a protective put position on that asset versus a fiduciary call position has a value that is:
    A. lower.
    B. the same.
    C. higher.

48. Based on put–call parity, which of the following combinations results in a synthetic long asset position?
    A. A long call, a short put, and a long bond
    B. A short call, a long put, and a short bond
    C. A long call, a short asset, and a long bond

49. For a holder of a European option, put–call–forward parity is based on the assumption that:
    A. no arbitrage is possible within the spot, forward, and option markets.
    B. the value of a European put at expiration is the greater of zero or the underlying value minus the exercise price.
    C. the value of a European call at expiration is the greater of zero or the exercise price minus the value of the underlying.

50. Under put–call–forward parity, which of the following transactions is risk free?
    A. Short call, long put, long forward contract, long risk-free bond
    B. Long call, short put, long forward contract, short risk-free bond
    C. Long call, long put, short forward contract, short risk-free bond

CHAPTER 3

PRICING AND VALUATION OF FORWARD COMMITMENTS

LEARNING OUTCOMES

The candidate should be able to:

- describe the carry arbitrage model without underlying cashflows and with underlying cashflows;
- describe how equity forwards and futures are priced, and calculate and interpret their no-arbitrage value;
- describe how interest rate forwards and futures are priced, and calculate and interpret their no-arbitrage value;
- describe how fixed-income forwards and futures are priced, and calculate and interpret their no-arbitrage value;
- describe how interest rate swaps are priced, and calculate and interpret their no-arbitrage value;
- describe how currency swaps are priced, and calculate and interpret their no-arbitrage value;
- describe how equity swaps are priced, and calculate and interpret their no-arbitrage value.

SUMMARY OVERVIEW

This reading on forward commitment pricing and valuation provides a foundation for understanding how forwards, futures, and swaps are both priced and valued.

Key points include the following:

- The arbitrageur would rather have more money than less and abides by two fundamental rules: Do not use your own money, and do not take any price risk.
- The no-arbitrage approach is used for the pricing and valuation of forward commitments and is built on the key concept of the law of one price, which states that if two investments

have the same future cash flows, regardless of what happens in the future, these two investments should have the same current price.

- Throughout this reading, the following key assumptions are made:
  - Replicating and offsetting instruments are identifiable and investable.
  - Market frictions are nil.
  - Short selling is allowed with full use of proceeds.
  - Borrowing and lending are available at a known risk-free rate.
- Carry arbitrage models used for forward commitment pricing and valuation are based on the no-arbitrage approach.
- With forward commitments, there is a distinct difference between pricing and valuation. Pricing involves the determination of the appropriate fixed price or rate, and valuation involves the determination of the contract's current value expressed in currency units.
- Forward commitment pricing results in determining a price or rate such that the forward contract value is equal to zero.
- Using the carry arbitrage model, the forward contract price (F_0) is:

$$F_0 = FV(S_0) = S_0(1 + r)^T \text{ (assuming annual compounding, r)}$$

$$F_0 = FV(S_0) = S_0 \exp^{r_c T} \text{ (assuming continuous compounding, } r_c)$$

- The key forward commitment pricing equations with carry costs (CC) and carry benefits (CB) are:

$$F_0 = FV[S_0 + CC_0 - CB_0] \text{ (with discrete compounding)}$$

$$F_0 = S_0 \exp^{(r_c + CC - CB)T} \text{ (with continuous compounding)}$$

Futures contract pricing in this reading can essentially be treated the same as forward contract pricing.

- The value of a forward commitment is a function of the price of the underlying instrument, financing costs, and other carry costs and benefits.
- The key forward commitment valuation equations are:

$$\text{Long Forward:} \quad V_t = PV[F_t - F_0] = \frac{[F_t - F_0]}{(1 + r)^{T-t}}$$

and

$$\text{Short Forward:} \quad -V_t = PV[F_0 - F_t] = \frac{[F_0 - F_t]}{(1 + r)^{T-t}},$$

With the PV of the difference in forward prices adjusted for carry costs and benefits. Alternatively,

$$\text{Long Forward:} \quad V_t = S_t - PV[F_0] = S_t - \frac{F_0}{(1 + r)^{T-t}}$$

and

$$\text{Short Forward:} - V_t = PV[F_0] - S_t = \frac{F_0}{(1 + r)^{T-t}} - S_t$$

- With equities and fixed-income securities, the forward price is determined such that the initial forward value is zero.
- A forward rate agreement (FRA) is a forward contract on interest rates. The FRA's fixed interest rate is determined such that the initial value of the FRA is zero.
- FRA settlements amounts at Time h are:

$$\text{Pay-fixed (Long): } NA \times \{[L_m - FRA_0] \, t_m\}/[1 + D_m t_m] \text{ and}$$

$$\text{Receive-fixed (Short): } NA \times \{FRA_0 - L_m] \, t_m\}/[1 + D_m t_m].$$

- The FRA's fixed interest rate (annualized) at contract initiation is:

$$FRA_0 = \{[1 + L_T t_T]/[1 + L_h t_h] - 1\}/t_m.$$

- The Time g value of an FRA initiated at Time 0 is:

$$\text{Long FRA: } V_g = NA \times \{[FRA_g - FRA_0] \, t_m\}/[1 + D_{(T-g)} \, t_{(T-g)}] \text{ and}$$

$$\text{Short FRA: } -V_g = NA \times \{[FRA_0 - FRA_g] \, t_m\}/[1 + D_{(T-g)} \, t_{(T-g)}].$$

- The fixed-income forward (or futures) price including conversion factor (i.e., adjusted price) is:

$$F_0 = Q_0 \times CF = FV[S_0 + CC_0 - CB_0] = FV[B_0 + AI_0 - PVCI],$$

and the conversion factor adjusted futures price (i.e., quoted futures price) is:

$$Q_0 = [1/CF] \, \{FV \, [B_0 + AI_0] - AI_T - FVCI\}.$$

- The general approach to pricing and valuing swaps as covered here is using a replicating portfolio or offsetting portfolio of comparable instruments, typically bonds for interest rate and currency swaps and equities plus bonds for equity swaps.
- The swap pricing equation, which sets r_{FIX} for the implied fixed bond in an interest rate swap, is:

$$r_{FIX} = \frac{1 - PV_n(1)}{\sum_{i=1}^{n} PV_i(1)}.$$

- The value of an interest rate swap at a point in Time t after initiation is the sum of the present values of the difference in fixed swap rates times the stated notional amount, or:

$$V_{SWAP,t} = NA \times (FS_0 - FS_t) \times \sum_{i=1}^{n} PV_i \text{ (Value of receive-fixed swap)}$$

and

$$-V_{SWAP,t} = NA \times (FS_t - FS_0) \times \sum_{i=1}^{n} PV_i \text{ (Value of pay-fixed swap)}.$$

- With a basic understanding of pricing and valuing a simple interest rate swap, it is a straightforward extension to pricing and valuing currency swaps and equity swaps.

- The solution for each of the three variables, one notional amount (NA_a) and two fixed rates (one for each currency, a and b), needed to price a fixed-for-fixed currency swap are:

$$NA_a = S_0 \times NA_b; \quad r_a = \frac{1 - PV_{n,a}(1)}{\sum_{i=1}^{n} PV_{i,a}(1)} \quad \text{and} \quad r_b = \frac{1 - PV_{n,b}(1)}{\sum_{i=1}^{n} PV_{i,b}(1)}.$$

- The currency swap valuation equation, for valuing the swap at time t (after initiation), can be expressed as:

$$V_{CS} = NA_a \left(r_{Fix,a} \sum_{i=1}^{n} PV_i(1) + PV_n(1) \right) - S_t NA_b \left(r_{Fix,b} \sum_{i=1}^{n} PV_i(1) + PV_n(1) \right).$$

- For a receive-fixed, pay equity swap, the fixed rate (r_{FIX}) for the implied fixed bond that makes the swap's value (V_{EQ}) equal to "0" at initiation is:

$$r_{FIX} = \frac{1 - PV_n(1)}{\sum_{i=1}^{n} PV_i(1)}.$$

- The value of an equity swap at Time t ($V_{EQ,t}$), after initiation, is:

$$V_{EQ,t} = V_{FIX}(C_0) - (S_t/S_{t-1})NA_E - PV(Par - NA_E)$$

where $V_{FIX}(C_0)$ is the Time t value of a fixed-rate bond initiated with coupon C_0 at Time 0, S_t is the current equity price, S_{t-1} is the equity price at the last reset date, and $PV()$ is the PV function from the swap maturity date to Time t.

PROBLEMS

The following information relates to Questions 1–5

Donald Troubadour is a derivatives trader for Southern Shores Investments. The firm seeks arbitrage opportunities in the forward and futures markets using the carry arbitrage model.

Troubadour identifies an arbitrage opportunity relating to a fixed-income futures contract and its underlying bond. Current data on the futures contract and underlying bond are presented in Exhibit 1. The current annual compounded risk-free rate is 0.30%.

EXHIBIT 1   Current Data for Futures and Underlying Bond

Futures Contract		Underlying Bond	
Quoted futures price	125.00	Quoted bond price	112.00
Conversion factor	0.90	Accrued interest since last coupon payment	0.08
Time remaining to contract expiration	Three months	Accrued interest at futures contract expiration	0.20
Accrued interest over life of futures contract	0.00		

Troubadour next gathers information on a Japanese equity index futures contract, the **Nikkei 225 Futures Contract**:

> Troubadour holds a long position in a Nikkei 225 futures contract that has a remaining maturity of three months. The continuously compounded dividend yield on the Nikkei 225 Stock Index is 1.1%, and the current stock index level is 16,080. The continuously compounded annual interest rate is 0.2996%.

Troubadour next considers an equity forward contract for Texas Steel, Inc. (TSI). Information regarding TSI common shares and a TSI equity forward contract is presented in Exhibit 2.

EXHIBIT 2   Selected Information for TSI

- The price per share of TSI's common shares is $250.
- The forward price per share for a nine-month TSI equity forward contract is $250.562289.
- Assume annual compounding.

Troubadour takes a short position in the TSI equity forward contract. His supervisor asks, "Under which scenario would our position experience a loss?"

Three months after contract initiation, Troubadour gathers information on TSI and the risk-free rate, which is presented in Exhibit 3.

EXHIBIT 3   Selected Data on TSI and the Risk-Free Rate (Three Months Later)

- The price per share of TSI's common shares is $245.
- The risk-free rate is 0.325% (quoted on an annual compounding basis).
- TSI recently announced its regular semiannual dividend of $1.50 per share that will be paid exactly three months before contract expiration.
- The market price of the TSI equity forward contract is equal to the no-arbitrage forward price.

1. Based on Exhibit 1 and assuming annual compounding, the arbitrage profit on the bond futures contract is *closest* to:
   A. 0.4158.
   B. 0.5356.
   C. 0.6195.
2. The current no-arbitrage futures price of the Nikkei 225 futures contract is *closest* to:
   A. 15,951.81.
   B. 16,047.86.
   C. 16,112.21.
3. Based on Exhibit 2, Troubadour should find that an arbitrage opportunity relating to TSI shares is
   A. not available.
   B. available based on carry arbitrage.
   C. available based on reverse carry arbitrage.
4. The *most appropriate* response to Troubadour's supervisor's question regarding the TSI forward contract is:
   A. a decrease in TSI's share price, all else equal.
   B. an increase in the risk-free rate, all else equal
   C. a decrease in the market price of the forward contract, all else equal.

5. Based on Exhibits 2 and 3, and assuming annual compounding, the per share value of Troubadour's short position in the TSI forward contract three months after contract initiation is *closest* to:
   A. $1.6549.
   B. $5.1561.
   C. $6.6549.

The following information relates to Questions 6–14

Sonal Johnson is a risk manager for a bank. She manages the bank's risks using a combination of swaps and forward rate agreements (FRAs).

Johnson prices a three-year Libor-based interest rate swap with annual resets using the present value factors presented in Exhibit 1.

EXHIBIT 1   Present Value Factors

Maturity (years)	Present Value Factors
1	0.990099
2	0.977876
3	0.965136

Johnson also uses the present value factors in Exhibit 1 to value an interest rate swap that the bank entered into one year ago as the pay-fixed (receive-floating) party. Selected data for the swap are presented in Exhibit 2. Johnson notes that the current equilibrium two-year fixed swap rate is 1.12%.

EXHIBIT 2   Selected Data on Fixed for Floating Interest Rate Swap

Swap notional amount	$50,000,000
Original swap term	Three years, with annual resets
Fixed swap rate (since initiation)	3.00%

One of the bank's investments is exposed to movements in the Japanese yen, and Johnson desires to hedge the currency exposure. She prices a one-year fixed-for-fixed currency swap involving yen and US dollars, with a quarterly reset. Johnson uses the interest rate data presented in Exhibit 3 to price the currency swap.

EXHIBIT 3   Selected Japanese and US Interest Rate Data

Days to Maturity	Yen Spot Interest Rates	US Dollar Spot Interest Rates
90	0.05%	0.20%
180	0.10%	0.40%
270	0.15%	0.55%
360	0.25%	0.70%

Johnson next reviews an equity swap with an annual reset that the bank entered into six months ago as the receive-fixed, pay-equity party. Selected data regarding the equity swap, which is linked to an equity index, are presented in Exhibit 4. At the time of initiation, the underlying equity index was trading at 100.00.

EXHIBIT 4   Selected Data on Equity Swap

Swap notional amount	$20,000,000
Original swap term	Five years, with annual resets
Fixed swap rate	2.00%

The equity index is currently trading at 103.00, and relevant US spot rates, along with their associated present value factors, are presented in Exhibit 5.

EXHIBIT 5   Selected US Spot Rates and Present Value Factors

Maturity (years)	Spot Rate	Present Value Factors
0.5	0.40%	0.998004
1.5	1.00%	0.985222
2.5	1.20%	0.970874
3.5	2.00%	0.934579
4.5	2.60%	0.895255

Johnson reviews a 6×9 FRA that the bank entered into 90 days ago as the pay-fixed/receive-floating party. Selected data for the FRA are presented in Exhibit 6, and current Libor (i.e., MRR) data are presented in Exhibit 7. Based on her interest rate forecast, Johnson also considers whether the bank should enter into new positions in 1×4 and 2×5 FRAs.

EXHIBIT 6 6×9 FRA Data

FRA term	6×9
FRA rate	0.70%
FRA notional amount	US$20,000,000
FRA settlement terms	Advanced set, advanced settle

EXHIBIT 7   Current Libor (Market Reference Rate)

30-day Libor	0.75%
60-day Libor	0.82%
90-day Libor	0.90%
120-day Libor	0.92%
150-day Libor	0.94%
180-day Libor	0.95%
210-day Libor	0.97%
270-day Libor	1.00%

Three months later, the 6 × 9 FRA in Exhibit 6 reaches expiration, at which time the three-month US dollar Libor is 1.10% and the six-month US dollar Libor is 1.20%. Johnson determines that the appropriate discount rate for the FRA settlement cash flows is 1.10%.

6. Based on Exhibit 1, Johnson should price the three-year Libor-based interest rate swap at a fixed rate *closest* to:
   A. 0.34%.
   B. 1.16%.
   C. 1.19%.

7. From the bank's perspective, using data from Exhibit 1, the current value of the swap described in Exhibit 2 is *closest* to:
   A. −$2,951,963.
   B. −$1,849,897.
   C. −$1,943,000.

8. Based on Exhibit 3, Johnson should determine that the annualized equilibrium fixed swap rate for Japanese yen is *closest* to:
   A. 0.0624%.
   B. 0.1375%.
   C. 0.2496%.

9. From the bank's perspective, using data from Exhibits 4 and 5, the fair value of the equity swap is *closest* to:
   A. −$1,139,425.
   B. −$781,322.
   C. −$181,323.

10. Based on Exhibit 5, the current value of the equity swap described in Exhibit 4 would be zero if the equity index was currently trading the *closest* to:
    A. 97.30.
    B. 99.09.
    C. 100.00.

11. From the bank's perspective, based on Exhibits 6 and 7, the value of the 6 × 9 FRA 90 days after inception is *closest* to:
    A. $14,820.
    B. $19,647.
    C. $29,635.

12. Based on Exhibit 7, the no-arbitrage fixed rate on a new 1 × 4 FRA is *closest* to:
    A. 0.65%.
    B. 0.73%.
    C. 0.98%.

13. Based on Exhibit 7, the fixed rate on a new 2 × 5 FRA is *closest* to:
    A. 0.61%.
    B. 1.02%.
    C. 1.71%.

14. Based on Exhibit 6 and the three-month US dollar Libor at expiration, the payment amount that the bank will receive to settle the 6 × 9 FRA is *closest* to:
    A. $19,945.
    B. $24,925.
    C. $39,781.

The following information relates to Questions 15–20

Tim Doyle is a portfolio manager at BestFutures Group, a hedge fund that frequently enters into derivative contracts either to hedge the risk of investments it holds or to speculate outside of those investments. Doyle works alongside Diane Kemper, a junior analyst at the hedge fund. They meet to evaluate new investment ideas and to review several of the firm's existing investments.

Carry Arbitrage Model

Doyle and Kemper discuss the carry arbitrage model and how they can take advantage of mispricing in bond markets. Specifically, they would like to execute an arbitrage transaction on a Eurodollar futures contract in which the underlying Eurodollar bond is expected to make an interest payment in two months. Doyle makes the following statements:

Statement 1: If the Eurodollar futures price is less than the price suggested by the carry arbitrage model, the futures contract should be purchased.

Statement 2: Based on the cost of carry model, the futures price would be higher if the underlying Eurodollar bond's upcoming interest payment was expected in five months instead of two.

Three-Year Treasury Note Futures Contract

Kemper then presents two investment ideas to Doyle. Kemper's first investment idea is to purchase a three-year Treasury note futures contract. The underlying 1.5%, semi-annual three-year Treasury note is quoted at a clean price of 101. It has been 60 days since the three-year Treasury note's last coupon payment, and the next coupon payment is payable in 120 days. Doyle asks Kemper to calculate the full spot price of the underlying three-year Treasury note.

10-Year Treasury Note Futures Contract

Kemper's second investment idea is to purchase a 10-year Treasury note futures contract. The underlying 2%, semi-annual 10-year Treasury note has a dirty price of 104.17. It has been 30 days since the 10-year Treasury note's last coupon payment. The futures contract expires in 90 days. The quoted futures contract price is 129. The current annualized three-month risk-free rate is 1.65%. The conversion factor is 0.7025. Doyle asks Kemper to calculate the equilibrium quoted futures contract price based on the carry arbitrage model.

Japanese Government Bonds

After discussing Kemper's new investment ideas, Doyle and Kemper evaluate one of their existing forward contract positions. Three months ago, BestFutures took a long position in eight 10-year Japanese government bond (JGB) forward contracts, with each contract having a contract notional value of 100 million yen. The contracts had a price of JPY153 (quoted as a percentage of par) when the contracts were purchased. Now, the contracts have six months left to expiration and have a price of JPY155. The annualized six-month interest rate is 0.12%. Doyle asks Kemper to value the JGB forward position.

Interest Rate Swaps

Additionally, Doyle asks Kemper to price a one-year plain vanilla swap. The spot rates and days to maturity at each payment date are presented in Exhibit 1.

EXHIBIT 1   Selected US Spot Rate Data

Days to Maturity	Spot Interest Rates (%)
90	1.90
180	2.00
270	2.10
360	2.20

Finally, Doyle and Kemper review one of BestFutures's pay-fixed interest rate swap positions. Two years ago, the firm entered into a JPY5 billion five-year interest rate swap, paying the fixed rate. The fixed rate when BestFutures entered into the swap two years ago was 0.10%. The current term structure of interest rates for JPY cash flows, which are relevant to the interest rate swap position, is presented in Exhibit 2.

EXHIBIT 2   Selected Japanese Interest Rate Data

Maturity (Years)	Yen Spot Interest Rates (%)	Present Value Factors
1	0.03	0.9997
2	0.06	0.9988
3	0.08	0.9976
Sum		2.9961

Doyle asks Kemper to calculate the value of the pay-fixed interest rate swap.

15. Which of Doyle's statements regarding the Eurodollar futures contract price is correct?
    A. Only Statement 1
    B. Only Statement 2
    C. Both Statement 1 and Statement 2
16. The full spot price of the three-year Treasury note is:
    A. 101.00.
    B. 101.25.
    C. 101.50.
17. The equilibrium 10-year Treasury note quoted futures contract price is *closest* to:
    A. 147.94.
    B. 148.89.
    C. 149.78.
18. The value of the JGB long forward position is *closest* to:
    A. JPY15,980,823.
    B. JPY15,990,409.
    C. JPY16,000,000.

19. Based on Exhibit 1, the fixed rate of the one-year plain vanilla swap is *closest* to:
    A. 0.12%.
    B. 0.55%.
    C. 0.72%.
20. Based on Exhibit 2, the value of the pay-fixed interest rate swap is *closest* to:
    A. –JPY6,491,550.
    B. –JPY2,980,500.
    C. –JPY994,793.

CHAPTER 4

VALUATION OF CONTINGENT CLAIMS

LEARNING OUTCOMES

The candidate should be able to:

- describe and interpret the binomial option valuation model and its component terms;
- calculate the no-arbitrage values of European and American options using a two-period binomial model;
- identify an arbitrage opportunity involving options and describe the related arbitrage;
- calculate and interpret the value of an interest rate option using a two-period binomial model;
- describe how the value of a European option can be analyzed as the present value of the option's expected payoff at expiration;
- identify assumptions of the Black–Scholes–Merton option valuation model;
- interpret the components of the Black–Scholes–Merton model as applied to call options in terms of a leveraged position in the underlying;
- describe how the Black–Scholes–Merton model is used to value European options on equities and currencies;
- describe how the Black model is used to value European options on futures;
- describe how the Black model is used to value European interest rate options and European swaptions;
- interpret each of the option Greeks;
- describe how a delta hedge is executed;
- describe the role of gamma risk in options trading;
- define implied volatility and explain how it is used in options trading.

SUMMARY OVERVIEW

This reading on the valuation of contingent claims provides a foundation for understanding how a variety of different options are valued. Key points include the following:

- The arbitrageur would rather have more money than less and abides by two fundamental rules: Do not use your own money and do not take any price risk.
- The no-arbitrage approach is used for option valuation and is built on the key concept of the law of one price, which says that if two investments have the same future cash flows regardless of what happens in the future, then these two investments should have the same current price.
- Throughout this reading, the following key assumptions are made:
  - Replicating instruments are identifiable and investable.
  - Market frictions are nil.
  - Short selling is allowed with full use of proceeds.
  - The underlying instrument price follows a known distribution.
  - Borrowing and lending is available at a known risk-free rate.
- The two-period binomial model can be viewed as three one-period binomial models, one positioned at Time 0 and two positioned at Time 1.
- In general, European-style options can be valued based on the expectations approach in which the option value is determined as the present value of the expected future option payouts, where the discount rate is the risk-free rate and the expectation is taken based on the risk-neutral probability measure.
- Both American-style options and European-style options can be valued based on the no-arbitrage approach, which provides clear interpretations of the component terms; the option value is determined by working backward through the binomial tree to arrive at the correct current value.
- For American-style options, early exercise influences the option values and hedge ratios as one works backward through the binomial tree.
- Interest rate option valuation requires the specification of an entire term structure of interest rates, so valuation is often estimated via a binomial tree.
- A key assumption of the Black–Scholes–Merton option valuation model is that the return of the underlying instrument follows geometric Brownian motion, implying a lognormal distribution of the price.
- The BSM model can be interpreted as a dynamically managed portfolio of the underlying instrument and zero-coupon bonds.
- BSM model interpretations related to $N(d_1)$ are that it is the basis for the number of units of underlying instrument to replicate an option, that it is the primary determinant of delta, and that it answers the question of how much the option value will change for a small change in the underlying.
- BSM model interpretations related to $N(d_2)$ are that it is the basis for the number of zero-coupon bonds to acquire to replicate an option and that it is the basis for estimating the risk-neutral probability of an option expiring in the money.
- The Black futures option model assumes the underlying is a futures or a forward contract.
- Interest rate options can be valued based on a modified Black futures option model in which the underlying is a forward rate agreement (FRA), there is an accrual period adjustment as well as an underlying notional amount, and that care must be given to day-count conventions.

- An interest rate cap is a portfolio of interest rate call options termed caplets, each with the same exercise rate and with sequential maturities.
- An interest rate floor is a portfolio of interest rate put options termed floorlets, each with the same exercise rate and with sequential maturities.
- A swaption is an option on a swap.
- A payer swaption is an option on a swap to pay fixed and receive floating.
- A receiver swaption is an option on a swap to receive fixed and pay floating.
- Long a callable fixed-rate bond can be viewed as long a straight fixed-rate bond and short a receiver swaption.
- Delta is a static risk measure defined as the change in a given portfolio for a given small change in the value of the underlying instrument, holding everything else constant.
- Delta hedging refers to managing the portfolio delta by entering additional positions into the portfolio.
- A delta neutral portfolio is one in which the portfolio delta is set and maintained at zero.
- A change in the option price can be estimated with a delta approximation.
- Because delta is used to make a linear approximation of the non-linear relationship that exists between the option price and the underlying price, there is an error that can be estimated by gamma.
- Gamma is a static risk measure defined as the change in a given portfolio delta for a given small change in the value of the underlying instrument, holding everything else constant.
- Gamma captures the non-linearity risk or the risk—via exposure to the underlying—that remains once the portfolio is delta neutral.
- A gamma neutral portfolio is one in which the portfolio gamma is maintained at zero.
- The change in the option price can be better estimated by a delta-plus-gamma approximation compared with just a delta approximation.
- Theta is a static risk measure defined as the change in the value of an option given a small change in calendar time, holding everything else constant.
- Vega is a static risk measure defined as the change in a given portfolio for a given small change in volatility, holding everything else constant.
- Rho is a static risk measure defined as the change in a given portfolio for a given small change in the risk-free interest rate, holding everything else constant.
- Although historical volatility can be estimated, there is no objective measure of future volatility.
- Implied volatility is the BSM model volatility that yields the market option price.
- Implied volatility is a measure of future volatility, whereas historical volatility is a measure of past volatility.
- Option prices reflect the beliefs of option market participant about the future volatility of the underlying.
- The volatility smile is a two dimensional plot of the implied volatility with respect to the exercise price.
- The volatility surface is a three dimensional plot of the implied volatility with respect to both expiration time and exercise prices.
- If the BSM model assumptions were true, then one would expect to find the volatility surface flat, but in practice, the volatility surface is not flat.

PROBLEMS

The following information relates to Questions 1–9

Bruno Sousa has been hired recently to work with senior analyst Camila Rocha. Rocha gives him three option valuation tasks.

Alpha Company

Sousa's first task is to illustrate how to value a call option on Alpha Company with a one-period binomial option pricing model. It is a non-dividend-paying stock, and the inputs are as follows.

- The current stock price is 50, and the call option exercise price is 50.
- In one period, the stock price will either rise to 56 or decline to 46.
- The risk-free rate of return is 5% per period.

    Based on the model, Rocha asks Sousa to estimate the hedge ratio, the risk-neutral probability of an up move, and the price of the call option. In the illustration, Sousa is also asked to describe related arbitrage positions to use if the call option is overpriced relative to the model.

Beta Company

Next, Sousa uses the two-period binomial model to estimate the value of a European-style call option on Beta Company's common shares. The inputs are as follows.

- The current stock price is 38, and the call option exercise price is 40.
- The up factor (u) is 1.300, and the down factor (d) is 0.800.
- The risk-free rate of return is 3% per period.

    Sousa then analyzes a put option on the same stock. All of the inputs, including the exercise price, are the same as for the call option. He estimates that the value of a European-style put option is 4.53. Exhibit 1 summarizes his analysis. Sousa next must determine whether an American-style put option would have the same value.
    Sousa makes two statements with regard to the valuation of a European-style option under the expectations approach.

    Statement 1:   The calculation involves discounting at the risk-free rate.
    Statement 2:   The calculation uses risk-neutral probabilities instead of true probabilities.

    Rocha asks Sousa whether it is ever profitable to exercise American options prior to maturity. Sousa answers, "I can think of two possible cases. The first case is the early exercise of an American call option on a dividend-paying stock. The second case is the early exercise of an American put option."

EXHIBIT 1   Two-Period Binomial European-Style Put Option on Beta Company

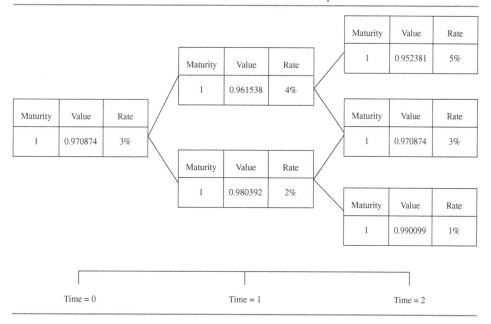

Item	Value
Underlying	64.22
Put	0

Item	Value
Underlying	49.4
Put	0.2517
Hedge Ratio	−0.01943

Item	Value
Underlying	39.52
Put	0.48

Item	Value
Underlying	38
Put	4.5346
Hedge Ratio	−0.4307

Item	Value
Underlying	30.4
Put	8.4350
Hedge Ratio	−1

Item	Value
Underlying	24.32
Put	15.68

Time = 0   Time = 1   Time = 2

Interest Rate Option

The final option valuation task involves an interest rate option. Sousa must value a two-year, European-style call option on a one-year spot rate. The notional value of the option is 1 million, and the exercise rate is 2.75%. The risk-neutral probability of an up move is 0.50. The current and expected one-year interest rates are shown in Exhibit 2, along with the values of a one-year zero-coupon bond of 1 notional value for each interest rate.

EXHIBIT 2   Two-Year Interest Rate Lattice for an Interest Rate Option

Maturity	Value	Rate
1	0.952381	5%

Maturity	Value	Rate
1	0.961538	4%

Maturity	Value	Rate
1	0.970874	3%

Maturity	Value	Rate
1	0.970874	3%

Maturity	Value	Rate
1	0.980392	2%

Maturity	Value	Rate
1	0.990099	1%

Time = 0   Time = 1   Time = 2

Rocha asks Sousa why the value of a similar in-the-money interest rate call option decreases if the exercise price is higher. Sousa provides two reasons.

Reason 1:   The exercise value of the call option is lower.
Reason 2:   The risk-neutral probabilities are changed.

1. The optimal hedge ratio for the Alpha Company call option using the one-period binomial model is *closest* to:
   A. 0.60.
   B. 0.67.
   C. 1.67.

2. The risk-neutral probability of the up move for the Alpha Company stock is *closest* to:
   A. 0.06.
   B. 0.40.
   C. 0.65.

3. The value of the Alpha Company call option is *closest* to:
   A. 3.71.
   B. 5.71.
   C. 6.19.

4. For the Alpha Company option, the positions to take advantage of the arbitrage opportunity are to write the call and:
   A. short shares of Alpha stock and lend.
   B. buy shares of Alpha stock and borrow.
   C. short shares of Alpha stock and borrow.

5. The value of the European-style call option on Beta Company shares is *closest* to:
   A. 4.83.
   B. 5.12.
   C. 7.61.

6. The value of the American-style put option on Beta Company shares is *closest* to:
   A. 4.53.
   B. 5.15.
   C. 9.32.

7. Which of Sousa's statements about binomial models is correct?
   A. Statement 1 only
   B. Statement 2 only
   C. Both Statement 1 and Statement 2

8. Based on Exhibit 2 and the parameters used by Sousa, the value of the interest rate option is *closest* to:
   A. 5,251.
   B. 6,236.
   C. 6,429.

9. Which of Sousa's reasons for the decrease in the value of the interest rate option is correct?
   A. Reason 1 only
   B. Reason 2 only
   C. Both Reason 1 and Reason 2

The following information relates to Questions 10–17

Trident Advisory Group manages assets for high-net-worth individuals and family trusts.

Alice Lee, chief investment officer, is meeting with a client, Noah Solomon, to discuss risk management strategies for his portfolio. Solomon is concerned about recent volatility and has asked Lee to explain options valuation and the use of options in risk management.

Options on Stock

Lee uses the BSM model to price TCB, which is one of Solomon's holdings. Exhibit 1 provides the current stock price (S), exercise price (X), risk-free interest rate (r), volatility (σ), and time to expiration (T) in years as well as selected outputs from the BSM model. TCB does not pay a dividend.

EXHIBIT 1   BSM Model for European Options on TCB

	BSM Inputs			
S	X	r	Σ	T
$57.03	55	0.22%	32%	0.25

		BSM Outputs			
d_1	$N(d_1)$	d_2	$N(d_2)$	BSM Call Price	BSM Put Price
0.3100	0.6217	0.1500	0.5596	$4.695	$2.634

Options on Futures

The Black model valuation and selected outputs for options on another of Solomon's holdings, the GPX 500 Index (GPX), are shown in Exhibit 2. The spot index level for the GPX is 187.95, and the index is assumed to pay a continuous dividend at a rate of 2.2% (δ) over the life of the options being valued, which expire in 0.36 years. A futures contract on the GPX also expiring in 0.36 years is currently priced at 186.73.

EXHIBIT 2   Black Model for European Options on the GPX Index

	Black Model Inputs				
GPX Index	X	r	σ	T	δ Yield
187.95	180	0.39%	24%	0.36	2.2%

Black Model Call Value	Black Model Put Value	Market Call Price	Market Put Price
$14.2089	$7.4890	$14.26	$7.20

		Option Greeks			
Delta (call)	Delta (put)	Gamma (call or put)	Theta (call) daily	Rho (call) per %	Vega per % (call or put)
0.6232	−0.3689	0.0139	−0.0327	0.3705	0.4231

After reviewing Exhibit 2, Solomon asks Lee which option Greek letter best describes the changes in an option's value as time to expiration declines.

Solomon observes that the market price of the put option in Exhibit 2 is $7.20. Lee responds that she used the historical volatility of the GPX of 24% as an input to the BSM model, and she explains the implications for the implied volatility for the GPX.

Options on Interest Rates

Solomon forecasts the three-month Libor will exceed 0.85% in six months and is considering using options to reduce the risk of rising rates. He asks Lee to value an interest rate call with a strike price of 0.85%. The current three-month Libor is 0.60%, and an FRA for a three-month Libor loan beginning in six months is currently 0.75%.

Hedging Strategy for the Equity Index

Solomon's portfolio currently holds 10,000 shares of an exchange-traded fund (ETF) that tracks the GPX. He is worried the index will decline. He remarks to Lee, "You have told me how the BSM model can provide useful information for reducing the risk of my GPX position." Lee suggests a delta hedge as a strategy to protect against small moves in the GPX Index.

Lee also indicates that a long position in puts could be used to hedge larger moves in the GPX. She notes that although hedging with either puts or calls can result in a delta-neutral position, they would need to consider the resulting gamma.

10. Based on Exhibit 1 and the BSM valuation approach, the initial portfolio required to replicate the long call option payoff is:
    A. long 0.3100 shares of TCB stock and short 0.5596 shares of a zero-coupon bond.
    B. long 0.6217 shares of TCB stock and short 0.1500 shares of a zero-coupon bond.
    C. long 0.6217 shares of TCB stock and short 0.5596 shares of a zero-coupon bond.
11. To determine the long put option value on TCB stock in Exhibit 1, the correct BSM valuation approach is to compute:
    A. 0.4404 times the present value of the exercise price minus 0.6217 times the price of TCB stock.
    B. 0.4404 times the present value of the exercise price minus 0.3783 times the price of TCB stock.
    C. 0.5596 times the present value of the exercise price minus 0.6217 times the price of TCB stock.
12. What are the correct spot value (S) and the risk-free rate (r) that Lee should use as inputs for the Black model?
    A. 186.73 and 0.39%, respectively
    B. 186.73 and 2.20%, respectively
    C. 187.95 and 2.20%, respectively
13. Which of the following is the correct answer to Solomon's question regarding the option Greek letter?
    A. Vega
    B. Theta
    C. Gamma

14. Based on Solomon's observation about the model price and market price for the put option in Exhibit 2, the implied volatility for the GPX is *most likely*:
    A. less than the historical volatility.
    B. equal to the historical volatility.
    C. greater than the historical volatility.

15. The valuation inputs used by Lee to price a call reflecting Solomon's interest rate views should include an underlying FRA rate of:
    A. 0.60% with six months to expiration.
    B. 0.75% with nine months to expiration.
    C. 0.75% with six months to expiration.

16. The strategy suggested by Lee for hedging small moves in Solomon's ETF position would *most likely* involve:
    A. selling put options.
    B. selling call options.
    C. buying call options.

17. Lee's put-based hedge strategy for Solomon's ETF position would *most likely* result in a portfolio gamma that is:
    A. negative.
    B. neutral.
    C. positive.

CHAPTER 5

CREDIT DEFAULT SWAPS

LEARNING OUTCOMES

The candidate should be able to:

- describe credit default swaps (CDS), single-name and index CDS, and the parameters that define a given CDS product;
- describe credit events and settlement protocols with respect to CDS;
- explain the principles underlying and factors that influence the market's pricing of CDS;
- describe the use of CDS to manage credit exposures and to express views regarding changes in the shape and/or level of the credit curve;
- describe the use of CDS to take advantage of valuation disparities among separate markets, such as bonds, loans, equities, and equity-linked instruments.

SUMMARY OVERVIEW

- A credit default swap (CDS) is a contract between two parties in which one party purchases protection from another party against losses from the default of a borrower for a defined period of time.
- A CDS is written on the debt of a third party, called the reference entity, whose relevant debt is called the reference obligation, typically a senior unsecured bond.
- A CDS written on a particular reference obligation normally provides coverage for all obligations of the reference entity that have equal or higher seniority.
- The two parties to the CDS are the credit protection buyer, who is said to be short the reference entity's credit, and the credit protection seller, who is said to be long the reference entity's credit.
- The CDS pays off upon occurrence of a credit event, which includes bankruptcy, failure to pay, and, in some countries, involuntary restructuring.
- Settlement of a CDS can occur through a cash payment from the credit protection seller to the credit protection buyer as determined by the cheapest-to-deliver obligation of the

reference entity or by physical delivery of the reference obligation from the protection buyer to the protection seller in exchange for the CDS notional.

- A cash settlement payoff is determined by an auction of the reference entity's debt, which gives the market's assessment of the likely recovery rate. The credit protection buyer must accept the outcome of the auction even though the ultimate recovery rate could differ.
- CDS can be constructed on a single entity or as indexes containing multiple entities. Bespoke CDS or baskets of CDS are also common.
- The fixed payments made from CDS buyer to CDS seller are customarily set at a fixed annual rate of 1% for investment-grade debt or 5% for high-yield debt.
- Valuation of a CDS is determined by estimating the present value of the payment leg, which is the series of payments made from the protection buyer to the protection seller, and the present value of the protection leg, which is the payment from the protection seller to the protection buyer in event of default. If the present value of the payment leg is greater than the present value of the protection leg, the protection buyer pays an upfront premium to the seller. If the present value of the protection leg is greater than the present value of the payment leg, the seller pays an upfront premium to the buyer.
- An important determinant of the value of the expected payments is the hazard rate, the probability of default given that default has not already occurred.
- CDS prices are often quoted in terms of credit spreads, the implied number of basis points that the credit protection seller receives from the credit protection buyer to justify providing the protection.
- Credit spreads are often expressed in terms of a credit curve, which expresses the relationship between the credit spreads on bonds of different maturities for the same borrower.
- CDS change in value over their lives as the credit quality of the reference entity changes, which leads to gains and losses for the counterparties, even though default may not have occurred or may never occur. CDS spreads approach zero as the CDS approaches maturity.
- Either party can monetize an accumulated gain or loss by entering into an offsetting position that matches the terms of the original CDS.
- CDS are used to increase or decrease credit exposures or to capitalize on different assessments of the cost of credit among different instruments tied to the reference entity, such as debt, equity, and derivatives of debt and equity.

PROBLEMS

The following information relates to Questions 1–6

UNAB Corporation

On 1 January 20X2, Deem Advisors purchased a $10 million six-year senior unsecured bond issued by UNAB Corporation. Six months later (1 July 20X2), concerned about the portfolio's credit exposure to UNAB, Doris Morrison, the chief investment officer at Deem Advisors, buys $10 million protection on UNAB with a standardized coupon rate of 5%. The reference obligation of the CDS is the UNAB bond owned by Deem Advisors. UNAB adheres to the ISDA CDS protocols.

On 1 January 20X3, Morrison asks Bill Watt, a derivatives analyst, to assess the current credit quality of UNAB bonds and the value of Deem Advisors' CDS on UNAB debt. Watt gathers the following information on UNAB's debt issues currently trading in the market:

Bond 1:   A two-year senior unsecured bond trading at 40% of par
Bond 2:   A five-year senior unsecured bond trading at 50% of par
Bond 3:   A five-year subordinated unsecured bond trading at 20% of par

With respect to the credit quality of UNAB, Watt makes the following statement:

"There is severe near-term stress in the financial markets, and UNAB's credit curve clearly reflects the difficult environment."

On 1 July 20X3, UNAB fails to make a scheduled interest payment on the outstanding subordinated unsecured obligation after a grace period; however, the company does not file for bankruptcy. Morrison asks Watt to determine if UNAB experienced a credit event and, if so, to recommend a settlement preference.

Kand Corporation

Morrison is considering purchasing protection on Kand Corporation debt to hedge the portfolio's position in Kand. She instructs Watt to determine if an upfront payment would be required and, if so, the amount of the premium. Watt presents the information for the CDS in Exhibit 1.

EXHIBIT 1   Summary Data for 10-year CDS on Kand Corporation

Credit spread	700 bps
Duration	7 years
Coupon rate	5%

Morrison purchases 10-year protection on Kand Corporation debt. Two months later the credit spread for Kand Corporation has increased by 200 bps. Morrison asks Watt to close out the firm's CDS position on Kand Corporation by entering into a new, offsetting contract.

Tollunt Corporation

Deem Advisors' chief credit analyst recently reported that Tollunt Corporation's five-year bond is currently yielding 7% and a comparable CDS contract has a credit spread of 4.25%. Since the current market reference rate is 2.5%, Watt has recommended executing a basis trade to take advantage of the pricing of Tollunt's bonds and CDS. The basis trade would consist of purchasing both the bond and the CDS contract.

1. If UNAB experienced a credit event on 1 July, Watt should recommend that Deem Advisors:
   A. prefer a cash settlement.
   B. prefer a physical settlement.
   C. be indifferent between a cash or a physical settlement.

2. According to Watt's statement, the shape of UNAB's credit curve is *most likely*:
   A. flat.
   B. upward-sloping.
   C. downward-sloping.

3. Should Watt conclude that UNAB experienced a credit event?
   A. Yes
   B. No, because UNAB did not file for bankruptcy
   C. No, because the failure to pay occurred on a subordinated unsecured bond

4. Based on Exhibit 1, the upfront premium as a percent of the notional for the CDS protection on Kand Corporation would be *closest* to:
   A. 2.0%.
   B. 9.8%.
   C. 14.0%.

5. If Deem Advisors enters into a new offsetting contract two months after purchasing protection on Kand Corporation, this action will *most likely* result in:
   A. a loss on the CDS position.
   B. a profit on the CDS position.
   C. neither a loss nor a profit on the CDS position.

6. If convergence occurs in the bond and CDS markets for Tollunt Corporation, a basis trade will capture a profit *closest* to:
   A. 0.25%.
   B. 1.75%.
   C. 2.75%.

The following information relates to Questions 7–14

John Smith, a fixed-income portfolio manager at a €10 billion sovereign wealth fund (the Fund), meets with Sofia Chan, a derivatives strategist with Shire Gate Securities (SGS), to discuss investment opportunities for the Fund. Chan notes that SGS adheres to ISDA (International Swaps and Derivatives Association) protocols for credit default swap (CDS) transactions and that any contract must conform to ISDA specifications. Before the Fund can engage in trading CDS products with SGS, the Fund must satisfy compliance requirements.

Smith explains to Chan that fixed-income derivatives strategies are being contemplated for both hedging and trading purposes. Given the size and diversified nature of the Fund, Smith asks Chan to recommend a type of CDS that would allow the Fund to simultaneously fully hedge multiple fixed-income exposures.

Smith and Chan discuss opportunities to add trading profits to the Fund. Smith asks Chan to determine the probability of default associated with a five-year investment-grade bond issued by Orion Industrial. Selected data on the Orion Industrial bond are presented in Exhibit 1.

EXHIBIT 1   Selected Data on Orion Industrial Five-Year Bond

Year	Hazard Rate
1	0.22%
2	0.35%
3	0.50%
4	0.65%
5	0.80%

Chan explains that a single-name CDS can also be used to add profit to the Fund over time. Chan describes a hypothetical trade in which the Fund sells £6 million of five-year CDS protection on Orion, where the CDS contract has a duration of 3.9 years. Chan assumes that the Fund closes the position six months later, after Orion's credit spread narrowed from 150 bps to 100 bps.

Chan discusses the mechanics of a long/short trade. In order to structure a number of potential trades, Chan and Smith exchange their respective views on individual companies and global economies. Chan and Smith agree on the following outlooks.

Outlook 1:   The European economy will weaken.
Outlook 2:   The US economy will strengthen relative to that of Canada.
Outlook 3:   The credit quality of electric car manufacturers will improve relative to that of traditional car manufacturers.

Chan believes US macroeconomic data are improving and that the general economy will strengthen in the short term. Chan suggests that a curve trade could be used by the Fund to capitalize on her short-term view of a steepening of the US credit curve.

Another short-term trading opportunity that Smith and Chan discuss involves the merger and acquisition market. SGS believes that Delta Corporation may make an unsolicited bid at a premium to the market price for all of the publicly traded shares of Zega, Inc. Zega's market capitalization and capital structure are comparable to Delta's; both firms are highly levered. It is anticipated that Delta will issue new equity along with 5- and 10-year senior unsecured debt to fund the acquisition, which will significantly increase its debt ratio.

7. To satisfy the compliance requirements referenced by Chan, the Fund is *most likely* required to:
   A. set a notional amount.
   B. post an upfront payment.
   C. sign an ISDA master agreement.
8. Which type of CDS should Chan recommend to Smith?
   A. CDS index
   B. Tranche CDS
   C. Single-name CDS
9. Based on Exhibit 1, the probability of Orion defaulting on the bond during the first three years is *closest* to:
   A. 1.07%.
   B. 2.50%.
   C. 3.85%.

10. To close the position on the hypothetical Orion trade, the Fund:
    A. sells protection at a higher premium than it paid at the start of the trade.
    B. buys protection at a lower premium than it received at the start of the trade.
    C. buys protection at a higher premium than it received at the start of the trade.
11. The hypothetical Orion trade generated an approximate:
    A. loss of £117,000.
    B. gain of £117,000.
    C. gain of £234,000.
12. Based on the three economic outlook statements, a profitable long/short trade would be to:
    A. sell protection using a Canadian CDX IG and buy protection using a US CDX IG.
    B. buy protection using an iTraxx Crossover and sell protection using an iTraxx Main.
    C. buy protection using an electric car CDS and sell protection using a traditional car CDS.
13. The curve trade that would *best* capitalize on Chan's view of the US credit curve is to:
    A. buy protection using a 20-year CDX and buy protection using a 2-year CDX.
    B. buy protection using a 20-year CDX and sell protection using a 2-year CDX.
    C. sell protection using a 20-year CDX and buy protection using a 2-year CDX.
14. A profitable equity-versus-credit trade involving Delta and Zega is to:
    A. short Zega shares and buy protection on Delta using the 10-year CDS.
    B. go long Zega shares and buy protection on Delta using 5-year CDS.
    C. go long Delta shares and buy protection on Delta using 5-year CDS.

CHAPTER 6

INTRODUCTION TO COMMODITIES AND COMMODITY DERIVATIVES

LEARNING OUTCOMES

The candidate should be able to:

- compare characteristics of commodity sectors;
- compare the life cycle of commodity sectors from production through trading or consumption;
- contrast the valuation of commodities with the valuation of equities and bonds;
- describe types of participants in commodity futures markets;
- analyze the relationship between spot prices and futures prices in markets in contango and markets in backwardation;
- compare theories of commodity futures returns;
- describe, calculate, and interpret the components of total return for a fully collateralized commodity futures contract;
- contrast roll return in markets in contango and markets in backwardation;
- describe how commodity swaps are used to obtain or modify exposure to commodities;
- describe how the construction of commodity indexes affects index returns.

SUMMARY OVERVIEW

- Commodities are a diverse asset class comprising various sectors: energy, grains, industrial (base) metals, livestock, precious metals, and softs (cash crops). Each of these sectors has a number of characteristics that are important in determining the supply and demand for each commodity, including ease of storage, geopolitics, and weather.

- Fundamental analysis of commodities relies on analyzing supply and demand for each of the products as well as estimating the reaction to the inevitable shocks to their equilibrium or underlying direction.
- The life cycle of commodities varies considerably depending on the economic, technical, and structural (i.e., industry, value chain) profile of each commodity as well as the sector. A short life cycle allows for relatively rapid adjustment to outside events, whereas a long life cycle generally limits the ability of the market to react.
- The valuation of commodities relative to that of equities and bonds can be summarized by noting that equities and bonds represent financial assets whereas commodities are physical assets. The valuation of commodities is not based on the estimation of future profitability and cash flows but rather on a discounted forecast of future possible prices based on such factors as the supply and demand of the physical item.
- The commodity trading environment is similar to other asset classes, with three types of trading participants: (1) informed investors/hedgers, (2) speculators, and (3) arbitrageurs.
- Commodities have two general pricing forms: spot prices in the physical markets and futures prices for later delivery. The spot price is the current price to deliver or purchase a physical commodity at a specific location. A futures price is an exchange-based price agreed on to deliver or receive a defined quantity and often quality of a commodity at a future date.
- The difference between spot and futures prices is generally called the basis. When the spot price is higher than the futures price, it is called backwardation, and when it is lower, it is called contango. Backwardation and contango are also used to describe the relationship between two futures contracts of the same commodity.
- Commodity contracts can be settled by either cash or physical delivery.
- There are three primary theories of futures returns.
  - In insurance theory, commodity producers who are long the physical good are motived to sell the commodity for future delivery to hedge their production price risk exposure.
  - The hedging pressure hypothesis describes when producers along with consumers seek to protect themselves from commodity market price volatility by entering into price hedges to stabilize their projected profits and cash flow.
  - The theory of storage focuses on supply and demand dynamics of commodity inventories, including the concept of "convenience yield."
- The total return of a fully collateralized commodity futures contract can be quantified as the spot price return plus the roll return plus the collateral return (risk-free rate return).
- The roll return is effectively the weighted accounting difference (in percentage terms) between the near-term commodity futures contract price and the farther-term commodity futures contract price.
- A commodity swap is a legal contract between two parties calling for the exchange of payments over multiple dates as determined by several reference prices or indexes.
- The most relevant commodity swaps include excess return swaps, total return swaps, basis swaps, and variance/volatility swaps.
- The five primary commodity indexes based on assets are (1) the S&P GSCI; (2) the Bloomberg Commodity Index, formerly the Dow Jones–UBS Commodity Index; (3) the Deutsche Bank Liquid Commodity Index; (4) the Thomson Reuters/CoreCommodity CRB Index; and (5) the Rogers International Commodities Index.
- The key differentiating characteristics of commodity indexes are
  - the breadth and selection methodology of coverage (number of commodities and sectors) included in each index, noting that some commodities have multiple reference contracts,

- the relative weightings assigned to each component/commodity and the related methodology for how these weights are determined,
- the methodology and frequency for rolling the individual futures contracts,
- the methodology and frequency for rebalancing the weights of the individual commodities and sectors, and
- the governance that determines which commodities are selected.

PROBLEMS

The following information relates to Questions 1–8

Raffi Musicale is the portfolio manager for a defined benefit pension plan. He meets with Jenny Brown, market strategist with Menlo Bank, to discuss possible investment opportunities. The investment committee for the pension plan has recently approved expanding the plan's permitted asset mix to include alternative asset classes.

Brown proposes the Apex Commodity Fund (Apex Fund) offered by Menlo Bank as a potentially suitable investment for the pension plan. The Apex Fund attempts to produce trading profits by capitalizing on the mispricing between the spot and futures prices of commodities. The fund has access to storage facilities, allowing it to take delivery of commodities when necessary. The Apex Fund's current asset allocation is presented in Exhibit 1.

EXHIBIT 1   Apex Fund's Asset Allocation

Commodity Sector	Allocation (%)
Energy	31.9
Livestock	12.6
Softs	21.7
Precious metals	33.8

Brown explains that the Apex Fund has had historically low correlations with stocks and bonds, resulting in diversification benefits. Musicale asks Brown, "Can you identify a factor that affects the valuation of financial assets like stocks and bonds but does not affect the valuation of commodities?"

Brown shares selected futures contract data for three markets in which the Apex Fund invests. The futures data are presented in Exhibit 2.

EXHIBIT 2   Selected Commodity Futures Data*

Month	Gold Price	Coffee Price	Gasoline Price
July	1,301.2	0.9600	2.2701
September	1,301.2	0.9795	2.2076
December	1,301.2	1.0055	2.0307

* Gold: US$/troy ounce; coffee: US$/pound; gasoline: US$/gallon.

Menlo Bank recently released a report on the coffee market. Brown shares the key conclusion from the report with Musicale: "The coffee market had a global harvest that was greater than expected. Despite the large harvest, coffee futures trading activity is balanced between producers and consumers. This balanced condition is not expected to change over the next year."

Brown shows Musicale the total return of a recent trade executed by the Apex Fund. Brown explains that the Apex Fund took a fully collateralized long futures position in nearby soybean futures contracts at the quoted futures price of 865.0 (US cents/bushel). Three months later, the entire futures position was rolled when the near-term futures price was 877.0 and the farther-term futures price was 883.0. During the three-month period between the time that the initial long position was taken and the rolling of the contract, the collateral earned an annualized rate of 0.60%.

Brown tells Musicale that the pension fund could alternatively gain long exposure to commodities using the swap market. Brown and Musicale analyze the performance of a long position in an S&P GSCI total return swap having monthly resets and a notional amount of $25 million. Selected data on the S&P GSCI are presented in Exhibit 3.

EXHIBIT 3   Selected S&P GSCI Data

Reference Date	Index Level
April (swap initiation)	2,542.35
May	2,582.23
June	2,525.21

1. The Apex Fund is *most likely* to be characterized as:
   A. a hedger.
   B. a speculator.
   C. an arbitrageur.
2. Which factor would *most likely* affect the supply or demand of all four sectors of the Apex Fund?
   A. Weather
   B. Spoilage
   C. Government actions
3. The *most appropriate* response to Musicale's question regarding the valuation factor is:
   A. storage costs.
   B. transportation costs.
   C. expected future cash flows.
4. Which futures market in Exhibit 2 is in backwardation?
   A. Gold
   B. Coffee
   C. Gasoline
5. Based on the key conclusion from the Menlo Bank coffee market report, the shape of the coffee futures curve in Exhibit 2 is *most consistent* with the:
   A. insurance theory.
   B. theory of storage.
   C. hedging pressure hypothesis.
6. Based on Exhibit 2, which commodity's roll returns will *most likely* be positive?
   A. Gold
   B. Coffee
   C. Gasoline

7. The Apex Fund's three-month total return on the soybean futures trade is *closest* to:
    A. 0.85%.
    B. 1.30%.
    C. 2.22%.
8. Based on Exhibit 3, on the June settlement date, the party that is long the S&P GSCI total return swap will:
    A. owe a payment of $552,042.23.
    B. receive a payment of $1,502,621.33.
    C. receive a payment of $1,971,173.60.

The following information relates to Questions 9–15

Jamal Nabli is a portfolio manager at NextWave Commodities (NWC), a commodity-based hedge fund located in the United States. NWC's strategy uses a fixed-weighting scheme to allocate exposure among 12 commodities, and it is benchmarked against the Thomson Reuters/CoreCommodity CRB Index (TR/CC CRB). Nabli manages the energy and livestock sectors with the help of Sota Yamata, a junior analyst.

Nabli and Yamata meet to discuss a variety of factors that affect commodity values in the two sectors they manage. Yamata tells Nabli the following:

Statement 1:   Storage costs are negatively related to futures prices.
Statement 2:   In contrast to stocks and bonds, most commodity investments are made by using derivatives.
Statement 3:   Commodities generate future cash flows beyond what can be realized through their purchase and sale.

Nabli and Yamata then discuss potential new investments in the energy sector. They review Brent crude oil futures data, which are presented in Exhibit 1.

Yamata presents his research related to the energy sector, which has the following conclusions:

EXHIBIT 1   Selected Data on Brent Crude Oil Futures

Spot Price	Near-Term Futures Price	Longer-Term Futures Price
77.56	73.64	73.59

- Consumers have been more concerned about prices than producers have.
- Energy is consumed on a real-time basis and requires minimal storage.

After concluding the discussion of the energy sector, Nabli reviews the performance of NWC's long position in lean hog futures contracts. Nabli notes that the portfolio earned a −12% price return on the lean hog futures position last year and a −24% roll return after the contracts were rolled forward. The position was held with collateral equal to 100% of the position at a risk-free rate of 1.2% per year.

Yamata asks Nabli to clarify how the state of the futures market affects roll returns. Nabli responds as follows:

Statement 4:   Roll returns are generally negative when a futures market is in contango.
Statement 5:   Roll returns are generally positive when a futures market is in backwardation.

As part of their expansion into new markets, NWC is considering changing its benchmark index. Nabli investigates two indexes as a possible replacement. These indexes both use similar weighting and rebalancing schemes. Index A includes contracts of commodities typically in contango, whereas Index B includes contracts of commodities typically in backwardation. Nabli asks Yamata how the two indexes perform relative to each other in a market that is trending upward.

Because of a substantial decline in drilling activity in the North Sea, Nabli believes the price of Brent crude oil will increase more than that of heavy crude oil. The actual price volatility of Brent crude oil has been lower than its expected volatility, and Nabli expects this trend to continue. Nabli also expects the level of the ICE Brent Index to increase from its current level. Nabli and Yamata discuss how to use swaps to take advantage of Nabli's expectations. The possible positions are (1) a basis swap long on Brent crude oil and short on heavy crude oil, (2) a long volatility swap on Brent crude oil, and (3) a short position in an excess return swap that is based on a fixed level (i.e., the current level) of the ICE Brent Index.

9. Which of Nabli's statements regarding the valuation and storage of commodities is correct?
    A. Statement 1
    B. Statement 2
    C. Statement 3
10. Based on Exhibit 1, Yamata should conclude that the:
    A. calendar spread for Brent crude oil is $3.97.
    B. Brent crude oil futures market is in backwardation.
    C. basis for the near-term Brent crude oil futures contract is $0.05 per barrel.
11. Based on Exhibit 1 and Yamata's research on the energy sector, the shape of the futures price curve for Brent crude oil is most consistent with the:
    A. insurance theory.
    B. theory of storage.
    C. hedging pressure hypothesis.
12. The total return (annualized excluding leverage) on the lean hog futures contract is:
    A. −37.2%.
    B. −36.0%.
    C. −34.8%.
13. Which of Nabli's statements about roll returns is correct?
    A. Only Statement 4
    B. Only Statement 5
    C. Both Statement 4 and Statement 5
14. The *best* response to Nabli's question about the relative performance of the two indexes is that Index B is *most likely* to exhibit returns that are:
    A. lower than those of Index A.
    B. the same as those of Index A.
    C. higher than those of index A.
15. Given Nabli's expectations for crude oil, the *most appropriate* swap position is the:
    A. basis swap.
    B. volatility swap.
    C. excess return swap.

The following information relates to Questions 16–22

Mary McNeil is the corporate treasurer at Farmhouse, which owns and operates several farms and ethanol production plants in the United States. McNeil's primary responsibility is risk management. Katrina Falk, a recently hired junior analyst at Farmhouse, works for McNeil in managing the risk of the firm's commodity price exposures. Farmhouse's risk management policy requires the use of futures to protect revenue from price volatility, regardless of forecasts of future prices, and prohibits risk managers from taking speculative positions.

McNeil meets with Falk to discuss recent developments in two of Farmhouse's commodity markets, grains and livestock. McNeil asks Falk about key characteristics of the two markets that affect revenues and costs. Falk tells McNeil the following:

Statement 1: The life cycle for livestock depends on the product and varies widely by product.

Statement 2: Grains have uniform, well-defined seasons and growth cycles specific to geographic regions.

A material portion of Farmhouse's revenue comes from livestock exports, and a major input cost is the cost of grains imported from outside the United States. Falk and McNeil next discuss three conclusions that Falk reached in an analysis of the grains and livestock markets:

Conclusion 1: Assuming demand for grains remains constant, extreme heat in the regions from which we import our grains will result in a benefit to us in the form of lower grain prices.

Conclusion 2: New tariffs on cattle introduced in our primary export markets will likely result in higher prices for our livestock products in our local market.

Conclusion 3: Major improvements in freezing technology allowing for longer storage will let us better manage the volatility in the prices of our livestock products.

McNeil asks Falk to gather spot and futures price data on live cattle, wheat, and soybeans, which are presented in Exhibit 1. Additionally, she observes that (1) the convenience yield of soybeans exceeds the costs of its direct storage and (2) commodity producers as a group are less interested in hedging in the forward market than commodity consumers are.

EXHIBIT 1   Selected Commodity Price Data*

Market	Live Cattle Price	Wheat Price	Soybeans Price
Spot	109	407	846
Futures	108	407	850

* Live cattle: US cents per pound; wheat and soybeans: US cents per bushel.

A key input cost for Farmhouse in producing ethanol is natural gas. McNeil uses positions in natural gas (NG) futures contracts to manage the risk of natural gas price volatility. Three months ago, she entered into a long position in natural gas futures at a futures price of $2.93 per million British thermal units (MMBtu). The current price of the same contract is $2.99. Exhibit 2 presents additional data about the three-month futures position.

EXHIBIT 2   Selected Information—Natural Gas Futures Three-Month Position*

| | | | Prices | |
| | Total Current $ | | Near-Term Futures | Farther-Term |
Commodity	Exposure	Position	(Current Price)	Futures
Natural Gas (NG)	5,860,000	Long	2.99	3.03

* NG: $ per MMBtu; 1 contract = 10,000 MMBtu.

The futures position is fully collateralized earning a 3% rate. McNeil decides to roll forward her current exposure in the natural gas position.

Each month, McNeil reports the performance of the energy futures positions, including details on price returns, roll returns, and collateral returns, to the firm's executive committee. A new committee member is concerned about the negative roll returns on some of the positions. In a memo to McNeil, the committee member asks her to explain why she is not avoiding positions with negative roll returns.

16. With respect to its risk management policy, Farmhouse can be *best* described as:
    A. a trader.
    B. a hedger.
    C. an arbitrageur.
17. Which of Falk's statements regarding the characteristics of the grains and livestock markets is correct?
    A. Only Statement 1
    B. Only Statement 2
    C. Both Statement 1 and Statement 2
18. Which of Falk's conclusions regarding commodity markets is correct?
    A. Conclusion 1
    B. Conclusion 2
    C. Conclusion 3
19. Which commodity market in Exhibit 1 is currently in a state of contango?
    A. Wheat
    B. Soybeans
    C. Live cattle
20. Based on Exhibit 1 and McNeil's two observations, the futures price of soybeans is *most* consistent with the:
    A. insurance theory.
    B. theory of storage.
    C. hedging pressure hypothesis.
21. Based on Exhibit 2, the total return from the long position in natural gas futures is *closest* to:
    A. 1.46%.
    B. 3.71%.
    C. 4.14%.
22. The *most appropriate* response to the new committee member's question is that:
    A. roll returns are negatively correlated with price returns.
    B. such roll returns are the result of futures markets in backwardation.
    C. such positions may outperform other positions that have positive roll returns.

CHAPTER 7

CURRENCY MANAGEMENT: AN INTRODUCTION

LEARNING OUTCOMES

The candidate should be able to:

- analyze the effects of currency movements on portfolio risk and return;
- discuss strategic choices in currency management;
- formulate an appropriate currency management program given financial market conditions and portfolio objectives and constraints;
- compare active currency trading strategies based on economic fundamentals, technical analysis, carry-trade, and volatility trading;
- describe how changes in factors underlying active trading strategies affect tactical trading decisions;
- describe how forward contracts and FX (foreign exchange) swaps are used to adjust hedge ratios;
- describe trading strategies used to reduce hedging costs and modify the risk–return characteristics of a foreign-currency portfolio;
- describe the use of cross-hedges, macro-hedges, and minimum-variance-hedge ratios in portfolios exposed to multiple foreign currencies;
- discuss challenges for managing emerging market currency exposures.

SUMMARY OVERVIEW

In this reading, we have examined the basic principles of managing foreign exchange risk within the broader investment process. International financial markets create a wide range of opportunities for investors, but they also create the need to recognize, measure, and control exchange rate risk. The management of this risk starts with setting the overall mandate for the portfolio, encoding the investors' investment objectives and constraints into the investment policy statement and providing strategic guidance on how currency risk will be managed in the portfolio. It extends to tactical positioning when portfolio managers translate market views into specific trading strategies within the overall risk management guidelines set by the IPS. We have examined some of these trading strategies, and how a range of portfolio management tools—positions in spot, forward, option, and FX swap contracts—can be used either to hedge away currency risk, or to express a market opinion on future exchange rate movements.

What we have emphasized throughout this reading is that there is no simple or single answer for the "best" currency management strategies. Different investors will have different strategic mandates (IPS), and different portfolio managers will have different market opinions and risk tolerances. There is a near-infinite number of possible currency trading strategies, each with its own benefits, costs, and risks. Currency risk management—both at the strategic and tactical levels—means having to manage the trade-offs between all of these various considerations.

Some of the main points covered in this reading are as follows:

- In professional FX markets, currencies are identified by standard three-letter codes, and quoted in terms of a price and a base currency (P/B).
- The spot exchange rate is typically for $T + 2$ delivery, and forward rates are for delivery for later periods. Both spot and forward rates are quoted in terms of a bid–offer price. Forward rates are quoted in terms of the spot rate plus forward points.
- An FX swap is a simultaneous spot and forward transaction; one leg of the swap is buying the base currency and the other is selling it. FX swaps are used to renew outstanding forward contracts once they mature, to "roll them forward."
- The domestic-currency return on foreign-currency assets can be broken into the foreign-currency asset return and the return on the foreign currency (the percentage appreciation or depreciation of the foreign currency against the domestic currency). These two components of the domestic-currency return are multiplicative.
- When there are several foreign-currency assets, the portfolio domestic-currency return is the weighted average of the individual domestic-currency returns (i.e., using the portfolio weights, which should sum to one).
- The risk of domestic-currency returns (its standard deviation) can be approximated by using a variance formula that recognizes the individual variances and covariances (correlations) among the foreign-currency asset returns and exchange rate movements.
- The calculation of the domestic-currency risk involves a large number of variables that must be estimated: the risks and correlations between all of the foreign-currency asset returns and their exchange rate risks.
- Guidance on where to target the portfolio along the risk spectrum is part of the IPS, which makes this a *strategic* decision based on the investment goals and constraints of the beneficial owners of the portfolio.
- If the IPS allows currency risk in the portfolio, the amount of desired currency exposure will depend on both portfolio diversification considerations and cost considerations.
  - Views on the diversifying effects of foreign-currency exposures depend on the time horizon involved, the type of foreign-currency asset, and market conditions.
  - Cost considerations also affect the hedging decision. Hedging is not free: It has both direct transactional costs as well as opportunity costs (the potential for favorable outcomes is foregone). Cost considerations make a perfect hedge difficult to maintain.

- Currency management strategies can be located along a spectrum stretching from:
  - passive, rules-based, complete hedging of currency exposures;
  - discretionary hedging, which allows the portfolio manager some latitude on managing currency exposures;
  - active currency management, which seeks out currency risk in order to manage it for profit; and to
  - currency overlay programs that aggressively manage currency "alpha."
- There are a variety of methods for forming market views.
  - The use of macroeconomic fundamentals to predict future currency movements is based on estimating the "fair value" for a currency with the expectation that spot rates will eventually converge on this equilibrium value.
  - Technical market indicators assume that, based on market psychology, historical price patterns in the data have a tendency to repeat. Technical indicators can be used to predict support and resistance levels in the market, as well as to confirm market trends and turning points.
  - The carry trade is based on violations of uncovered interest rate parity, and is also based on selling low-yield currencies in order to invest in high-yield currencies. This approach is equivalent to trading the forward rate bias, which means selling currencies trading at a forward premium and buying currencies trading at a forward discount.
  - Volatility trading uses the option market to express views on the distribution of future exchange rates, not their levels.
- Passive hedging will typically use forward contracts (rather than futures contracts) because they are more flexible. However, currency futures contracts are an option for smaller trading sizes and are frequently used in private wealth management.
- Forward contracts have the possibility of negative roll yield (the forward points embedded in the forward price can work for or against the hedge). The portfolio manager will have to balance the advantages and costs of hedging with forward contracts.
- Foreign-currency options can reduce opportunity costs (they allow the upside potential for favorable foreign-currency movements). However, the upfront option premiums must be paid.
- There are a variety of means to reduce the cost of the hedging with either forward or option contracts, but these cost-reduction measures always involve some combination of less downside protection and/or less upside potential.
- Hedging multiple foreign currencies uses the same tools and strategies used in hedging a single foreign-currency exposure; except now the correlation between residual currency exposures in the portfolio should be considered.
- Cross hedges introduce basis risk into the portfolio, which is the risk that the correlation between exposure and its cross hedging instrument may change in unexpected ways. Forward contracts typically have very little basis risk compared with movements in the underlying spot rate.
- The number of trading strategies that can be used, for hedging or speculative purposes, either for a single foreign currency or multiple foreign currencies, is near infinite. The manager must assess the costs, benefits, and risks of each in the context of the investment goals and constraints of the portfolio. There is no single "correct" approach.

PROBLEMS

The following information relates to Questions 1–9

Kamala Gupta, a currency management consultant, is hired to evaluate the performance of two portfolios. Portfolio A and Portfolio B are managed in the United States and performance is measured in terms of the US dollar (USD). Portfolio A consists of British pound (GBP) denominated bonds and Portfolio B holds euro (EUR) denominated bonds.

Gupta calculates a 19.5% domestic-currency return for Portfolio A and 0% domestic-currency return for Portfolio B.

1. **Analyze** the movement of the USD against the foreign currency for Portfolio A. **Justify** your choice.

Template for Question 1

Asset	Foreign-Currency Portfolio Return	USD Relative to Foreign-Currency (circle one)
Portfolio A	15%	Appreciated
		Depreciated

Justification

2. **Analyze** the foreign-currency return for Portfolio B. **Justify** your choice.

Template for Question 2

Asset	Percentage Movement in the Spot Exchange Rate	Foreign-Currency Portfolio Return (circle one)
Portfolio B	EUR appreciated 5% against the USD	Positive
		Negative

Justification

The fund manager of Portfolio B is evaluating an internally-managed 100% foreign-currency hedged strategy.

3. **Discuss** *two* forms of trading costs associated with this currency management strategy.
    Gupta tells the fund manager of Portfolio B:

    "We need to seriously consider the potential costs associated with favorable currency rate movements, given that a 100% hedge-ratio strategy is being applied to this portfolio."

4. **Explain** Gupta's statement in light of the strategic choices in currency management available to the portfolio manager.
    The investment policy statement (IPS) for Portfolio A provides the manager with discretionary authority to take directional views on future currency movements. The fund manager believes the foreign currency assets of the portfolio could be fully hedged internally. However, the manager also believes existing firm personnel lack the expertise to actively manage foreign-currency movements to generate currency alpha.

5. **Recommend** a solution that will provide the fund manager the opportunity to earn currency alpha through active foreign exchange management.
    Gupta and the fund manager of Portfolio A discuss the differences among several active currency management methods.

6. **Evaluate** each statement independently and select the active currency approach it *best* describes. **Justify** each choice.

Template for Question 6

Gupta's Statements	Active Currency Approach (circle one)	Justification
"Many traders believe that it is not necessary to examine factors like the current account deficit, inflation, and interest rates because current exchange rates already reflect the market view on how these factors will affect future exchange rates."	Carry trade Technical analysis Economic fundamental	
"The six-month interest rate in India is 8% compared to 1% in the United States. This presents a yield pick-up opportunity."	Carry trade Technical analysis Economic fundamental	
"The currency overlay manager will estimate the fair value of the currencies with the expectation that observed spot rates will converge to long-run equilibrium values described by parity conditions."	Carry trade Technical analysis Economic fundamental	

The following information is used for Question 7

Gupta interviews a currency overlay manager on behalf of Portfolio A. The foreign currency overlay manager describes volatility-based trading, compares volatility-based trading strategies and explains how the firm uses currency options to establish positions in the foreign exchange market. The overlay manager states:

Statement 1: "Given the current stability in financial markets, several traders at our firm take advantage of the fact that most options expire out-of-the money and therefore are net-short volatility."

Statement 2: "Traders that want to minimize the impact of unanticipated price volatility are net-long volatility."

7. **Compare** Statement 1 and Statement 2 and **identify** which *best* explains the view of a speculative volatility trader and which best explains the view of a hedger of volatility. **Justify** your response.

The following information is used for Questions 8 and 9

The fund manager of Portfolio B believes that setting up a full currency hedge requires a simple matching of the *current* market value of the foreign-currency exposure in the portfolio with an equal and offsetting position in a forward contract.

8. **Explain** how the hedge, as described by the fund manager, will eventually expose the portfolio to currency risk.
9. **Recommend** an alternative hedging strategy that will keep the hedge ratio close to the target hedge ratio. **Identify** the main disadvantage of implementing such a strategy.

The following information relates to Questions 10–15

Guten Investments GmbH, based in Germany and using the EUR as its reporting currency, is an asset management firm providing investment services for local high net worth and institutional investors seeking international exposures. The firm invests in the Swiss, UK, and US markets, after conducting fundamental research in order to select individual investments. Exhibit 1 presents recent information for exchange rates in these foreign markets.

EXHIBIT 1   Exchange Rate Data

	One Year Ago	Today
Euro-dollar (USD/EUR)*	1.2730	1.2950
Euro-sterling (GBP/EUR)	0.7945	0.8050
Euro-Swiss (CHF/EUR)	1.2175	1.2080

* The amount of USD required to buy one EUR

In prior years, the correlation between movements in the foreign-currency asset returns for the USD-denominated assets and movements in the exchange rate was estimated to be +0.50. After analyzing global financial markets, Konstanze Ostermann, a portfolio manager at Guten Investments, now expects that this correlation will increase to +0.80, although her forecast for foreign-currency asset returns is unchanged.

Ostermann believes that currency markets are efficient and hence that long-run gains cannot be achieved from active currency management, especially after netting out management and transaction costs. She uses this philosophy to guide hedging decisions for her discretionary accounts, unless instructed otherwise by the client.

Ostermann is aware, however, that some investors hold an alternative view on the merits of active currency management. Accordingly, their portfolios have different investment guidelines. For these accounts, Guten Investments employs a currency specialist firm, Umlauf Management, to provide currency overlay programs specific to each client's investment objectives. For most hedging strategies, Umlauf Management develops a market view based on underlying fundamentals in exchange rates. However, when directed by clients, Umlauf Management uses options and a variety of trading strategies to unbundle all of the various risk factors (the "Greeks") and trade them separately.

Ostermann conducts an annual review for three of her clients and gathers the summary information presented in Exhibit 2.

EXHIBIT 2   Select Clients at Guten Investments

Client	Currency Management Objectives
Adele Kastner – A high net worth individual with a low risk tolerance.	Keep the portfolio's currency exposures close, if not equal to, the benchmark so that the domestic-currency return is equal to the foreign-currency return.
Braunt Pensionskasse – A large private-company pension fund with a moderate risk tolerance.	Limited discretion which allows the actual portfolio currency risk exposures to vary plus-or-minus 5% from the neutral position.
Franz Trading GmbH – An exporting company with a high risk tolerance.	Discretion with respect to currency exposure is allowed in order to add alpha to the portfolio.

10. Based on Exhibit 1, the domestic-currency return over the last year (measured in EUR terms) was *higher* than the foreign-currency return for:
    A. USD-denominated assets.
    B. GBP-denominated assets.
    C. CHF-denominated assets.
11. Based on Ostermann's correlation forecast, the expected domestic-currency return (measured in EUR terms) on USD-denominated assets will *most* likely:
    A. increase.
    B. decrease.
    C. remain unchanged.
12. Based on Ostermann's views regarding active currency management, the percentage of currency exposure in her discretionary accounts that is hedged is *most likely:*
    A. 0%.
    B. 50%.
    C. 100%.
13. The active currency management approach that Umlauf Management is *least* likely to employ is based on:
    A. volatility trading.
    B. technical analysis.
    C. economic fundamentals.
14. Based on Exhibit 2, the currency overlay program *most* appropriate for Braunt Pensionskasse would:
    A. be fully passive.
    B. allow limited directional views.
    C. actively manage foreign exchange as an asset class.

15. Based on Exhibit 2, the client *most likely* to benefit from the introduction of an additional overlay manager is:
    A. Adele Kastner.
    B. Braunt Pensionskasse.
    C. Franz Trading GmbH.

The following information relates to Questions 16–19

Li Jiang is an international economist operating a subscription website through which she offers financial advice on currency issues to retail investors. One morning she receives four subscriber e-mails seeking guidance.

Subscriber 1	"As a French national now working in the United States, I hold US dollar-denominated assets currently valued at USD 700,000. The USD/EUR exchange rate has been quite volatile and now appears oversold based on historical price trends. With my American job ending soon, I will return to Europe. I want to protect the value of my USD holdings, measured in EUR terms, before I repatriate these funds back to France. To reduce my currency exposure I am going to use currency futures contracts. Can you explain the factors most relevant to implementing this strategy?"
Subscriber 2	"I have observed that many of the overseas markets for Korean export goods are slowing, while the United States is experiencing a rise in exports. Both trends can combine to possibly affect the value of the won (KRW) relative to the US dollar. As a result, I am considering a speculative currency trade on the KRW/USD exchange rate. I also expect the volatility in this exchange rate to increase."
Subscriber 3	"India has relatively high interest rates compared to the United States and my market view is that this situation is likely to persist. As a retail investor actively trading currencies, I am considering borrowing in USD and converting to the Indian rupee (INR). I then intend to invest these funds in INR-denominated bonds, but without using a currency hedge."
Subscriber 4	"I was wondering if trading in emerging market currencies provides the more opportunities for superior returns through active management than trading in Developed Market currencies."

16. For Subscriber 1, the *most* significant factor to consider would be:
    A. margin requirements.
    B. transaction costs of using futures contracts.
    C. different quoting conventions for future contracts.
17. For Subscriber 2, and assuming all of the choices relate to the KRW/USD exchange rate, the *best* way to implement the trading strategy would be to:
    A. write a straddle.
    B. buy a put option.
    C. use a long NDF position.

18. Which of the following market developments would be *most* favorable for Subscriber 3's trading plan?
    A. A narrower interest rate differential.
    B. A higher forward premium for INR/USD.
    C. Higher volatility in INR/USD spot rate movements.
19. Jiang's *best* response to Subscriber 4 would be that active trading in trading in emerging market currencies:
    A. typically leads to return distributions that are positively skewed.
    B. should not lead to higher returns because FX markets are efficient.
    C. often leads to higher returns through carry trades, but comes with higher risks and trading costs.

The following information relates to Questions 20–23

Rika Björk runs the currency overlay program at a large Scandinavian investment fund, which uses the Swedish krona (SEK) as its reporting currency. She is managing the fund's exposure to GBP-denominated assets, which are currently hedged with a GBP 100,000,000 forward contract (on the SEK/GBP cross rate, which is currently at 10.6875 spot). The maturity for the forward contract is December 1, which is still several months away. However, since the contract was initiated the value of the fund's assets has declined by GBP 7,000,000. As a result, Björk wants to rebalance the hedge immediately.

Next Björk turns her attention to the fund's Swiss franc (CHF) exposures. In order to maintain some profit potential Björk wants to hedge the exposure using a currency option, but at the same time, she wants to reduce hedging costs. She believes that there is limited upside for the SEK/CHF cross rate.

Björk then examines the fund's EUR-denominated exposures. Due to recent monetary tightening by the Riksbank (the Swedish central bank) forward points for the SEK/EUR rate have swung to a premium. The fund's EUR-denominated exposures are hedged with forward contracts.

Finally Björk turns her attention to the fund's currency exposures in several emerging markets. The fund has large positions in several Latin American bond markets, but Björk does not feel that there is sufficient liquidity in the related foreign exchange derivatives to easily hedge the fund's Latin American bond markets exposures. However, the exchange rates for these countries, measured against the SEK, are correlated with the MXN/SEK exchange rate. (The MXN is the Mexican peso, which is considered to be among the most liquid Latin American currencies). Björk considers using forward positions in the MXN to cross-hedge the fund's Latin American currency exposures.

20. To rebalance the SEK/GBP hedge, and assuming all instruments are based on SEK/GBP, Björk would buy:
    A. GBP 7,000,000 spot.
    B. GBP 7,000,000 forward to December 1.
    C. SEK 74,812,500 forward to December 1.
21. Given her investment goals and market view, and assuming all options are based on SEK/ CHF, the *best* strategy for Björk to manage the fund's CHF exposure would be to buy an:
    A. ATM call option.
    B. ITM call option and write an OTM call option.
    C. OTM put option and write an OTM call option.

22. Given the recent movement in the forward premium for the SEK/EUR rate, Björk can expect that the hedge will experience higher:
    A. basis risk.
    B. roll yield.
    C. premia income.
23. The *most* important risk to Björk's Latin American currency hedge would be changes in:
    A. forward points.
    B. exchange rate volatility.
    C. cross-currency correlations.

The following information relates to Question 24

Kalila Al-Khalili has been hired as a consultant to a Middle Eastern sovereign wealth fund. The fund's oversight committee has asked her to examine the fund's financial characteristics and recommend an appropriate currency management strategy given the fund's Investment Policy Statement. After a thorough study of the fund and its finances, Al-Khalili reaches the following conclusions:

- The fund's mandate is focused on the long-term development of the country, and the royal family (who are very influential on the fund's oversight committee) are prepared to take a long-term perspective on the fund's investments.
- The fund's strategic asset allocation is tilted towards equity rather than fixed-income assets.
- Both its fixed-income and equity portfolios have a sizeable exposure to emerging market assets.
- Currently, about 90% of exchange rate exposures are hedged although the IPS allows a range of hedge ratios.
- Liquidity needs of the fund are minimal, since the government is running a balanced budget and is unlikely to need to dip into the fund in the near term to cover fiscal deficits. Indeed, the expected lifetime of country's large oil reserves has been greatly extended by recent discoveries, and substantial oil royalties are expected to persist into the future.

24. Based on her investigation, Al-Khalili would *most* likely recommend:
    A. active currency management.
    B. a hedging ratio closer to 100%.
    C. a narrow discretionary band for currency exposures.

The following information relates to Questions 25–27

Mason Darden is an adviser at Colgate & McIntire (C&M), managing large-cap global equity separate accounts. C&M's investment process restricts portfolio positions to companies based in the United States, Japan, and the eurozone. All C&M clients are US-domiciled, with client reporting in US dollars.

Darden manages Ravi Bhatt's account, which had a total (US dollar) return of 7.0% last year. Darden must assess the contribution of foreign currency to the account's total return. Exhibit 1 summarizes the account's geographic portfolio weights, asset returns, and currency returns for last year.

EXHIBIT 1   Performance Data for Bhatt's Portfolio Last Year

Geography	Portfolio Weight	Asset Return	Currency Return
United States	50%	10.0%	NA
Eurozone	25%	5.0%	2.0%
Japan	25%	–3.0%	4.0%
Total	100%		

25. **Calculate** the contribution of foreign currency to the Bhatt account's total return. **Show** your calculations.

Darden meets with Bhatt and learns that Bhatt will be moving back to his home country of India next month to resume working as a commodity trader. Bhatt is concerned about a possible US recession. His investment policy statement (IPS) allows for flexibility in managing currency risk. Overall returns can be enhanced by capturing opportunities between the US dollar and the Indian rupee (INR) within a range of plus or minus 25% from the neutral position using forward contracts on the currency pair. C&M has a currency overlay team that can appropriately manage currency risk for Bhatt's portfolio.

26. **Determine** the *most appropriate* currency management strategy for Bhatt. **Justify** your response.

Determine the *most appropriate* currency management strategy for Bhatt. (Circle one.)

Passive hedging	Discretionary hedging	Active currency management

Justify your response.

Following analysis of Indian economic fundamentals, C&M's currency team expects continued stability in interest rate and inflation rate differentials between the United States and India. C&M's currency team strongly believes the US dollar will appreciate relative to the Indian rupee.

C&M would like to exploit the perceived alpha opportunity using forward contracts on the USD10,000,000 Bhatt portfolio.

27. **Recommend** the trading strategy C&M should implement. **Justify** your response.

The following information relates to Questions 28–29

Renita Murimi is a currency overlay manager and market technician who serves institutional investors seeking to address currency-specific risks associated with investing in international assets. Her firm also provides volatility overlay programs. She is developing a volatility-based strategy for Emil Konev, a hedge fund manager focused on option trading. Konev seeks to implement an "FX as an asset class" approach distinct to his portfolio to realize speculative gains and believes the long-term strength of the US dollar is peaking.

28. **Describe** how a volatility-based strategy for Konev would *most likely* contrast with Murimi's other institutional investors. **Justify** your response.

29. **Discuss** how Murimi can use her technical skills to devise the strategy.

30. Carnoustie Capital Management, Ltd. (CCM), a UK-based global investment advisory firm, is considering adding an emerging market currency product to its offerings. CCM has for the past three years managed a "model" portfolio of emerging market currencies using the same investment approach as its developed economy currency products. The risk and return measures of the "model" portfolio compare favorably with the one- and three-year emerging market benchmark performance net of CCM's customary advisory fee and estimated trading costs. Mindful of the higher volatility of emerging market currencies, CCM management is particularly pleased with the "model" portfolio's standard deviation, Sharpe ratio, and value at risk (VAR) in comparison to those of its developed economy products.

Recognizing that market conditions have been stable since the "model" portfolio's inception, CCM management is sensitive to the consequences of extreme market events for emerging market risk and return.

Evaluate the application of emerging market and developed market investment return probability distributions for CCM's potential new product.

The following information relates to Questions 31–32

Wilson Manufacturing (Wilson) is an Australian institutional client of Ethan Lee, who manages a variety of portfolios across asset classes. Wilson prefers a neutral benchmark over a rules-based approach, with its investment policy statement (IPS) requiring a currency hedge ratio between 97% and 103% to protect against currency risk. Lee has assessed various currency management strategies for Wilson's US dollar-denominated fixed-income portfolio to optimally locate it along the currency risk spectrum. The portfolio is currently in its flat natural neutral position because of Lee's lack of market conviction.

31. **Identify** the *most likely* approach for Lee to optimally locate Wilson's portfolio on the currency risk spectrum, consistent with the IPS. **Justify** your response with *two* reasons supporting the approach.

Identify the *most likely* approach for Lee to optimally locate Wilson's portfolio on the currency risk spectrum, consistent with IPS. (Circle one.)

Passive Hedging	Discretionary Hedging	Active Currency Management	Currency Overlay

Justify your response with *two* reasons supporting the approach.

1.	2.

Lee and Wilson recently completed the annual portfolio review and determined the IPS is too short-term focused and excessively risk averse. Accordingly, the IPS is revised and foreign currency is introduced as a separate asset class. Lee hires an external foreign exchange sub-adviser to implement a currency overlay program, emphasizing that it is important to structure the program so that the currency overlay is allowed in terms of strategic portfolio positioning.

32. **Discuss** a key attribute of the currency overlay that would *increase* the likelihood it would be allowed in terms of strategic portfolio positioning.

The following information relates to Questions 33–35

Rosario Delgado is an investment manager in Spain. Delgado's client, Max Rivera, seeks assistance with his well-diversified investment portfolio denominated in US dollars.

Rivera's reporting currency is the euro, and he is concerned about his US dollar exposure. His portfolio IPS requires monthly rebalancing, at a minimum. The portfolio's market value is USD2.5 million. Given Rivera's risk aversion, Delgado is considering a monthly hedge using either a one-month forward contract or one-month futures contract.

33. **Determine** which type of hedge instrument combination is *most* appropriate for Rivera's situation. **Justify** your selection.

Determine which type of hedge instrument combination is *most* appropriate for Rivera's situation. (Circle one.)

Static Forward	Static Futures	Dynamic Forward	Dynamic Futures

Justify your selection.

Assume Rivera's portfolio was perfectly hedged. It is now time to rebalance the portfolio and roll the currency hedge forward one month. The relevant data for rebalancing are provided in Exhibit 1.

EXHIBIT 1   Portfolio and Relevant Market Data

	One Month Ago	Today
Portfolio value of assets (USD)	2,500,000	2,650,000
USD/EUR spot rate (bid–offer)	0.8913/0.8914	0.8875/0.8876
One-month forward points (bid–offer)	25/30	20/25

34. **Calculate** the net cash flow (in euros) to maintain the desired hedge. **Show** your calculations.

With the US dollar currently trading at a forward premium and US interest rates lower than Spanish rates, Delgado recommends trading against the forward rate bias to earn additional return from a positive roll yield.

35. **Identify** *two* strategies Delgado should use to earn a positive roll yield. **Describe** the specific steps needed to execute each strategy.

Identify *two* strategies Delgado should use to earn a positive roll yield.	**Describe** the specific steps needed to execute *each* strategy.
1.	
2.	

CHAPTER 8

OPTIONS STRATEGIES

LEARNING OUTCOMES

The candidate should be able to:

- demonstrate how an asset's returns may be replicated by using options;
- discuss the investment objective(s), structure, payoff, risk(s), value at expiration, profit, maximum profit, maximum loss, and breakeven underlying price at expiration of a covered call position;
- discuss the investment objective(s), structure, payoff, risk(s), value at expiration, profit, maximum profit, maximum loss, and breakeven underlying price at expiration of a protective put position;
- compare the delta of covered call and protective put positions with the position of being long an asset and short a forward on the underlying asset;
- compare the effect of buying a call on a short underlying position with the effect of selling a put on a short underlying position;
- discuss the investment objective(s), structure, payoffs, risk(s), value at expiration, profit, maximum profit, maximum loss, and breakeven underlying price at expiration of the following option strategies: bull spread, bear spread, straddle, and collar;
- describe uses of calendar spreads;
- discuss volatility skew and smile;
- identify and evaluate appropriate option strategies consistent with given investment objectives;
- demonstrate the use of options to achieve targeted equity risk exposures.

SUMMARY OVERVIEW

This reading on options strategies shows a number of ways in which market participants might use options to enhance returns or to reduce risk to better meet portfolio objectives. The following are the key points.

- Buying a call and writing a put on the same underlying with the same strike price and expiration creates a synthetic long position (i.e., a synthetic long forward position).
- Writing a call and buying a put on the same underlying with the same strike price and expiration creates a synthetic short position (i.e., a synthetic short forward position).
- A synthetic long put position consists of a short stock and long call position in which the call strike price equals the price at which the stock is shorted.
- A synthetic long call position consists of a long stock and long put position in which the put strike price equals the price at which the stock is purchased.
- Delta is the change in an option's price for a change in price of the underlying, all else equal.
- Gamma is the change in an option's delta for a change in price of the underlying, all else equal.
- Vega is the change in an option's price for a change in volatility of the underlying, all else equal.
- Theta is the daily change in an option's price, all else equal.
- A covered call, in which the holder of a stock writes a call giving someone the right to buy the shares, is one of the most common uses of options by individual investors.
- Covered calls can be used to change an investment's risk–reward profile by effectively enhancing yield or reducing/exiting a position when the shares hit a target price.
- A covered call position has a limited maximum return because of the transfer of the right tail of the return distribution to the option buyer.
- The maximum loss of a covered call position is less than the maximum loss of the underlying shares alone, but the covered call carries the potential for an opportunity loss if the underlying shares rise sharply.
- A protective put is the simultaneous holding of a long stock position and a long put on the same asset. The put provides protection or insurance against a price decline.
- The continuous purchase of protective puts maintains the upside potential of the portfolio, while limiting downside volatility. The cost of the puts must be carefully considered, however, because this activity may be expensive. Conversely, the occasional purchase of a protective put to deal with a bearish short-term outlook can be a reasonable risk-reducing strategy.
- The maximum loss with a protective put is limited because the downside risk is transferred to the option writer in exchange for the payment of the option premium.
- With an option spread, an investor buys one option and writes another of the same type. This approach reduces the position cost but caps the maximum payoff.
- A bull spread expresses a bullish view on the underlying and is normally constructed by buying a call option and writing another call option with a higher exercise price (both options have same underlying and same expiry).
- A bear spread expresses a bearish view on the underlying and is normally constructed by buying a put option and writing another put option with a lower exercise price (both options have same underlying and same expiry).
- With either a bull spread or a bear spread, both the maximum gain and the maximum loss are known and limited.

- A long (short) straddle is an option combination in which the investor buys (sells) puts and calls with the same exercise price and expiration date. The long (short) straddle investor expects increased (stable/decreased) volatility and typically requires a large (small/no) price movement in the underlying asset in order to make a profit.
- A collar is an option position in which the investor is long shares of stock and simultaneously writes a call with an exercise price above the current stock price and buys a put with an exercise price below the current stock price. A collar limits the range of investment outcomes by sacrificing upside gain in exchange for providing downside protection.
- A long (short) calendar spread involves buying (selling) a long-dated option and writing (buying) a shorter-dated option of the same type with the same exercise price. A long (short) calendar spread is used when the investment outlook is flat (volatile) in the near term but greater (lesser) return movements are expected in the future.
- Implied volatility is the expected volatility an underlying asset's return and is derived from an option pricing model (i.e., the Black–Scholes–Merton model) as the value that equates the model price of an option to its market price.
- When implied volatilities of OTM options exceed those of ATM options, the implied volatility curve is a volatility smile. The more common shape is a volatility skew, in which implied volatility increases for OTM puts and decreases for OTM calls, as the strike price moves away from the current price.
- The implied volatility surface is a 3-D plot, for put and call options on the same underlying, showing expiration time (*x*-axis), strike prices (*y*-axis), and implied volatilities (*z*-axis). It simultaneously displays volatility skew and the term structure of implied volatility.
- Options, like all derivatives, should always be used in connection with a well-defined investment objective. When using options strategies, it is important to have a view on the expected change in implied volatility and the direction of movement of the underlying asset.

PROBLEMS

The following information relates to Questions 1–10

Aline Nuñes, a junior analyst, works in the derivatives research division of an international securities firm. Nuñes's supervisor, Cátia Pereira, asks her to conduct an analysis of various option trading strategies relating to shares of three companies: IZD, QWY, and XDF. On 1 February, Nuñes gathers selected option premium data on the companies, presented in Exhibit 1.

EXHIBIT 1 Share Price and Option Premiums as of 1 February (share prices and option premiums in €)

Company	Share Price	Call Premium	Option Date/ Strike	Put Premium
		9.45	April/87.50	1.67
IZD	93.93	2.67	April/95.00	4.49
		1.68	April/97.50	5.78

(continued)

EXHIBIT 1   (Continued)

Company	Share Price	Call Premium	Option Date/ Strike	Put Premium
		4.77	April/24.00	0.35
QWY	28.49	3.96	April/25.00	0.50
		0.32	April/31.00	3.00
		0.23	February/80.00	5.52
XDF	74.98	2.54	April/75.00	3.22
		2.47	December/80.00	9.73

Nuñes considers the following option strategies relating to IZD:

Strategy 1: Constructing a synthetic long put position in IZD
Strategy 2: Buying 100 shares of IZD and writing the April €95.00 strike call option on IZD
Strategy 3: Implementing a covered call position in IZD using the April €97.50 strike option

Nuñes next reviews the following option strategies relating to QWY:

Strategy 4: Implementing a protective put position in QWY using the April €25.00 strike option
Strategy 5: Buying 100 shares of QWY, buying the April €24.00 strike put option, and writing the April €31.00 strike call option
Strategy 6: Implementing a bear spread in QWY using the April €25.00 and April €31.00 strike options

Finally, Nuñes considers two option strategies relating to XDF:

Strategy 7: Writing both the April €75.00 strike call option and the April €75.00 strike put option on XDF
Strategy 8: Writing the February €80.00 strike call option and buying the December €80.00 strike call option on XDF

1. Strategy 1 would require Nuñes to buy:
   A. shares of IZD.
   B. a put option on IZD.
   C. a call option on IZD.
2. Based on Exhibit 1, Nuñes should expect Strategy 2 to be *least* profitable if the share price of IZD at option expiration is:
   A. less than €91.26.
   B. between €91.26 and €95.00.
   C. more than €95.00.

3. Based on Exhibit 1, the breakeven share price of Strategy 3 is *closest* to:
   A. €92.25.
   B. €95.61.
   C. €95.82.
4. Based on Exhibit 1, the maximum loss per share that would be incurred by implementing Strategy 4 is:
   A. €2.99.
   B. €3.99.
   C. unlimited.
5. Strategy 5 is *best* described as a:
   A. collar.
   B. straddle.
   C. bear spread.
6. Based on Exhibit 1, Strategy 5 offers:
   A. unlimited upside.
   B. a maximum profit of €2.48 per share.
   C. protection against losses if QWY's share price falls below €28.14.
7. Based on Exhibit 1, the breakeven share price for Strategy 6 is *closest* to:
   A. €22.50.
   B. €28.50.
   C. €33.50.
8. Based on Exhibit 1, the maximum gain per share that could be earned if Strategy 7 is implemented is:
   A. €5.74.
   B. €5.76.
   C. unlimited.
9. Based on Exhibit 1, the *best* explanation for Nuñes to implement Strategy 8 would be that, between the February and December expiration dates, she expects the share price of XDF to:
   A. decrease.
   B. remain unchanged.
   C. increase.
10. Over the past few months, Nuñes and Pereira have followed news reports on a proposed merger between XDF and one of its competitors. A government antitrust committee is currently reviewing the potential merger. Pereira expects the share price to move sharply upward or downward depending on whether the committee decides to approve or reject the merger next week. Pereira asks Nuñes to recommend an option trade that might allow the firm to benefit from a significant move in the XDF share price regardless of the direction of the move.

    The option trade that Nuñes should recommend relating to the government committee's decision is a:
    A. collar.
    B. bull spread.
    C. long straddle.

The following information relates to Questions 11–16

Stanley Kumar Singh, CFA, is the risk manager at SKS Asset Management. He works with individual clients to manage their investment portfolios. One client, Sherman Hopewell, is worried about how short-term market fluctuations over the next three months might impact his equity position in Walnut Corporation. Although Hopewell is concerned about short-term downside price movements, he wants to remain invested in Walnut shares because he remains positive about its long-term performance. Hopewell has asked Singh to recommend an option strategy that will keep him invested in Walnut shares while protecting against a short-term price decline. Singh gathers the information in Exhibit 1 to explore various strategies to address Hopewell's concerns.

Another client, Nigel French, is a trader who does not currently own shares of Walnut Corporation. French has told Singh that he believes that Walnut shares will experience a large move in price after the upcoming quarterly earnings release in two weeks. French also tells Singh, however, that he is unsure which direction the stock will move. French asks Singh to recommend an option strategy that would allow him to profit should the share price move in either direction.

A third client, Wanda Tills, does not currently own Walnut shares and has asked Singh to explain the profit potential of three strategies using options in Walnut: a long straddle, a bull call spread, and a bear put spread. In addition, Tills asks Singh to explain the gamma of a call option. In response, Singh prepares a memo to be shared with Tills that provides a discussion of gamma and presents his analysis on three option strategies:

Strategy 1: A long straddle position at the $67.50 strike option
Strategy 2: A bull call spread using the $65 and $70 strike options
Strategy 3: A bear put spread using the $65 and $70 strike options

EXHIBIT 1   Walnut Corporation Current Stock Price: $67.79
Walnut Corporation European Options

Exercise Price	Market Call Price	Call Delta	Market Put Price	Put Delta
$55.00	$12.83	1.00	$0.24	−0.05
$65.00	$3.65	0.91	$1.34	−0.29
$67.50	$1.99	0.63	$2.26	−0.42
$70.00	$0.91	0.37	$3.70	−0.55
$80.00	$0.03	0.02	$12.95	−0.76

Note: Each option has 106 days remaining until expiration.

11. The option strategy Singh is *most likely* to recommend to Hopewell is a:
    A. collar.
    B. covered call.
    C. protective put.

12. The option strategy that Singh is *most likely* to recommend to French is a:
    A. straddle.
    B. bull spread.
    C. collar.

13. Based on Exhibit 1, Strategy 1 is profitable when the share price at expiration is *closest* to:
    A. $63.00.
    B. $65.24.
    C. $69.49.
14. Based on Exhibit 1, the maximum profit, on a per share basis, from investing in Strategy 2, is *closest* to:
    A. $2.26.
    B. $2.74.
    C. $5.00.
15. Based on Exhibit 1, and assuming the market price of Walnut's shares at expiration is $66, the profit or loss, on a per share basis, from investing in Strategy 3, is *closest* to:
    A. $2.36.
    B. $1.64.
    C. $2.64.
16. Based on the data in Exhibit 1, Singh would advise Tills that the call option with the *largest* gamma would have a strike price *closest* to:
    A. $ 55.00.
    B. $ 67.50.
    C. $ 80.00.

The following information relates to Questions 17–23

Anneke Ngoc is an analyst who works for an international bank, where she advises high-net-worth clients on option strategies. Ngoc prepares for a meeting with a US-based client, Mani Ahlim.

Ngoc notes that Ahlim recently inherited an account containing a large Brazilian real (BRL) cash balance. Ahlim intends to use the inherited funds to purchase a vacation home in the United States with an expected purchase price of US$750,000 in six months. Ahlim is concerned that the Brazilian real will weaken against the US dollar over the next six months. Ngoc considers potential hedge strategies to reduce the risk of a possible adverse currency movement over this time period.

Ahlim holds shares of Pselftarô Ltd. (PSÔL), which has a current share price of $37.41. Ahlim is bullish on PSÔL in the long term. He would like to add to his long position but is concerned about a moderate price decline after the quarterly earnings announcement next month, in April. Ngoc recommends a protective put position with a strike price of $35 using May options and a $40/$50 bull call spread using December options. Ngoc gathers selected PSÔL option prices for May and December, which are presented in Exhibit 1.

EXHIBIT 1 Selected PSÔL Option Prices (all prices in US dollars)

Exercise Price	Expiration Month	Call Price	Put Price
35	May	3.00	1.81
40	December	6.50	10.25
50	December	4.25	20.50

Ahlim also expresses interest in trading options on India's NIFTY 50 (National Stock Exchange Fifty) Index. Ngoc gathers selected one-month option prices and implied volatility data, which are presented in Exhibit 2. India's NIFTY 50 Index is currently trading at a level of 11,610.

EXHIBIT 2   Selected One-Month Option Prices and Implied Volatility Data: NIFTY 50 Index (all prices in Indian rupees)

Exercise Price	Market Call Price	Market Put Price	Implied Call Volatility	Implied Put Volatility
11,200	526.00	61.90	5.87	17.72
11,400	365.45	102.60	10.80	17.01
11,600	240.00	165.80	12.26	16.44
11,800	135.00	213.00	12.14	16.39
12,000	65.80	370.00	11.98	16.56

Ngoc reviews a research report that includes a one-month forecast of the NIFTY 50 Index. The report's conclusions are presented in Exhibit 3.

EXHIBIT 3   Research Report Conclusions: NIFTY 50 Index

One-month forecast:

- We have a neutral view on the direction of the index's move over the next month.
- The rate of the change in underlying prices (vega) is expected to increase.
- The implied volatility of index options is expected to be above the consensus forecast.

Based on these conclusions, Ngoc considers various NIFTY 50 Index option strategies for Ahlim.

17. Which of the following positions would best mitigate Ahlim's concern regarding the purchase of his vacation home in six months?
    A. Sell an at-the-money six-month BRL/USD call option.
    B. Purchase an at-the-money six-month USD/BRL put option.
    C. Take a short position in a six-month BRL/USD futures contract.
18. Based on Exhibit 1, the maximum loss per share of Ngoc's recommended PSÔL protective put position is:
    A. $0.60.
    B. $2.41.
    C. $4.22.
19. Based on Exhibit 1, the breakeven price per share of Ngoc's recommended PSÔL protective put position is:
    A. $35.60.
    B. $36.81.
    C. $39.22.
20. Based on Exhibit 1, the maximum profit per share of Ngoc's recommended PSÔL bull call spread is:
    A. $2.25.
    B. $7.75.
    C. $12.25.

21. Based on Exhibit 1, the breakeven price per share of Ngoc's recommended PSÔL bull call spread is:
    A. $42.25.
    B. $47.75.
    C. $52.25.
22. Based on Exhibit 2, the NIFTY 50 Index implied volatility data *most likely* indicate a:
    A. risk reversal.
    B. volatility skew.
    C. volatility smile.
23. Based on Exhibit 3, which of the following NIFTY 50 Index option strategies should Ngoc recommend to Ahlim?
    A. Buy a straddle.
    B. Buy a call option.
    C. Buy a calendar spread.

CHAPTER 9

SWAPS, FORWARDS, AND FUTURES STRATEGIES

LEARNING OUTCOMES

The candidate should be able to:

- demonstrate how interest rate swaps, forwards, and futures can be used to modify a portfolio's risk and return;
- demonstrate how currency swaps, forwards, and futures can be used to modify a portfolio's risk and return;
- demonstrate how equity swaps, forwards, and futures can be used to modify a portfolio's risk and return;
- demonstrate the use of volatility derivatives and variance swaps;
- demonstrate the use of derivatives to achieve targeted equity and interest rate risk exposures;
- demonstrate the use of derivatives in asset allocation, rebalancing, and inferring market expectations.

SUMMARY OVERVIEW

This reading on swap, forward, and futures strategies shows a number of ways in which market participants might use these derivatives to enhance returns or to reduce risk to better meet portfolio objectives. Following are the key points.

- Interest rate, currency, and equity swaps, forwards, and futures can be used to modify risk and return by altering the characteristics of the cash flows of an investment portfolio.
- An interest rate swap is an OTC contract in which two parties agree to exchange cash flows on specified dates, one based on a floating interest rate and the other based on a fixed rate (swap rate), determined at swap initiation. Both rates are applied to the swap's notional value to determine the size of the payments, which are typically netted. Interest rate swaps enable a party with a fixed (floating) risk or obligation to effectively convert it into a floating (fixed) one.

- Investors can use short-dated interest rate futures and forward rate agreements or longer-dated fixed-income (bond) futures contracts to modify their portfolios' interest rate risk exposure.
- When hedging interest rate risk with bond futures, one must determine the basis point value of the portfolio to be hedged, the target basis point value, and the basis point value of the futures, which itself is determined by the basis point value of the cheapest-to-deliver bond and its conversion factor. The number of bond futures to buy or sell to reach the target basis point value is then determined by the basis point value hedge ratio: $BPVHR = \left(\dfrac{BPV_T - BPV_P}{BPV_{CTD}}\right) \times CF.$
- Cross-currency basis swaps help parties in the swap to hedge against the risk of exchange rate fluctuations and to achieve better rate outcomes. Firms that need foreign-denominated cash can obtain funding in their local currency (likely at a more favorable rate) and then swap the local currency for the required foreign currency using a cross-currency basis swap.
- Equity risk in a portfolio can be managed using equity swaps and total return swaps. There are three main types of equity swap: (1) receive-equity return, pay-fixed; (2) receive-equity return, pay-floating; and (3) receive-equity return, pay-another equity return. A total return swap is a modified equity swap; it also includes in the performance any dividends paid by the underlying stocks or index during the period until the swap maturity.
- Equity risk in a portfolio can also be managed using equity futures and forwards. Equity futures are standardized, exchange-listed contracts, and when the underlying is a stock index, only cash settlement is available at contract expiration. The number of equity futures contracts to buy or sell is determined by $N_f = \left(\dfrac{\beta_T - \beta_S}{\beta_f}\right)\left(\dfrac{S}{F}\right).$
- Cash equitization is a strategy designed to boost returns by finding ways to "equitize" unintended cash holdings. It is typically done using stock index futures and interest rate futures.
- Derivatives on volatility include VIX futures and options and variance swaps. Importantly, VIX option prices are determined from VIX futures, and both instruments allow an investor to implement a view depending on her expectations about the timing and magnitude of a change in implied volatility.
- In a variance swap, the buyer of the contract will pay the difference between the fixed variance strike specified in the contract and the realized variance (annualized) on the underlying over the period specified and applied to a variance notional. Thus, variance swaps allow directional bets on implied versus realized volatility.
- Derivatives can be used to infer market participants' current expectations for changes over the short term in inflation (e.g., CPI swaps) and market volatility (e.g., VIX futures). Another common application is using fed funds futures prices to derive the probability of a central bank move in the federal funds rate target at the FOMC's next meeting.

PROBLEMS

1. A US bond portfolio manager wants to hedge a long position in a 10-year Treasury bond against a potential rise in domestic interest rates. He would *most likely:*
   A. sell fixed-income (bond) futures.
   B. enter a receive-fixed 10-year interest rate swap.
   C. sell a strip of 90-day Eurodollar futures contracts.

2. A European bond portfolio manager wants to increase the modified duration of his €30 million portfolio from 3 to 5. She would *most likely* enter a receive-fixed interest rate swap that has principal notional of €20 million and:

   A. a modified duration of 2.

   B. a modified duration of 3.

   C. a modified duration of 4.

3. The CIO of a Canadian private equity company wants to lock in the interest on a three-month "bridge" loan his firm will take out in six months to complete an LBO deal. He sells the relevant interest rate futures contracts at 98.05. In six-months' time, he initiates the loan at 2.70% and unwinds the hedge at 97.30. The effective interest rate on the loan is:

   A. 0.75%.

   B. 1.95%.

   C. 2.70%.

4. A US institutional investor in search of yield decides to buy Italian government bonds for her portfolio but wants to hedge against the risk of exchange rate fluctuations. She enters a cross-currency basis swap, with the same payment dates as the bonds, where at inception she delivers US dollars in exchange for euros for use in purchasing the Italian bonds. The notional principals on the swap are *most likely* exchanged:

   A. at inception only.

   B. at maturity only.

   C. both at inception and at maturity.

5. Continuing from the previous question, assume demand for US dollars is strong relative to demand for euros, so there is a positive basis for "lending" US dollars. By hedging the position in Italian government bonds with the currency basis swap, the US investor will *most likely* increase the periodic net interest payments received from the swap counter-party in:

   A. euros only.

   B. US dollars only.

   C. both euros and US dollars.

6. An equity portfolio manager is invested 100% in US large-cap stocks, but he wants to reduce the current allocation by 20%, to 80%, and allocate 20% to US small caps. He decides not to sell the stocks because of the high transaction costs. Rather, he will use S&P 500 Index futures and Russell 2000 Index futures for achieving the desired exposure in, respectively, US large caps and small caps. To achieve the new allocation, he will for an equivalent of 20% of the portfolio value:

   A. purchase Russell 2000 futures only.

   B. purchase Russell 2000 futures and sell S&P 500 futures.

   C. sell Russell 2000 futures and purchase S&P 500 futures.

7. A volatility trader observes that the VIX term structure is upward sloping. In particular, the VIX is at 13.50, the front-month futures contract trades at 14.10, and the second-month futures contract trades at 15.40. Assuming the shape of the VIX term structure will remain constant over the next three-month period, the trader decides to implement a trade that would profit from the VIX carry roll down. She will *most likely* purchase the:

   A. VIX and sell the VIX second-month futures.

   B. VIX and sell the VIX front-month futures.

   C. VIX front-month futures and sell the VIX second-month futures.

8. The CEO of a corporation owns 100 million shares of his company's stock, which is currently priced at €30 a share. Given the huge exposure of his personal wealth to this one company, he has decided to sell 10% of his position and invest the funds in a floating interest rate instrument. A derivatives dealer suggests that he do so using an equity swap.

    Explain how to structure such a swap.

9. A $30 million investment account of a bank trust fund is allocated one-third to stocks and two-thirds to bonds. The portfolio manager wants to change the overall allocation to 50% stock and 50% bonds and the allocation within the stock fund from 70% domestic stock and 30% foreign stock to 60% domestic and 40% foreign. The bond allocation will remain entirely invested in domestic corporate issues.

    Explain how swaps can be used to implement this adjustment. The market reference rate is assumed to be flat for all swaps, and you do not need to refer to specific stock and bond indexes.

10. Sarah Ko, a private wealth adviser in Singapore, is developing a short-term interest rate forecast for her private wealth clients who have holdings in the US fixed-income markets. Ko needs to understand current market expectations for possible upcoming central bank (i.e., US Federal Reserve Board) rate actions. The current price for the fed funds futures contract expiring after the next FOMC meeting is 97.175. The current federal funds rate target range is set between 2.50% and 2.75%.

    Explain how Ko can use this information to understand potential movements in the current federal funds rate.

The following information relates to Questions 11–17

Global Mega (Global) is a diversified financial services firm. Yasuko Regan, senior trader, and Marcus Whitacre, junior trader, both work on the firm's derivatives desk. Regan and Whitacre assist in structuring and implementing trades for clients in the financial services industry that have limited derivatives expertise. Regan and Whitacre are currently assisting one of Global's clients—Monatize, an asset management firm—with two of its portfolios: Portfolio A and Portfolio B.

Portfolio A is a bond portfolio composed solely of US Treasury bonds. Monatize has asked Global to quote the number of Treasury futures contracts necessary to fully hedge this bond portfolio against a rise in interest rates. Exhibit 1 presents selected data on Portfolio A, the relevant Treasury futures contract, and the cheapest-to-deliver (CTD) bond.

EXHIBIT 1   Selected Data on Portfolio A, the Treasury Futures Contract, and the CTD Bond

Portfolio A		Futures Contract and CTD Bond	
Market value	$143,234,000	Price	145.20
Modified duration	9.10	Modified duration	8.75
Basis point value	$130,342.94	Basis point value	$127.05
		Conversion factor	0.72382
		Contract size	$100,000

After an internal discussion, Monatize elects to not hedge Portfolio A but rather decrease the portfolio's modified duration to 3.10. Regan asks Whitacre to compute the number of

Treasury futures contracts to sell in order to achieve this objective. Regan tells Whitacre to assume the yield curve is flat.

Portfolio B is a $100,000,000 equity portfolio indexed to the S&P 500 Index, with excess cash of $4,800,000. Monatize is required to equitize its excess cash to be fully invested, and the firm directs Global to purchase futures contracts to do so. To replicate the return of Portfolio B's target index, Whitacre purchases S&P 500 futures contracts, at a price of 3,300 per contract, that have a multiplier of $250 per index point and a beta of 1.00.

Monatize's CFO and Regan discuss two potential hedging strategies for Portfolio B to protect against a hypothetical extreme sell-off in equities. Regan first suggests that Monatize could enter into a total return equity swap, whereby Monatize agrees to pay the return on the S&P 500 and receive a fixed interest rate at pre-specified dates in exchange for a fee.

Regan next suggests that Monatize could alternatively hedge Portfolio B using variance swaps. Monatize's CFO asks Regan to calculate what the gain would be in five months on a purchase of $1,000,000 vega notional of a one-year variance swap on the S&P 500 at a strike of 15% (quoted as annual volatility), assuming the following:

- Over the next five months, the S&P 500 experiences a realized volatility of 20%;
- At the end of the five-month period, the fair strike of a new seven-month variance swap on the S&P 500 will be 18%; and
- The annual interest rate is 1.50%.

Regan and Whitacre discuss the use of federal funds futures contracts to infer probabilities of future monetary policy changes. Whitacre makes the following three statements about fed funds futures contracts:

Statement 1:   Typical end-of-month activity by large financial and banking institutions often induces "dips" in the effective fed funds rate.

Statement 2:   Especially for the longer-term horizon, the probabilities inferred from the pricing of fed funds futures usually have strong predictive power.

Statement 3:   To derive probabilities of Federal Reserve interest rate actions, market participants look at the pricing of fed funds futures, which are tied to the Federal Reserve's target fed funds rate.

Whitacre then proposes to Regan that Global explore opportunities in bond futures arbitrage. Whitacre makes the following two statements:

Statement 4:   If the basis is positive, a trader would make a profit by "selling the basis."

Statement 5:   If the basis is negative, a trader would make a profit by selling the bond and buying the futures.

11. Based on Exhibit 1, the number of Treasury futures contracts Whitacre should sell to fully hedge Portfolio A is *closest* to:
    A. 650.
    B. 743.
    C. 1,026.

12. Based on Exhibit 1, the number of Treasury futures contracts Whitacre should sell to achieve Monetize's objective with respect to Portfolio A is *closest* to:
    A. 490.
    B. 518.
    C. 676.

13. The number of S&P 500 futures contracts that Whitacre should buy to equitize Portfolio B's excess cash position is *closest* to:
    A. 6.
    B. 121.
    C. 1,455.

14. The derivative product first suggested by Regan as a potential hedge strategy for Portfolio B:
    A. is a relatively liquid contract.
    B. eliminates counterparty credit risk.
    C. allows Monetize to keep voting rights on its equity portfolio.

15. Based on the CFO's set of assumptions, the gain on the purchase of the variance swap on the S&P 500 in five months would be *closest* to:
    A. $4,317,775.
    B. $4,355,556.
    C. $4,736,334.

16. Which of Whitacre's three statements about fed funds futures is correct?
    A. Statement 1
    B. Statement 2
    C. Statement 3

17. Which of Whitacre's two statements regarding bond futures arbitrage is correct?
    A. Only Statement 4
    B. Only Statement 5
    C. Both Statement 4 and Statement 5

The following information relates to Questions 18–20

Nisqually Uff is the portfolio manager for the Chehalis Fund (the Fund), which holds equities and bonds in its portfolio. Uff focuses on tactical portfolio strategies and uses derivatives to implement his strategies.

Uff has a positive short-term outlook for equities relative to bonds and decides to temporarily increase the beta of the portfolio's equity allocation from 0.9 to 1.2. He will use three-month equity index futures contracts to adjust the beta. Exhibit 1 displays selected data for the Fund's current equity allocation and the relevant futures contract.

EXHIBIT 1   Selected Data for the Fund's Current Equity Allocation and Futures Contract

Current value of the Fund's equity allocation	€168,300,000
Current portfolio beta	0.9
Target portfolio beta	1.2
Index futures contract value	€45,000
Beta of futures contract	1.0

18. Determine the appropriate number of equity index futures contracts that Uff should use to achieve the target portfolio beta. Identify whether the equity index futures contracts should be bought or sold.

One month later, Uff expects interest rates to rise. He decides to reduce the modified duration of the bond allocation of the Fund's portfolio without selling any of its existing bonds. To do so, Uff adds a negative-duration position by entering into an interest rate swap in which he pays the fixed rate and receives the floating rate. Exhibit 2 presents selected data for the Fund's bond allocation and the relevant swap contract.

EXHIBIT 2   Selected Data for the Fund's Bond Allocation and Swap Contract

Current value of the Fund's bond allocation	€90,100,000
Current portfolio average modified duration	7.8000
Target portfolio modified duration	5.0000
Swap modified duration for fixed-rate payer	−2.4848

19. Determine the required notional principal for the interest rate swap in order to achieve the target modified duration for the portfolio.

Six months later, Uff has since closed out both the equity index futures contract position and the interest rate swap position. In response to market movements, he now wants to implement a tactical rebalancing of the Fund's portfolio. Exhibit 3 presents the current and target asset allocations for the Fund's portfolio.

EXHIBIT 3   Current and Target Asset Allocations for the Fund's Portfolio

Asset Class	Current	Target
Equities	€201,384,000 (69.56%)	€188,181,500 (65.0%)
Bonds	€88,126,000 (30.44%)	€101,328,500 (35.0%)
Total	**€289,510,000**	**€289,510,000**

Uff decides to use equity index and bond futures contracts to rebalance the portfolio. Exhibit 4 shows selected data on the Fund's portfolio and the relevant futures contracts.

EXHIBIT 4   Selected Data on Fund's Portfolio and Relevant Futures Contracts

Beta of the Fund's equities relative to index	1.28
Modified duration of the Fund's bonds	4.59
Equity index futures contract value	€35,000
Beta of equity index futures contract	1.00
Basis point value of cheapest-to-deliver (CTD) bond	€91.26
Conversion factor (CF) for CTD bond	0.733194

20. Determine how many equity index and bond futures contracts Uff should use to rebalance the Fund's portfolio to the target allocation. Identify whether the futures contracts should be bought or sold.

The following information relates to Questions 21–22

Canawacta Tioga is the CFO for Wyalusing Corporation, a multinational manufacturing company based in Canada. One year ago, Wyalusing issued fixed-rate coupon bonds in Canada. Tioga now expects Canadian interest rates to fall and remain low for three years. During this three-year period, Tioga wants to use a par interest rate swap to effectively convert the fixed-rate bond coupon payments into floating-rate payments.

21. Explain how to construct the swap that Tioga wants to use with regard to the swap:
    i. tenor
    ii. cash flows
    iii. notional value
    iv. settlement dates

Wyalusing will soon be building a new manufacturing plant in the United States. To fund construction of the plant, the company will borrow in its home currency of CAD because of favorable interest rates. Tioga plans to use a cross-currency basis swap so that Wyalusing will borrow in CAD but make interest payments in USD.

22. Describe how the swap will function, from the perspective of Wyalusing, in terms of the:
    i. cash flows at inception.
    ii. periodic cash flows.
    iii. cash flows at maturity.

The following information relates to Questions 23–24

Southern Sloth Sanctuary (Sanctuary) is a charitable organization that cares for orphaned and injured sloths from the rain forest in the country of Lushland. The organization is supported by both domestic and international contributions. The Sanctuary's CFO typically invests any funds that are not immediately needed for short-term operational expenses into a domestic index fund that tracks the Lushland 100 stock index, which is denominated in Lushland dollars (LLD).

The Sanctuary just received a large contribution from a local benefactor in the amount of LLD1,000,000. These funds are not needed for short-term operational expenses. The CFO intends to equitize this excess cash position using futures contracts to replicate the return on the Lushland 100 stock index. Exhibit 1 shows selected data for the Lushland 100 Index futures contract.

EXHIBIT 1   Selected Data for Lushland 100 Index Futures Contract

Quoted price of futures contract	1,247
Contract multiplier	LLD 200
Contract beta	1.00

23. Determine the appropriate number of futures contracts that the CFO should buy to equitize the excess cash position.

A Japanese benefactor recently donated a plot of land in Japan to the Sanctuary. Ownership of the land has been transferred to the Sanctuary, which has a binding contract to sell the property for JPY500,000,000. The property sale will be completed in 30 days. The Sanctuary's CFO wants to hedge the risk of JPY depreciation using futures contracts. The CFO assumes a hedge ratio of 1.

24. Describe a strategy to implement the CFO's desired hedge.

CHAPTER 10

INTRODUCTION TO RISK MANAGEMENT

LEARNING OUTCOMES

The candidate should be able to:

- define risk management;
- describe features of a risk management framework;
- define risk governance and describe elements of effective risk governance;
- explain how risk tolerance affects risk management;
- describe risk budgeting and its role in risk governance;
- identify financial and non-financial sources of risk and describe how they may interact;
- describe methods for measuring and modifying risk exposures and factors to consider in choosing among the methods.

SUMMARY OVERVIEW

Success in business and investing requires the skillful selection and management of risks. A well-developed risk management process ties together an organization's goals, strategic competencies, and tools to create value to help it both thrive and survive. Good risk management results in better decision making and a keener assessment of the many important trade-offs in business and investing, helping managers maximize value.

- Risk and risk management are critical to good business and investing. Risk management is *not* only about avoiding risk.
- Taking risk is an active choice by boards and management, investment managers, and individuals. Risks must be understood and carefully chosen and managed.
- Risk exposure is the extent to which an organization's value may be affected through sensitivity to underlying risks.
- Risk management is a process that defines risk tolerance and measures, monitors, and modifies risks to be in line with that tolerance.

- A risk management framework is the infrastructure, processes, and analytics needed to support effective risk management; it includes risk governance, risk identification and measurement, risk infrastructure, risk policies and processes, risk mitigation and management, communication, and strategic risk analysis and integration.
- Risk governance is the top-level foundation for risk management, including risk oversight and setting risk tolerance for the organization.
- Risk identification and measurement is the quantitative and qualitative assessment of all potential sources of risk and the organization's risk exposures.
- Risk infrastructure comprises the resources and systems required to track and assess the organization's risk profile.
- Risk policies and processes are management's complement to risk governance at the operating level.
- Risk mitigation and management is the active monitoring and adjusting of risk exposures, integrating all the other factors of the risk management framework.
- Communication includes risk reporting and active feedback loops so that the risk process improves decision making.
- Strategic risk analysis and integration involves using these risk tools to rigorously sort out the factors that are and are not adding value as well as incorporating this analysis into the management decision process, with the intent of improving outcomes.
- Employing a risk management committee, along with a chief risk officer (CRO), are hallmarks of a strong risk governance framework.
- Governance and the entire risk process should take an enterprise risk management perspective to ensure that the value of the entire enterprise is maximized.
- Risk tolerance, a key element of good risk governance, delineates which risks are acceptable, which are unacceptable, and how much risk the overall organization can be exposed to.
- Risk budgeting is any means of allocating investments or assets by their risk characteristics.
- Financial risks are those that arise from activity in the financial markets.
- Non-financial risks arise from actions within an organization or from external origins, such as the environment, the community, regulators, politicians, suppliers, and customers.
- Financial risks consist of market risk, credit risk, and liquidity risk.
- Market risk arises from movements in stock prices, interest rates, exchange rates, and commodity prices.
- Credit risk is the risk that a counterparty will not pay an amount owed.
- Liquidity risk is the risk that, as a result of degradation in market conditions or the lack of market participants, one will be unable to sell an asset without lowering the price to less than the fundamental value.
- Non-financial risks consist of a variety of risks, including settlement risk, legal risk, regulatory risk, accounting risk, tax risk, model risk, tail risk, and operational risk.
- Operational risk is the risk that arises either from within the operations of an organization or from external events that are beyond the control of the organization but affect its operations. Operational risk can be caused by employees, the weather and natural disasters, vulnerabilities of IT systems, or terrorism.
- Solvency risk is the risk that the organization does not survive or succeed because it runs out of cash to meet its financial obligations.
- Individuals face many of the same organizational risks outlined here but also face health risk, mortality or longevity risk, and property and casualty risk.
- Risks are not necessarily independent because many risks arise as a result of other risks; risk interactions can be extremely non-linear and harmful.

- Risk drivers are the fundamental global and domestic macroeconomic and industry factors that create risk.
- Common measures of risk include standard deviation or volatility; asset-specific measures, such as beta or duration; derivative measures, such as delta, gamma, vega, and rho; and tail measures such as value at risk, CVaR and expected loss given default.
- Risk can be modified by prevention and avoidance, risk transfer (insurance), or risk shifting (derivatives).
- Risk can be mitigated internally through self-insurance or diversification.
- The primary determinants of which method is best for modifying risk are the benefits weighed against the costs, with consideration for the overall final risk profile and adherence to risk governance objectives.

PROBLEMS

1. Risk management in the case of individuals is *best* described as concerned with:
   A. hedging risk exposures.
   B. maximizing utility while bearing a tolerable level of risk.
   C. maximizing utility while avoiding exposure to undesirable risks.
2. Which of the following may be controlled by an investor?
   A. Risk
   B. Raw returns
   C. Risk-adjusted returns
3. The process of risk management includes:
   A. minimizing risk.
   B. maximizing returns.
   C. defining and measuring risks being taken.
4. Risk governance:
   A. aligns risk management activities with the goals of the overall enterprise.
   B. defines the qualitative assessment and evaluation of potential sources of risk in an organization.
   C. delegates responsibility for risk management to all levels of the organization's hierarchy.
5. The factors a risk management framework should address include all of the following *except*:
   A. communications.
   B. policies and processes.
   C. names of responsible individuals.
6. Which of the following is the correct sequence of events for risk governance and management that focuses on the entire enterprise? Establishing:
   A. risk tolerance, then risk budgeting, and then risk exposures.
   B. risk exposures, then risk tolerance, and then risk budgeting.
   C. risk budgeting, then risk exposures, and then risk tolerance.
7. Which of the following *best* describes activities that are supported by a risk management infrastructure?
   A. Risk tolerance, budgeting, and reporting
   B. Risk tolerance, measurement, and monitoring
   C. Risk identification, measurement, and monitoring

8. Effective risk governance in an enterprise provides guidance on all of the following *except*:
   A. unacceptable risks.
   B. worst losses that may be tolerated.
   C. specific methods to mitigate risk for each subsidiary in the enterprise.

9. A firm's risk management committee would be expected to do all of the following *except*:
   A. approving the governing body's proposed risk policies.
   B. deliberating the governing body's risk policies at the operational level.
   C. providing top decision-makers with a forum for considering risk management issues.

10. Once an enterprise's risk tolerance is determined, the role of risk management is to:
    A. analyze risk drivers.
    B. align risk exposures with risk appetite.
    C. identify the extent to which the enterprise is willing to fail in meeting its objectives.

11. Which factor should *most* affect a company's ability to tolerate risk?
    A. A stable market environment
    B. The beliefs of the individual board members
    C. The ability to dynamically respond to adverse events

12. Risk budgeting includes all of the following *except*:
    A. determining the target return.
    B. quantifying tolerable risk by specific metrics.
    C. allocating a portfolio by some risk characteristics of the investments.

13. A benefit of risk budgeting is that it:
    A. considers risk tradeoffs.
    B. establishes a firm's risk tolerance.
    C. reduces uncertainty facing the firm.

14. Which of the following risks is *best* described as a financial risk?
    A. Credit
    B. Solvency
    C. Operational

15. Liquidity risk is *most* associated with:
    A. the probability of default.
    B. a widening bid–ask spread.
    C. a poorly functioning market.

16. An example of a non-financial risk is:
    A. market risk.
    B. liquidity risk.
    C. settlement risk.

17. If a company has a one-day 5% Value at Risk of $1 million, this means:
    A. 5% of the time the firm is expected to lose at least $1 million in one day.
    B. 95% of the time the firm is expected to lose at least $1 million in one day.
    C. 5% of the time the firm is expected to lose no more than $1 million in one day.

18. An organization choosing to accept a risk exposure may:
    A. buy insurance.
    B. enter into a derivative contract.
    C. establish a reserve fund to cover losses.

19. The choice of risk-modification method is based on:
    A. minimizing risk at the lowest cost.
    B. maximizing returns at the lowest cost.
    C. weighing costs versus benefits in light of the organization's risk tolerance.

CHAPTER 11

MEASURING AND MANAGING MARKET RISK

LEARNING OUTCOMES

The candidate should be able to:

- explain the use of value at risk (VaR) in measuring portfolio risk;
- compare the parametric (variance–covariance), historical simulation, and Monte Carlo simulation methods for estimating VaR;
- estimate and interpret VaR under the parametric, historical simulation, and Monte Carlo simulation methods;
- describe advantages and limitations of VaR;
- describe extensions of VaR;
- describe sensitivity risk measures and scenario risk measures and compare these measures to VaR;
- demonstrate how equity, fixed-income, and options exposure measures may be used in measuring and managing market risk and volatility risk;
- describe the use of sensitivity risk measures and scenario risk measures;
- describe advantages and limitations of sensitivity risk measures and scenario risk measures;
- explain constraints used in managing market risks, including risk budgeting, position limits, scenario limits, and stop-loss limits;
- explain how risk measures may be used in capital allocation decisions;
- describe risk measures used by banks, asset managers, pension funds, and insurers.

SUMMARY OVERVIEW

This reading on market risk management models covers various techniques used to manage the risk arising from market fluctuations in prices and rates. The key points are summarized as follows:

- Value at risk (VaR) is the minimum loss in either currency units or as a percentage of portfolio value that would be expected to be incurred a certain percentage of the time over a certain period of time given assumed market conditions.
- VaR requires the decomposition of portfolio performance into risk factors.
- The three methods of estimating VaR are the parametric method, the historical simulation method, and the Monte Carlo simulation method.
- The parametric method of VaR estimation typically provides a VaR estimate from the left tail of a normal distribution, incorporating the expected returns, variances, and covariances of the components of the portfolio.
- The parametric method exploits the simplicity of the normal distribution but provides a poor estimate of VaR when returns are not normally distributed, as might occur when a portfolio contains options.
- The historical simulation method of VaR estimation uses historical return data on the portfolio's current holdings and allocation.
- The historical simulation method has the advantage of incorporating events that actually occurred and does not require the specification of a distribution or the estimation of parameters, but it is only useful to the extent that the future resembles the past.
- The Monte Carlo simulation method of VaR estimation requires the specification of a statistical distribution of returns and the generation of random outcomes from that distribution.
- The Monte Carlo simulation method is extremely flexible but can be complex and time consuming to use.
- There is no single right way to estimate VaR.
- The advantages of VaR include the following: It is a simple concept; it is relatively easy to understand and easily communicated, capturing much information in a single number. It can be useful in comparing risks across asset classes, portfolios, and trading units and, as such, facilitates capital allocation decisions. It can be used for performance evaluation and can be verified by using backtesting. It is widely accepted by regulators.
- The primary limitations of VaR are that it is a subjective measure and highly sensitive to numerous discretionary choices made in the course of computation. It can underestimate the frequency of extreme events. It fails to account for the lack of liquidity and is sensitive to correlation risk. It is vulnerable to trending or volatility regimes and is often misunderstood as a worst-case scenario. It can oversimplify the picture of risk and focuses heavily on the left tail.
- There are numerous variations and extensions of VaR, including conditional VaR (CVaR), incremental VaR (IVaR), and marginal VaR (MVaR), that can provide additional useful information.
- Conditional VaR is the average loss conditional on exceeding the VaR cutoff.
- Incremental VaR measures the change in portfolio VaR as a result of adding or deleting a position from the portfolio or if a position size is changed relative to the remaining positions.
- MVaR measures the change in portfolio VaR given a small change in the portfolio position. In a diversified portfolio, MVaRs can be summed to determine the contribution of each asset to the overall VaR.
- *Ex ante* tracking error measures the degree to which the performance of a given investment portfolio might deviate from its benchmark.

- Sensitivity measures quantify how a security or portfolio will react if a single risk factor changes. Common sensitivity measures are beta for equities; duration and convexity for bonds; and delta, gamma, and vega for options. Sensitivity measures do not indicate which portfolio has greater loss potential.
- Risk managers can use deltas, gammas, vegas, durations, convexities, and betas to get a comprehensive picture of the sensitivity of the entire portfolio.
- Stress tests apply extreme negative stress to a particular portfolio exposure.
- Scenario measures, including stress tests, are risk models that evaluate how a portfolio will perform under certain high-stress market conditions.
- Scenario measures can be based on actual historical scenarios or on hypothetical scenarios.
- Historical scenarios are scenarios that measure the portfolio return that would result from a repeat of a particular period of financial market history.
- Hypothetical scenarios model the impact of extreme movements and co-movements in different markets that have not previously occurred.
- Reverse stress testing is the process of stressing the portfolio's most significant exposures.
- Sensitivity and scenario risk measures can complement VaR. They do not need to rely on history, and scenarios can be designed to overcome an assumption of normal distributions.
- Limitations of scenario measures include the following: Historical scenarios are unlikely to re-occur in exactly the same way. Hypothetical scenarios may incorrectly specify how assets will co-move and thus may get the magnitude of movements wrong. And, it is difficult to establish appropriate limits on a scenario analysis or stress test.
- Constraints are widely used in risk management in the form of risk budgets, position limits, scenario limits, stop-loss limits, and capital allocation.
- Risk budgeting is the allocation of the total risk appetite across sub-portfolios.
- A scenario limit is a limit on the estimated loss for a given scenario, which, if exceeded, would require corrective action in the portfolio.
- A stop-loss limit either requires a reduction in the size of a portfolio or its complete liquidation (when a loss of a particular size occurs in a specified period).
- Position limits are limits on the market value of any given investment.
- Risk measurements and constraints in and of themselves are not restrictive or unrestrictive; it is the limits placed on the measures that drive action.
- The degree of leverage, the mix of risk factors to which the business is exposed, and accounting or regulatory requirements influence the types of risk measures used by different market participants.
- Banks use risk tools to assess the extent of any liquidity and asset/liability mismatch, the probability of losses in their investment portfolios, their overall leverage ratio, interest rate sensitivities, and the risk to economic capital.
- Asset managers' use of risk tools focuses primarily on volatility, probability of loss, or the probability of underperforming a benchmark.
- Pension funds use risk measures to evaluate asset/liability mismatch and surplus at risk.
- Property and casualty insurers use sensitivity and exposure measures to ensure exposures remain within defined asset allocation ranges. They use economic capital and VaR measures to estimate the impairment in the event of a catastrophic loss. They use scenario analysis to stress the market risks and insurance risks simultaneously.
- Life insurers use risk measures to assess the exposures of the investment portfolio and the annuity liability, the extent of any asset/liability mismatch, and the potential stress losses based on the differences between the assets in which they have invested and the liabilities resulting from the insurance contracts they have written.

PROBLEMS

The following information relates to Questions 1–5

Randy Gorver, chief risk officer at Eastern Regional Bank, and John Abell, assistant risk officer, are currently conducting a risk assessment of several of the bank's independent investment functions. These reviews include the bank's fixed-income investment portfolio and an equity fund managed by the bank's trust department. Gorver and Abell are also assessing Eastern Regional's overall risk exposure.

Eastern Regional Bank Fixed-Income Investment Portfolio

The bank's proprietary fixed-income portfolio is structured as a barbell portfolio: About half of the portfolio is invested in zero-coupon Treasuries with maturities in the 3- to 5-year range (Portfolio P_1), and the remainder is invested in zero-coupon Treasuries with maturities in the 10- to 15-year range (Portfolio P_2). Georges Montes, the portfolio manager, has discretion to allocate between 40% and 60% of the assets to each maturity "bucket." He must remain fully invested at all times. Exhibit 1 shows details of this portfolio.

EXHIBIT 1   US Treasury Barbell Portfolio

	Maturity	
	P_1	P_2
	3–5 Years	10–15 Years
Average duration	3.30	11.07
Average yield to maturity	1.45%	2.23%
Market value	$50.3 million	$58.7 million

Trust Department's Equity Fund

A. **Use of Options:** The trust department of Eastern Regional Bank manages an equity fund called the Index Plus Fund, with $325 million in assets. This fund's objective is to track the S&P 500 Index price return while producing an income return 1.5 times that of the S&P 500. The bank's chief investment officer (CIO) uses put and call options on S&P 500 stock index futures to adjust the risk exposure of certain client accounts that have an investment in this fund. The portfolio of a 60-year-old widow with a below-average risk tolerance has an investment in this fund, and the CIO has asked his assistant, Janet Ferrell, to propose an options strategy to bring the portfolio's delta to 0.90.

B. **Value at Risk:** The Index Plus Fund has a value at risk (VaR) of $6.5 million at 5% for one day. Gorver asks Abell to write a brief summary of the portfolio VaR for the report he is preparing on the fund's risk position.

Combined Bank Risk Exposures

The bank has adopted a new risk policy, which requires forward-looking risk assessments in addition to the measures that look at historical risk characteristics. Management has also become very focused on tail risk since the subprime crisis and is evaluating the bank's capital allocation to certain higher-risk lines of business. Gorver must determine what additional risk metrics to include in his risk reporting to address the new policy. He asks Abell to draft a section of the risk report that will address the risk measures' adequacy for capital allocation decisions.

1. If Montes is expecting a 50 bp increase in yields at all points along the yield curve, which of the following trades is he *most likely* to execute to minimize his risk?
   A. Sell $35 million of P_2 and reinvest the proceeds in three-year bonds
   B. Sell $15 million of P_2 and reinvest the proceeds in three-year bonds
   C. Reduce the duration of P_2 to 10 years and reduce the duration of P_1 to 3 years
2. Which of the following options strategies is Ferrell *most likely* to recommend for the client's portfolio?
   A. Long calls
   B. Short calls
   C. Short puts
3. Which of the following statements regarding the VaR of the Index Plus Fund is correct?
   A. The expected maximum loss for the portfolio is $6.5 million.
   B. Five percent of the time, the portfolio can be expected to experience a loss of at least $6.5 million.
   C. Ninety-five percent of the time, the portfolio can be expected to experience a one-day loss of no more than $6.5 million.
4. To comply with the new bank policy on risk assessment, which of the following is the *best* set of risk measures to add to the chief risk officer's risk reporting?
   A. Conditional VaR, stress test, and scenario analysis
   B. Monte Carlo VaR, incremental VaR, and stress test
   C. Parametric VaR, marginal VaR, and scenario analysis
5. Which of the following statements should *not* be included in Abell's report to management regarding the use of risk measures in capital allocation decisions?
   A. VaR measures capture the increased liquidity risk during stress periods.
   B. Stress tests and scenario analysis can be used to evaluate the effect of outlier events on each line of business.
   C. VaR approaches that can accommodate a non-normal distribution are critical to understand relative risk across lines of business.

The following information relates to Questions 6–11

Hiram Life (Hiram), a large multinational insurer located in Canada, has received permission to increase its ownership in an India-based life insurance company, LICIA, from 26% to 49%. Before completing this transaction, Hiram wants to complete a risk assessment of LICIA's investment portfolio. Judith Hamilton, Hiram's chief financial officer, has been asked to brief the management committee on investment risk in its India-based insurance operations.

LICIA's portfolio, which has a market value of CAD260 million, is currently structured as shown in Exhibit 1. Despite its more than 1,000 individual holdings, the portfolio is invested predominantly in India. The Indian government bond market is highly liquid, but the country's mortgage and infrastructure loan markets, as well as the corporate bond market, are relatively illiquid. Individual mortgage and corporate bond positions are large relative to the normal trading volumes in these securities. Given the elevated current and fiscal account deficits, Indian investments are also subject to above-average economic risk.

Hamilton begins with a summary of the India-based portfolio. Exhibit 1 presents the current portfolio composition and the risk and return assumptions used to estimate value at risk (VaR).

EXHIBIT 1   Selected Assumptions for LICIA's Investment Portfolio

	Allocation	Average Daily Return	Daily Standard Deviation
India government securities	50%	0.015%	0.206%
India mortgage/infrastructure loans	25%	0.045%	0.710%
India corporate bonds	15%	0.025%	0.324%
India equity	10%	0.035%	0.996%

Infrastructure is a rapidly growing asset class with limited return history; the first infrastructure loans were issued just 10 years ago.

Hamilton's report to the management committee must outline her assumptions and provide support for the methods she used in her risk assessment. If needed, she will also make recommendations for rebalancing the portfolio to ensure its risk profile is aligned with that of Hiram.

Hamilton develops the assumptions shown in Exhibit 2, which will be used for estimating the portfolio VaR.

EXHIBIT 2   VaR Input Assumptions for Proposed CAD260 Million Portfolio

Method	Average Return Assumption	Standard Deviation Assumption
Monte Carlo simulation	0.026%	0.501%
Parametric approach	0.026%	0.501%
Historical simulation	0.023%	0.490%

Hamilton elects to apply a one-day, 5% VaR limit of CAD2 million in her risk assessment of LICIA's portfolio. This limit is consistent with the risk tolerance the committee has specified for the Hiram portfolio.

The markets' volatility during the last 12 months has been significantly higher than the historical norm, with increased frequency of large daily losses, and Hamilton expects the next 12 months to be equally volatile.

She estimates the one-day 5% portfolio VaR for LICIA's portfolio using three different approaches:

EXHIBIT 3   VaR Results over a One-Day Period for Proposed Portfolio

Method	5% VaR
Monte Carlo simulation	CAD2,095,565
Parametric approach	CAD2,083,610
Historical simulation	CAD1,938,874

The committee is likely to have questions in a number of key areas—the limitations of the VaR report, potential losses in an extreme adverse event, and the reliability of the VaR numbers if the market continues to exhibit higher-than-normal volatility. Hamilton wants to be certain that she has thoroughly evaluated the risks inherent in the LICIA portfolio and compares them with the risks in Hiram's present portfolio.

Hamilton believes the possibility of a ratings downgrade on Indian sovereign debt is high and not yet fully reflected in securities prices. If the rating is lowered, many of the portfolio's holdings will no longer meet Hiram's minimum ratings requirement. A downgrade's effect is unlikely to be limited to the government bond portfolio. All asset classes can be expected to be affected to some degree. Hamilton plans to include a scenario analysis that reflects this possibility to ensure that management has the broadest possible view of the risk exposures in the India portfolio.

6. Given Hamilton's expectations, which of the following models is *most appropriate* to use in estimating portfolio VaR?
   A. Parametric method
   B. Historical simulation method
   C. Monte Carlo simulation method
7. Which risk measure is Hamilton *most likely* to present when addressing the committee's concerns regarding potential losses in extreme stress events?
   A. Relative VaR
   B. Incremental VaR
   C. Conditional VaR
8. The scenario analysis that Hamilton prepares for the committee is *most likely* a:
   A. stress test.
   B. historical scenario.
   C. hypothetical scenario.
9. The scenario analysis that Hamilton prepares for the committee is a valuable tool to supplement VaR *because* it:
   A. incorporates historical data to evaluate the risk in the tail of the VaR distribution.
   B. enables Hamilton to isolate the risk stemming from a single risk factor—the ratings downgrade.
   C. allows the committee to assess the effect of low liquidity in the event of a ratings downgrade.
10. Using the data in Exhibit 2, the portfolio's annual 1% parametric VaR is *closest* to:
   A. CAD17 million.
   B. CAD31 million.
   C. CAD48 million.

11. What additional risk measures would be most appropriate to add to Hamilton's risk assessment?
    A. Delta
    B. Duration
    C. Tracking error

The following information relates to Questions 12–19

Tina Ming is a senior portfolio manager at Flusk Pension Fund (Flusk). Flusk's portfolio is composed of fixed-income instruments structured to match Flusk's liabilities. Ming works with Shrikant McKee, Flusk's risk analyst.

Ming and McKee discuss the latest risk report. McKee calculated value at risk (VaR) for the entire portfolio using the historical method and assuming a lookback period of five years and 250 trading days per year. McKee presents VaR measures in Exhibit 1.

EXHIBIT 1 Flusk Portfolio VaR (in $ millions)

Confidence Interval	Daily VaR	Monthly VaR
95%	1.10	5.37

After reading McKee's report, Ming asks why the number of daily VaR breaches over the last year is zero even though the portfolio has accumulated a substantial loss.

Next, Ming requests that McKee perform the following two risk analyses on Flusk's portfolio:

Analysis 1: Use scenario analysis to evaluate the impact on risk and return of a repeat of the last financial crisis.

Analysis 2: Estimate over one year, with a 95% level of confidence, how much Flusk's assets could underperform its liabilities.

Ming recommends purchasing newly issued emerging market corporate bonds that have embedded options. Prior to buying the bonds, Ming wants McKee to estimate the effect of the purchase on Flusk's VaR. McKee suggests running a stress test using a historical period specific to emerging markets that encompassed an extreme change in credit spreads.

At the conclusion of their conversation, Ming asks the following question about risk management tools: "What are the advantages of VaR compared with other risk measures?"

12. Based on Exhibit 1, Flusk's portfolio is expected to experience:
    A. a minimum daily loss of $1.10 million over the next year.
    B. a loss over one month equal to or exceeding $5.37 million 5% of the time.
    C. an average daily loss of $1.10 million 5% of the time during the next 250 trading days.
13. The number of Flusk's VaR breaches *most likely* resulted from:
    A. using a standard normal distribution in the VaR model.
    B. using a 95% confidence interval instead of a 99% confidence interval.
    C. lower market volatility during the last year compared with the lookback period.

14. To perform Analysis 1, McKee should use historical bond:
    A. prices.
    B. yields.
    C. durations.
15. The limitation of the approach requested for Analysis 1 is that it:
    A. omits asset correlations.
    B. precludes incorporating portfolio manager actions.
    C. assumes no deviation from historical market events.
16. The estimate requested in Analysis 2 is *best* described as:
    A. liquidity gap.
    B. surplus at risk.
    C. maximum drawdown.
17. Which measure should McKee use to estimate the effect on Flusk's VaR from Ming's portfolio recommendation?
    A. Relative VaR
    B. Incremental VaR
    C. Conditional VaR
18. When measuring the portfolio impact of the stress test suggested by McKee, which of the following is *most likely* to produce an accurate result?
    A. Marginal VaR
    B. Full revaluation of securities
    C. The use of sensitivity risk measures
19. The risk management tool referenced in Ming's question:
    A. is widely accepted by regulators.
    B. takes into account asset liquidity.
    C. usually incorporates right-tail events.

The following information relates to questions 20–26

Carol Kynnersley is the chief risk officer at Investment Management Advisers (IMA). Kynnersley meets with IMA's portfolio management team and investment advisers to discuss the methods used to measure and manage market risk and how risk metrics are presented in client reports.

The three most popular investment funds offered by IMA are the Equity Opportunities, the Diversified Fixed Income, and the Alpha Core Equity. The Equity Opportunities Fund is composed of two exchange-traded funds: a broadly diversified large-cap equity product and one devoted to energy stocks. Kynnersley makes the following statements regarding the risk management policies established for the Equity Opportunities portfolio:

Statement 1: IMA's preferred approach to model value at risk (VaR) is to estimate expected returns, volatilities, and correlations under the assumption of a normal distribution.

Statement 2: In last year's annual client performance report, IMA stated that a hypothetical $6 million Equity Opportunities Fund account had a daily 5% VaR of approximately 1.5% of portfolio value.

Kynnersley informs the investment advisers that the risk management department recently updated the model for estimating the Equity Opportunities Fund VaR based on the information presented in Exhibit 1.

EXHIBIT 1   Equity Opportunities Fund—VaR Model Input Assumptions

	Large-Cap ETF	Energy ETF	Total Portfolio
Portfolio weight	65.0%	35.0%	100.0%
Expected annual return	12.0%	18.0%	14.1%
Standard deviation	20.0%	40.0%	26.3%

Correlation between ETFs: 0.90
Number of trading days/year: 250

For clients interested in fixed-income products, IMA offers the Diversified Fixed-Income Fund. Kynnersley explains that the portfolio's bonds are all subject to interest rate risk. To demonstrate how fixed-income exposure measures can be used to identify and manage interest rate risk, Kynnersley distributes two exhibits featuring three hypothetical Treasury coupon bonds (Exhibit 2) under three interest rate scenarios (Exhibit 3).

EXHIBIT 2   Fixed-Income Risk Measure

Hypothetical Bond	Duration
Bond 1	1.3
Bond 2	3.7
Bond 3	10.2

EXHIBIT 3   Interest Rate Scenarios

Scenario	Interest Rate Environment
Scenario 1	Rates increase 25 bps
Scenario 2	Rates increase 10 bps
Scenario 3	Rates decrease 20 bps

One of the investment advisers comments that a client recently asked about the performance of the Diversified Fixed-Income Fund relative to its benchmark, a broad fixed-income index. Kynnersley informs the adviser as follows:

Statement 3:   The Diversified Fixed-Income Fund manager monitors the historical deviation between portfolio returns and benchmark returns. The fund prospectus stipulates a target deviation from the benchmark of no more than 5 bps.

Kynnersley concludes the meeting by reviewing the constraints IMA imposes on securities included in the Alpha Core Equity Fund. The compliance department conducts daily oversight using numerous risk screens and, when indicated, notifies portfolio managers to make adjustments. Kynnersley makes the following statement:

Statement 4: It is important that all clients investing in the fund be made aware of IMA's compliance measures. The Alpha Core Equity Fund restricts the exposure of individual securities to 1.75% of the total portfolio.

20. Based on Statement 1, IMA's VaR estimation approach is *best* described as the:
    A. parametric method.
    B. historical simulation method.
    C. Monte Carlo simulation method.
21. In Statement 2, Kynnersley implies that the portfolio:
    A. is at risk of losing $4,500 each trading day.
    B. value is expected to decline by $90,000 or more once in 20 trading days.
    C. has a 5% chance of falling in value by a maximum of $90,000 on a single trading day.
22. Based *only* on Statement 2, the risk measurement approach:
    A. ignores right-tail events in the return distribution.
    B. is similar to the Sharpe ratio because it is backward looking.
    C. provides a relatively accurate risk estimate in both trending and volatile regimes.
23. Based on Exhibit 1, the daily 5% VaR estimate is *closest* to:
    A. 1.61%.
    B. 2.42%.
    C. 2.69%.
24. Based *only* on Exhibits 2 and 3, it is *most likely* that under:
    A. Scenario 1, Bond 2 outperforms Bond 1.
    B. Scenario 2, Bond 1 underperforms Bond 3.
    C. Scenario 3, Bond 3 is the best performing security.
25. The risk measure referred to in Statement 3 is:
    A. active share.
    B. beta sensitivity
    C. *ex post* tracking error.
26. In Statement 4, Kynnersley describes a constraint associated with a:
    A. risk budget.
    B. position limit.
    C. stop-loss limit.

CHAPTER 12

RISK MANAGEMENT FOR INDIVIDUALS

LEARNING OUTCOMES

The candidate should be able to:

- compare the characteristics of human capital and financial capital as components of an individual's total wealth;
- discuss the relationships among human capital, financial capital, and economic net worth;
- discuss the financial stages of life for an individual;
- describe an economic (holistic) balance sheet;
- discuss risks (earnings, premature death, longevity, property, liability, and health risks) in relation to human and financial capital;
- describe types of insurance relevant to personal financial planning;
- describe the basic elements of a life insurance policy and how insurers price a life insurance policy;
- discuss the use of annuities in personal financial planning;
- discuss the relative advantages and disadvantages of fixed and variable annuities;
- analyze and evaluate an insurance program;
- discuss how asset allocation policy may be influenced by the risk characteristics of human capital;
- recommend and justify appropriate strategies for asset allocation and risk reduction when given an investor profile of key inputs.

SUMMARY OVERVIEW

The risk management process for individuals is complex given the variety of potential risks that may be experienced over the life cycle and the differences that exist across households. In this reading, key concepts related to risk management and individuals include the following:

- The two primary asset types for most individuals can be described broadly as human capital and financial capital. Human capital is the net present value of the individual's future expected labor income, whereas financial capital consists of assets currently owned by the individual and can include such items as a bank account, individual securities, pooled funds, a retirement account, and a home.
- Economic net worth is an extension of traditional balance sheet net worth that includes claims to future assets that can be used for consumption, such as human capital, as well as the present value of pension benefits.
- There are typically four key steps in the risk management process for individuals: Specify the objective, identify risks, evaluate risks and select appropriate methods to manage the risks, and monitor outcomes and risk exposures and make appropriate adjustments in methods.
- The financial stages of life for adults can be categorized in the following seven periods: education phase, early career, career development, peak accumulation, pre-retirement, early retirement, and late retirement.
- The primary goal of an economic (holistic) balance sheet is to arrive at an accurate depiction of an individual's overall financial health by accounting for the present value of all available marketable and non-marketable assets, as well as all liabilities. An economic (holistic) balance sheet includes traditional assets and liabilities, as well as human capital and pension value, as assets and includes consumption and bequests as liabilities.
- The total economic wealth of an individual changes throughout his or her lifetime, as do the underlying assets that make up that wealth. The total economic wealth of younger individuals is typically dominated by the value of their human capital. As individuals age, earnings will accumulate, increasing financial capital.
- Earnings risk refers to the risks associated with the earnings potential of an individual—that is, events that could negatively affect someone's human and financial capital.
- Premature death risk relates to the death of an individual, such as a family member, whose future earnings (human capital) were expected to help pay for the financial needs and aspirations of the family.
- Longevity risk is the risk of reaching an age at which one's income and financial assets are insufficient to provide adequate support.
- Property risk relates to the possibility that one's property may be damaged, destroyed, stolen, or lost. There are different types of property insurance, depending on the asset, such as automobile insurance and homeowner's insurance.
- Liability risk refers to the possibility that an individual or other entity may be held legally liable for the financial costs of property damage or physical injury.
- Health risk refers to the risks and implications associated with illness or injury. Health risks manifest themselves in different ways over the life cycle and can have significant implications for human capital.
- The primary purpose of life insurance is to help replace the economic value of an individual to a family or a business in the event of that individual's death. The family's need for life insurance is related to the potential loss associated with the future earnings power of that individual.

- The two main types of life insurance are temporary and permanent. Temporary life insurance, or term life insurance, provides insurance for a certain period of time specified at purchase, whereas permanent insurance, or whole life insurance, is used to provide lifetime coverage, assuming the premiums are paid over the entire period.

- Fixed annuities provide a benefit that is fixed (or known) for life, whereas variable annuities have a benefit that can change over time and that is generally based on the performance of some underlying portfolio or investment. When selecting between fixed and variable annuities, there are a number of important considerations, such as the volatility of the benefit, flexibility, future market expectations, fees, and inflation concerns.

- Among the factors that would likely increase demand for an annuity are the following: longer-than-average life expectancy, greater preference for lifetime income, less concern for leaving money to heirs, more conservative investing preferences, and lower guaranteed income from other sources (such as pensions).

- Techniques for managing a risk include risk avoidance, risk reduction, risk transfer, and risk retention. The most appropriate choice among these techniques often is related to consideration of the frequency and severity of losses associated with the risk.

- The decision to retain risk or buy insurance is determined by a household's risk tolerance. At the same level of wealth, a more risk-tolerant household will prefer to retain more risk, either through higher insurance deductibles or by simply not buying insurance, than will a less risk-tolerant household. Insurance products that have a higher load will encourage a household to retain more risk.

- An individual's total economic wealth affects portfolio construction through asset allocation, which includes the overall allocation to risky assets, as well as the underlying asset classes, such as stocks and bonds, selected by the individual.

- Investment risk, property risk, and human capital risk can be either idiosyncratic or systematic. Examples of idiosyncratic risks include the risks of a specific occupation, the risk of living a very long life or experiencing a long-term illness, and the risk of premature death or loss of property. Systematic risks affect all households.

PROBLEMS

The following information relates to Questions 1–8

Richard Lansky is an insurance and wealth adviser for individuals. Lansky's first meeting of the day is with Gregory Zavris, age 27, a new client who works as a journalist. Gregory's only asset is $5,000 in savings; he has $67,000 in liabilities. During the conversation, Lansky describes the concepts of financial capital and human capital, as well as the components of economic and traditional balance sheets. Gregory asks Lansky:

> *On which balance sheet are my future earnings reflected?*

Gregory does not have medical insurance. He asks Lansky for advice regarding a policy that potentially would allow him to avoid paying for office visits related to minor medical problems.

In the afternoon, Lansky meets with Gregory's parents, Molly and Kirk, ages 53 and 60. Molly is a tenured university professor and provides consulting services to local businesses. Kirk is a senior manager for an investment bank. Lansky determines that Molly's income is more stable than Kirk's.

Kirk and Molly discuss estate planning, and Lansky recommends a whole life insurance policy on Kirk's life, with Molly responsible for paying the premiums. In the event of Kirk's death, Gregory would be entitled to the proceeds from the policy. Lansky explains that one feature of the policy provides for a portion of the benefits to be paid even if a premium payment is late or missed.

Molly tells Lansky that she has recently been reading about annuities and would like to clarify her understanding. Molly makes the following statements.

Statement 1: Both deferred and immediate annuities provide the same flexibility concerning access to invested funds.

Statement 2: The income yield for a given amount invested in a life-only immediate annuity is higher for an older person than for a younger person.

At the end of the consultation, Molly asks Lansky for advice regarding her retired aunt, Rose Gabriel, age 69. Molly believes that Gabriel's life annuity and pension benefits will provide enough income to meet her customary lifestyle needs. Gabriel lives in her mortgage-free home; her medical insurance plan covers basic health care expenses. Women in Gabriel's family generally have long life spans but often experience chronic health problems requiring extended nursing at home. Therefore, Molly is concerned that medical expenses might exceed Gabriel's net worth during her final years.

1. Gregory's human capital is:
   A. lower than his financial capital.
   B. equal to his financial capital.
   C. higher than his financial capital.
2. The *most* appropriate response to Gregory's balance sheet question is:
   A. the economic balance sheet only.
   B. the traditional balance sheet only.
   C. both the economic and the traditional balance sheets.
3. Given Gregory's policy preference, which type of medical insurance should Lansky recommend?
   A. Indemnity plan
   B. Preferred provider plan
   C. Health maintenance organization plan
4. In estimating Molly's human capital value, Lansky should apply an income volatility adjustment that is:
   A. less than Kirk's.
   B. the same as Kirk's.
   C. greater than Kirk's.
5. Regarding the whole life insurance policy recommended by Lansky, Kirk would be the:
   A. owner.
   B. insured.
   C. beneficiary.

6. The whole life insurance policy feature described by Lansky is a:
   A. non-forfeiture clause.
   B. waiver-of-premium rider.
   C. guaranteed insurability rider.
7. Which of Molly's statements about annuities is/are correct?
   A. Statement 1 only
   B. Statement 2 only
   C. Both Statement 1 and Statement 2
8. The type of insurance that will *best* address Molly's concern about Gabriel is:
   A. disability insurance.
   B. longevity insurance.
   C. long-term care insurance.

The following information relates to Questions 9–15

Henri Blanc is a financial adviser serving high-net-worth individuals in the United States. Alphonse Perrin, age 55, meets with Blanc for advice about coordinating his employee benefits with his investment and retirement planning strategies.

Perrin has adopted a life-cycle portfolio strategy and plans to retire in 10 years. Recently, he received a promotion and $50,000 salary increase to manage a regional distribution center for a national retail firm. Perrin's spending needs are currently less than his annual income, and he has no debt. His investment assets consist of $2,000,000 in marketable securities (90% equity/10% fixed income) and a vineyard with winery valued at $1,500,000.

Blanc leads Perrin through a discussion of the differences between his financial capital and his human capital, as well as between his traditional balance sheet and his economic balance sheet. Perrin is vested in a defined benefit pension plan based on years of service and prior salary levels. Future benefits will vest annually based on his new salary. Perrin makes the following statements regarding his understanding of pension benefits.

Statement 1: Unvested pension benefits should be classified as human capital.

Statement 2: Vested pension benefits should not be classified as financial capital until payments begin.

Perrin asks Blanc to compare his traditional and economic balance sheets. Blanc calculates that the sum of the present values of Perrin's consumption goals and bequests exceeds that of his unvested pension benefits and future earnings.

Perrin tells Blanc that he expects a slower rate of growth in the US economy. Perrin expresses the following concerns to Blanc.

Concern 1   Holding all else equal, I wonder what the effect will be on my human capital if the nominal risk-free rate declines?

Concern 2   My employer projects a slower rate of sales growth in my region; therefore, I am anxious about losing my job.

Perrin is a widower with three adult children who live independently. Perrin's oldest son wishes to inherit the vineyard; the two other children do not want to be involved. Perrin would like to accommodate his children's wishes; however, he wants each child to inherit equal value from his estate. Blanc explains potential uses of life insurance to Perrin and suggests that one of these uses best meets Perrin's immediate needs.

Perrin expresses a preference for a life insurance policy that provides a range of investment options. Perrin selects a policy and asks Blanc to calculate the net payment cost index (per $1,000 of face value, per year), using a life expectancy of 20 years and a discount rate of 5%. Table 1 provides information about Perrin's policy.

TABLE 1   Perrin's Life Insurance Policy

Face value	$500,000
Annual premium (paid at beginning of the year)	$12,000
Policy dividends anticipated per year (paid at end of the year)	$2,000
Cash value projected at the end of 20 years	$47,000

9. Which of Perrin's statements regarding his pension is/are correct?
   A. Statement 1 only
   B. Statement 2 only
   C. Both Statement 1 and Statement 2
10. Blanc's calculations show that Perrin's economic net worth is:
    A. less than his net worth.
    B. equal to his net worth.
    C. greater than his net worth.
11. In response to Perrin's Concern #1, human capital will *most likely*:
    A. decrease.
    B. remain the same.
    C. increase.
12. Perrin's Concern #2 identifies a risk related to:
    A. human capital only.
    B. financial capital only.
    C. both human and financial capital.
13. Which of the following uses of life insurance *best* meets Perrin's immediate needs?
    A. Provides estate liquidity
    B. Acts as a tax-sheltered savings instrument
    C. Replaces lost earning power for dependents
14. The type of life insurance *most appropriate* for Perrin is:
    A. term.
    B. universal.
    C. whole life.
15. The net payment cost index that Blanc should calculate is *closest* to:
    A. $17.48.
    B. $20.00.
    C. $20.19.

The following information relates to Questions 16–23

Adrian and Olivia Barksdale live in Australia with their 16-year-old twins. Adrian, 47, works in a highly cyclical industry as an engineering manager at a bauxite mine. Olivia, 46, is an accountant. The Barksdales are saving for their retirement and college funding for both children. Adrian's annual salary is A$190,000; Olivia's annual salary is A$85,000. The family's living expenses are currently A$95,000 per year.

Both Adrian and Olivia plan to work 18 more years, and they depend on their combined income and savings to fund their goals. The Barksdales' new financial adviser, Duncan Smith, recommends an appropriate disability insurance policy to cover Adrian, given his large salary. Because he has a highly specialized job, Adrian is willing to pay for the most comprehensive policy available.

Smith is also concerned about the Barksdales' existing life insurance coverage. Currently, the Barksdales have a term life policy insuring Adrian with a death benefit of A$100,000. Smith assesses the family's insurance needs in the event Adrian were to die this year. To do so, Smith uses the needs analysis method based on the financial data presented in Exhibit 1 and the following assumptions:

- The discount rate is 6.0%, and the tax rate is 30%.
- Salary and living expenses grow at 3.5% annually.
- Salary and living expenses occur at the beginning of each year.
- The following assumptions apply in the event of Adrian's death:
  - Olivia will continue to work until retirement;
  - Family living expenses will decline by $30,000 per year;
  - Olivia's projected living expense will be $50,000 per year for 44 years; and
  - The children's projected living expenses will be $15,000 per year for 6 years.

EXHIBIT 1   Barksdale Family Financial Needs Worksheet

Cash Needs	AUD (A$)
Final expenses and taxes payable	20,000
Mortgage retirement	400,000
Education fund	300,000
Emergency fund	30,000
Total cash needs	750,000
Capital Available	
Cash and investments	900,000
Adrian: Life insurance	100,000
Total capital available	1,000,000

Next, Smith discusses the advantages and disadvantages of annuities. The Barksdales are interested in purchasing an annuity that offers the following characteristics:

- a payout that begins at retirement,
- the ability to invest in a menu of investment options, and
- a payout that continues as long as either Olivia or Adrian is living.

Olivia's mother, Sarah Brown, is also a client of Smith. She is age 75 and retired, and she needs a known income stream to assist her with current and future expenses. Brown's parents both lived longer than average, and she is concerned about outliving her assets. Smith recommends an annuity.

The Barksdales also worry about longevity risk given their family history and healthy life-style. Both spouses want an annuity for their later years (beginning in 40 years) that will ensure the greatest supplemental, level income stream relative to the cost. The Barksdales are willing to forgo the right to cash out the policy.

Smith turns to a discussion about the Barksdales' investment portfolio and how total eco-nomic wealth (human capital plus financial capital) might affect asset allocation decisions. The Barksdales' human capital is valued at $2.9 million and estimated to be 35% equity-like. Smith determines that an overall target allocation of 40% equity is appropriate for the Barksdales' total assets on the economic balance sheet.

Smith makes two recommendations regarding the Barksdales' investment portfolio.

Recommendation 1   The portfolio should have lower risk than a portfolio for similar investors in the same lifestyle stage.

Recommendation 2   The portfolio should underweight securities having a high correlation with bauxite demand.

16. Based on Adrian's job and salary, the *most appropriate* disability policy would define dis-ability as the inability to perform duties of:
    A. any occupation.
    B. Adrian's regular occupation.
    C. any occupation for which Adrian is suited by education and experience.
17. Based on the given assumptions and the data in Exhibit 1, the additional amount of life insurance coverage needed is *closest* to:
    A. A$0.
    B. A$331,267.
    C. A$2,078,101.
18. Based on the Barksdales' annuity preferences, which type of annuity should they purchase?
    A. Deferred fixed
    B. Deferred variable
    C. Immediate variable
19. Based on the Barksdales' annuity preferences, which annuity payout method should they choose?
    A. Joint life annuity
    B. Life annuity with refund
    C. Life annuity with period certain
20. Based on Brown's goals and concerns, which type of annuity should Smith recommend for her?
    A. Deferred fixed
    B. Immediate fixed
    C. Immediate variable
21. Which type of annuity *best* satisfies the Barksdales' desire for supplemental income in their later years?
    A. Deferred fixed
    B. Deferred variable
    C. Advanced life deferred

22. Based on Exhibit 1, and meeting the Barksdales' target equity allocation for total economic wealth, the financial capital equity allocation should be *closest* to:
    A. 35.0%.
    B. 54.5%.
    C. 56.1%.

23. Which of Smith's recommendations regarding the Barksdales' investment portfolio is/are correct?
    A. Recommendation 1 only
    B. Recommendation 2 only
    C. Both Recommendation 1 and Recommendation 2

CHAPTER 13

CASE STUDY IN RISK MANAGEMENT: PRIVATE WEALTH

LEARNING OUTCOMES

The candidate should be able to:

- identify and analyze a family's risk exposures during the early career stage;
- recommend and justify methods to manage a family's risk exposures during the early career stage;
- identify and analyze a family's risk exposures during the career development stage;
- recommend and justify methods to manage a family's risk exposures during the career development stage;
- identify and analyze a family's risk exposures during the peak accumulation stage;
- recommend and justify methods to manage a family's risk exposures during the peak accumulation stage;
- identify and analyze a family's risk exposures during the early retirement stage;
- recommend and justify a plan to manage risks to an individual's retirement lifestyle goals.

SUMMARY OVERVIEW

This case study follows a family from the early career to the retirement stage. It touches on a small and simplified selection of a wide range of issues and considerations that a family may face. A great range of skills and competencies is required to provide financial advice, ranging from the ability to conduct in-depth risk analysis, all the way to making recommendations on risk mitigation strategies, including the choice of insurance products, to perform asset allocation, tax optimization, retirement planning, and estate planning. All of this must be done with a clear understanding of the applicable legal environment and of the level of access and the cost of accessing financial products. In practice, it is very unlikely that a single financial professional can master all the foregoing competencies. The key to success is to understand at what point the generalist needs to bring in, or refer the client to, a subject matter expert.

In this case study:

- We identify and analyze the Schmitts' risk exposures. We observed that the types of risk exposure change substantially from the early career stage to the early retirement stage. We conducted the analysis holistically, starting from the economic balance sheet, including human capital.
- We recommend and justify methods to manage the Schmitt family's risk exposures at different stages of their professional life. We use insurance, self-insurance, and adjustments to their investment portfolio.
- We prepare summaries of the Schmitts' risk exposures and the selected methods of managing those risk exposures.
- We recommend and justify modifications to the Schmitts' life and disability insurance at different stages of the income earners' lives.
- Finally, we recommend a justified a plan to manage risk to the Schmitts' retirement lifestyle goals.

PROBLEMS

The following information relates to Questions 1–2

Recently married, Jennifer and Ron Joseph live in the United States. Jennifer, age 26, and Ron, age 28, both earned master's degrees in the high-demand field of computer science. The young couple are in their early career stage and have combined savings of $50,000 with no other financial assets.

Both Jennifer and Ron are in good health and have been working for a few years. Ron works in the private sector as a programmer for a large information technology company, and Jennifer works in the state sector as a public high school teacher. Jennifer benefits from excellent job security with limited earnings risk from unemployment; however, any salary increases over time are expected to be modest. In contrast, Ron faces significant uncertainties in his future employment income, although he could benefit from significant upside in income if he and his employer achieve performance targets.

The Josephs seek financial advice and ask Jeff Berger, a long-time adviser to Ron's parents, to plan a wealth management strategy. Berger explains the concept of an economic balance sheet and the importance of the value of human capital in meeting their financial objectives.

1. **Discuss** key factors that affect the value of the Josephs' human capital.

Berger is concerned about possible financial difficulties for the surviving spouse in the event of the other's premature death. He advises the Josephs to consider mitigating this risk by purchasing life insurance policies.

Berger suggests using the needs analysis method to determine the required insurance amount. He first estimates cash needs for Jennifer and Ron and then estimates that the surviving spouse would live until age 85 and require $35,000 annually for living expenses, and that those expenses would increase 2% annually in nominal terms. He assumes a 2.5% discount rate. Berger also estimates the present value of the surviving spouse's salary income until retirement at age 65 for both Jennifer and Ron. Exhibit 1 presents an abbreviated life insurance worksheet.

EXHIBIT 1   Joseph Family Financial Needs: Life Insurance Worksheet

Cash needs	Ron	Jennifer
Funeral and burial costs plus taxes	$20,000	$20,000
Emergency fund	$15,000	$15,000
Debts to be repaid	$0	$0
Total cash needs	**$35,000**	**$35,000**
Total capital needs	?	?
Total financial needs	?	?
Capital available:		
Cash and investments	$50,000	$50,000
Total capital available	**$50,000**	**$50,000**
Supplemental information:		
PV of surviving spouse's income until retirement at age 65	$748,837 (based on $25,000 starting salary for Jennifer)	$1,304,662 (based on $45,000 starting salary for Ron)

2. **Calculate** the amount of life insurance needs for both Jennifer and Ron individually, based on Berger's assumptions and Exhibit 1.

The following information relates to Questions 3–5

Susan and Robert Hunter, both age 47, live in the United States with their two children, ages 10 and 12. The Hunters both plan to retire at age 67. Susan works as a petroleum engineer at a small oil company, and Robert is a nurse at a local state-owned hospital. The Hunters are saving for retirement and for their children's college education expenses. Susan's annual salary is $135,000 ($90,000 after taxes), and Robert's annual salary is $55,000 ($36,000 after taxes). Their annual household living expenses are $90,000.

The Hunters have $50,000 in their bank account. They also have a stock portfolio consisting of five microcap energy stocks worth around $150,000, which they plan to use to partially fund their retirement needs. The Hunters plan to meet their retirement needs through contributions to pension plans offered by their employers, supplemented by government Social Security income payments starting at age 67. Both contribute 5% of their salaries to their respective defined contribution (DC) plans, but only Susan's company offers a matching contribution up to 10% of her base salary. Susan's DC plan has a current value of $80,000, while Robert's plan has a current value of $40,000. Income and capital gain distributions within the plan are tax free.

The Hunters meet with Helen Chapman seeking financial advice. After reviewing the Hunters' financial objectives, which include funding their retirement and the college education for their two children, Chapman discusses several risks facing the Hunters in their efforts to achieve those objectives.

3. **Evaluate** *each* of the following risks facing the Hunters:
   i.   Premature death risk
   ii. Investment portfolio risk
   iii. Risk to their retirement lifestyle goals
   iv. Earnings risk resulting from potential loss of employment

Chapman reviews the Hunters' existing life insurance policies. Susan Hunter informs Chapman that she currently has a life insurance policy of $200,000 and his wife has a life insurance policy of $300,000. Only Susan has life insurance coverage at work, with coverage at two times her annual salary.

Chapman believes that the Hunters' current coverage is insufficient to provide support for their family in the event of a death. She suggests using the human life value method to estimate the amount of life insurance required. Chapman estimates the present value of the pretax income needed to replace after-tax income to be $1,700,000 for Susan and $394,000 for Robert.

4. **Recommend** the additional life insurance the Hunters need. **Justify** your recommendation.

Chapman reviews the Hunters' expected spending needs in retirement and is concerned they will not have saved enough by retirement to support their lifestyle thereafter. Chapman recommends that the Hunters raise their DC plan contributions to 10% of their salaries. The Hunters are reluctant to do so, however, telling Chapman that they would rather save the additional funds to continue building up their bank account balance. The bank account savings are readily accessible compared with the contribution to the DC funds, which will be unavailable until they retire.

5. **Discuss** the advantages of the recommendation made by Chapman.

The following information relates to Question 6

James and Wendy Chang, both age 58, plan to retire in nine years. James is a human resource manager for a large US company with a defined contribution (DC) pension plan to which he regularly contributes. Wendy is a freelance computer programmer who works out of a home-based office. She contributes to a private DC plan. Both expect to start receiving Social Security income benefits when they retire at age 67. Their long-term goal is for a comfortable retirement and to provide an inheritance for their two children. The Changs believe they will need to maintain, in real terms, their current level of spending of $100,000 when they retire.

The Changs meet with their financial adviser, Lucie Timan, to discuss the risks to their retirement lifestyle goal. She estimates their Social Security benefit amounts at age 67. In her estimation calculations, Timan assumes a 25% tax rate and a 3% inflation rate. Based on his estimates, the Changs will have total annual pretax retirement income, including Social Security benefits, of $194,500 when they retire at age 67. The Changs tell Timan that they plan to use their DC plans' balances at age 67 to buy an immediate fixed annuity with no inflation adjustment.

6. **Discuss** how *each* of the following risk factors could affect the Changs' projected retirement income:
   i.   inflation risk
   ii. loss of employment
   iii. poor investment returns

CHAPTER 14

INTEGRATED CASES IN RISK MANAGEMENT: INSTITUTIONAL

LEARNING OUTCOMES

The candidate should be able to:

- discuss financial risks associated with the portfolio strategy of an institutional investor;
- discuss environmental and social risks associated with the portfolio strategy of an institutional investor;
- analyze and evaluate the financial and non-financial risk exposures in the portfolio strategy of an institutional investor;
- discuss various methods to manage the risks that arise on long-term direct investments of an institutional investor;
- evaluate strengths and weaknesses of an enterprise risk management system and recommend improvements.

PART **II**

SOLUTIONS

CHAPTER 1

DERIVATIVE MARKETS AND INSTRUMENTS

SOLUTIONS

1. C is correct. A derivative is a financial instrument that transforms the performance of the underlying. The transformation of performance function of derivatives is what distinguishes it from mutual funds and exchange traded funds that pass through the returns of the underlying.

   A is incorrect because derivatives, in contrast to mutual funds and exchange traded funds, do not simply pass through the returns of the underlying at payout. B is incorrect because a derivative transforms rather than replicates the performance of the underlying.

2. B is correct. Insurance is a financial contract that provides protection against loss. The party bearing the risk purchases an insurance policy, which transfers the risk to the other party, the insurer, for a specified period of time. The risk itself does not change, but the party bearing it does. Derivatives allow for this same type of risk transfer.

   A is incorrect because derivatives, like insurance, have a definite, as opposed to indefinite, life span and expire on a specified date.

   C is incorrect because both derivatives and insurance allow for the transfer of risk from one party (the purchaser of the insurance policy or of a derivative) to another party (the insurer or a derivative seller), for a specified period of time. The risk itself does not change, but the party bearing it does.

3. A is correct. Derivatives allow market participants to practice more effective risk management, a process by which an organization, or individual, defines the level of risk it wishes to take, measures the level of risk it is taking, and adjusts the latter to equal the former.

   B is incorrect because derivatives are characterized by a relatively high degree of leverage, meaning that participants in derivatives transactions usually have to invest only a small amount, as opposed to a large amount, of their own capital relative to the value of the underlying. This allows participants to generate returns that are disproportional, as opposed to proportional, to movements in the underlying.

C is incorrect because derivatives are not needed to copy strategies that can be implemented with the underlying on a standalone basis. Rather, derivatives can be used to create strategies that cannot be implemented with the underlying alone. Simultaneously taking long positions in multiple highly liquid fixed-income securities is a strategy that can be implemented with the underlying securities on a standalone basis.

4. B is correct. Over-the counter-derivatives markets are customized and mostly unregulated. As a result, over-the-counter markets are less transparent in comparison with the high degree of transparency and standardization associated with exchange-traded derivative markets.

A is incorrect because exchange-traded derivatives are standardized, whereas over-the-counter derivatives are customized. C is incorrect because exchange-traded derivatives are characterized by a high degree of transparency because all transactions are disclosed to exchanges and regulatory agencies, whereas over-the-counter derivatives are relatively opaque.

5. C is correct. Exchanged-traded derivatives are guaranteed by a clearinghouse against default.

A is incorrect because traded derivatives are characterized by a relatively high degree of regulation. B is incorrect because the terms of exchange-traded derivatives terms are specified by the exchange.

6. A is correct. The clearing and settlement process of derivative transactions provides a credit guarantee.

B is incorrect because although the exchange markets are said to have transparency, they also involve standardization. That entails a loss of flexibility, with participants limited to only those transactions permitted on the exchange.

C is incorrect because derivatives exchanges clear and settle all contracts overnight, which is faster than most securities exchanges, which require two business days.

7. B is correct. With full implementation of these regulations in the OTC derivatives market, most OTC transactions need to be reported to regulators.

A is incorrect because although under full implementation of the regulations information on most OTC transactions needs to be reported to regulators, many transactions retain a degree of privacy with lower transparency.

C is incorrect because although under full implementation of new regulations a number of OTC transactions have to be cleared through central clearing agencies, there are exemptions that cover a significant percentage of derivative transactions.

8. A is correct because forward commitments provide linear payoffs.

B is incorrect because forward commitments depend on the outcome or payoff of an underlying asset.

C is incorrect because forward commitments obligate parties to make (not provide the right to engage) a final payment contingent on the performance of the underlying.

9. B is correct. In a forward contract, either party could default, whereas in a contingent claim, default is possible only from the short to the long.

A is incorrect because the forward price is set in the pricing of the contract such that the starting contract value is zero, unlike contingent claims, under which parties can select any starting value.

C is incorrect because both forward contracts and contingent claims can be settled by either physical or cash delivery.

10. B is correct. The buyer is obligated to pay the forward price $F_0(T)$ at expiration and receives an asset worth S_T, the price of the underlying. The contract effectively pays off $S_T - F_0(T)$, the value of the contract at expiration. The buyer therefore profits if $S_T > F_0(T)$.

    A is incorrect because the long and the short are engaged in a zero-sum game. This is a type of competition in which one participant's gains are the other's losses, with their payoffs effectively being mirror images.

    C is incorrect because although the gain from owning the underlying and the gain from owning the forward are both driven by S_T, the price of the underlying at expiration, they are not the same value. The gain from owning the underlying would be $S_T - S_0$, the change in its price, whereas the gain from owning the forward would be $S_T - F_0(T)$, the value of the forward at expiration.

11. C is correct. In the case of cash settlement, the long can acquire the asset, effectively paying the forward price, $F_0(T)$.

    A is incorrect because forward contracts settled by cash or by delivery have the same economic effect.

    B is incorrect because both non-deliverable forwards and contracts for differences can settle by an exchange of cash.

12. A is correct. A futures contract is a standardized derivative contract.

    B is incorrect because through its clearinghouse the futures exchange provides a credit guarantee that it will make up a loss in the event a losing party cannot pay.

    C is incorrect because a futures contract is marked to market at the end of each day, a process in which the futures clearinghouse determines an average of the final futures trade of the day and designates that price as the settlement price.

13. A is correct. Price limits are important in helping the clearinghouse manage its credit exposure. Sharply moving prices make it more difficult for the clearinghouse to collect from parties losing money.

    B is incorrect because typically the exchange rules allow for an expansion of price limits the next day (not intra-day) if traders are willing.

    C is incorrect because price limits establish a band relative to the previous day's settlement price (not final trade).

14. A is correct. The maintenance margin is always significantly lower than the initial margin.

    B is incorrect because the initial margin required is typically at most (not at least) 10% of the futures price.

    C is incorrect because a margin call requires a deposit large enough to bring the balance up to the initial (not maintenance) margin.

15. C is correct. Comparing the derivatives, forward and futures contracts have nearly equivalent profits by the time of expiration of the forward.

    A is incorrect because the timing of profits for a futures contract is different from that of forwards. Forwards realize the full amount at expiration, whereas futures contracts realize their profit in parts on a day-to-day basis.

    B is incorrect because the settlement arrangements for the forwards can be agreed on at initiation and written in the contract based on the desires of the engaged parties. However, in the case of a futures contract, the exchange (not the engaged parties) specifies whether physical delivery or cash settlement applies.

16. C is correct. A credit default swap (CDS) is a derivative in which the credit protection seller provides protection to the credit protection buyer against the credit risk of a separate party. CDS are classified as a contingent claim.

A is incorrect because futures contracts are classified as forward commitments. B is incorrect because interest rate swaps are classified as forward commitments.

17. B is correct. Forward commitments represent an obligation to buy or sell the underlying asset at an agreed upon price at a future date.

    A is incorrect because the right to buy or sell the underlying asset is a characteristic of contingent claims, not forward commitments. C is incorrect because a credit default swap provides a promise to provide credit protection to the credit protection buyer in the event of a credit event such as a default or credit downgrade and is classified as a contingent claim.

18. A is correct. Options are classified as a contingent claim, which provides payoffs that are non-linearly related to the performance of the underlying.

    B is incorrect because forwards are classified as a forward commitment, which provides payoffs that are linearly related to the performance of the underlying. C is incorrect because interest-rate swaps are classified as a forward commitment, which provides payoffs that are linearly related to the performance of the underlying.

19. A is correct. An interest rate swap is defined as a derivative in which two parties agree to exchange a series of cash flows: One set of cash flows is variable, and the other set can be variable or fixed.

    B is incorrect because a credit derivative is a derivative contract in which the credit protection seller provides protection to the credit protection buyer. C is incorrect because a call option gives the buyer the right to purchase the underlying from the seller.

20. C is correct. Interest rate swaps and forwards are over-the-counter contracts that are privately negotiated and are both subject to default. Futures contracts are traded on an exchange, which provides a credit guarantee and protection against default.

    A is incorrect because futures are exchange-traded contracts that provide daily settlement of gains and losses and a credit guarantee by the exchange through its clearinghouse. B is incorrect because futures are exchange-traded contracts that provide daily settlement of gains and losses and a credit guarantee by the exchange through its clearinghouse.

21. A is correct. A swap is a bit more like a forward contract than a futures contract in that it is an OTC contract, so it is privately negotiated and subject to default.

    B is incorrect because in a swap, although either party can default, only one party can do so at a particular time. Money owed is based on the net owed by one party to the other, and only the party owing the greater amount can default to the counterparty owing the lesser amount.

    C is incorrect because a swap involves an exchange between parties in which at least one party pays a variable series of cash flows determined by an underlying asset or rate.

22. B is correct. A plain vanilla swap is a fixed-for-floating interest rate swap, which is the most common type of swap.

    A is incorrect because a basis swap is a transaction based on the TED spread (T-bills versus Eurodollars) and is not the same as a plain vanilla swap.

    C is incorrect because an overnight indexed swap is a swap that is tied to a federal funds type of rate, reflecting the rate at which banks borrow overnight, and is not the same as a plain vanilla swap.

23. A is correct. The notional principal of a swap is not exchanged in the case of an interest rate swap.

    B is incorrect because an amortizing loan will be matched with a swap with a pre-specified declining (not fixed) notional principal that matches the loan balance.

C is incorrect because the notional principal is equal to the loan balance. Although the loan has an actual balance (the amount owed by the borrower to the creditor), the swap does not have such a balance owed by one swap party to the other.

24. B is correct. The buyer of the option pays the option premium to the seller of the option at the initiation of the contract. The option premium represents the value of the option, whereas futures and forwards have a value of zero at the initiation of the contract.

    A is incorrect because no money changes hands between parties at the initiation of the futures contract, thus the value of the futures contract is zero at initiation. C is incorrect because no money changes hands between parties at the initiation of the forward contract, thus the value of the forward contract is zero at initiation.

25. A is correct. A contingent claim, a derivative in which the outcome or payoff depends on the outcome or payoff of an underlying asset, has come to be associated with a right, but not an obligation, to make a final payment contingent on the performance of the underlying.

    B is incorrect because an option, as a contingent claim, grants the right but not the obligation to buy or sell the underlying at a later date.

    C is incorrect because the holder of an option has a choice of whether to exercise the option. This choice creates a payoff that transforms the underlying payoff in a more pronounced manner than does a forward, futures, or swap, which provide linear payoffs. Options are different in that they limit losses in one direction.

26. C is correct. The right to buy the underlying is referred to as a call option. Furthermore, options that can be exercised prior to the expiration date are referred to as American-style options.

    A is incorrect because a put option grants the holder the right to sell, as opposed to buy, the underlying.

    B is incorrect because European-style options can only be exercised at expiration.

27. B is correct. A credit derivative is a derivative contract in which the credit protection seller provides protection to the credit protection buyer against the credit risk of a third party.

    A is incorrect because the clearinghouse provides a credit guarantee to both the buyer and the seller of a futures contract, whereas a credit derivative is between two parties, in which the credit protection seller provides a credit guarantee to the credit protection buyer. C is incorrect because futures contracts require that both the buyer and the seller of the futures contract provide a cash deposit for a portion of the futures transaction into a margin account, often referred to as a performance bond or good faith deposit.

28. C is correct. An asset-backed security is a derivative contract in which a portfolio of debt instruments is assembled and claims are issued on the portfolio in the form of tranches, which have different priorities of claims on the payments made by the debt securities such that prepayments or credit losses are allocated to the most junior tranches first and the most senior tranches last.

    A is incorrect because the expected returns of the tranches vary according to the perceived credit risk, with the senior tranches having the highest credit quality and the junior tranches the lowest. Thus, the senior tranches have the lowest expected returns and the junior tranches have the highest. Notably, in a bond mutual fund or an ETF, all investors in the fund have equal claims, and so the rate of return earned by each investor is the same.

    B is incorrect because an asset-backed security is a derivative contract in which a single portfolio of securities is assembled and claims are issued on the portfolio in the form of tranches.

29. A is correct. Lower interest rates entice homeowners to pay off their mortgages early because they can refinance at lower rates. The most junior tranche in a CMO will bear the first wave of prepayments until that tranche has been completely repaid its full principal investment. At that point, the next tranche will bear prepayments until that tranche has been fully repaid. Therefore, the Class C tranche of a CMO will be repaid before the more senior Class A tranche.

    B is incorrect because the tranches, which have different priorities of claims on the principal payments made by the underlying mortgages, will see prepayments allocated to the most junior tranches first and the most senior tranches last.

    C is incorrect because the most junior tranche in a CMO will bear the first wave of prepayments until that tranche has been completely repaid its full principal investment. At that point, the next tranche will bear prepayments until that tranche has been fully repaid. Therefore, the Class C tranche will be repaid prior to, not after, the Class A tranche.

30. A is correct. The expected returns of the tranches vary according to the perceived credit risk, with the senior tranches having the highest credit quality and the junior tranches the lowest. Thus, the senior tranches have the lowest expected returns and the junior tranches have the highest. The most junior tranche is sometimes called the "equity tranche."

    B is incorrect because the senior tranches in a CDO have the lowest expected returns and the junior (or equity) tranches have the highest.

    C is incorrect because the senior tranches in a CDO have the lowest expected returns and the junior (or equity) tranches have the highest. A mezzanine tranche is intermediate between the senior and junior tranches.

31. A is correct. Equity swaps, also known as index swaps, are quite popular and permit investors to pay the return on one stock index and receive the return on another index or a fixed rate.

    B is incorrect because warrants are options that are sold directly to the public, allowing holders to exercise and buy shares directly from the company as opposed to using stock indexes to determine returns.

    C is incorrect because although index derivatives in the form of options, forwards, futures, and swaps are very popular, paying the return on a stock index and receiving a fixed rate describes an equity swap (or index swap), not a futures contract.

32. A is correct. In a plain vanilla interest rate swap, an interest rate, such as Libor, serves as the underlying. A plain vanilla interest rate swap is one of many derivatives in which a rate, not the instrument that pays the rate, is the underlying.

    B is incorrect because a plain vanilla interest rate swap is one of many derivatives in which a rate, not an instrument that pays a rate, is the underlying.

    C is incorrect because a plain vanilla interest rate swap is one of many derivatives in which a rate, not an instrument (or index) that pays a rate, is the underlying.

33. B is correct. Because interest rates and currencies are both subject to change, a currency swap has two sources of risk. Furthermore, companies operating across borders are subject to both interest rate risk and currency risk, and currency swaps are commonly used to manage these risks.

    A is incorrect because currency risk is a major factor in global financial markets, and the currency derivatives market is extremely large, as opposed to small.

    C is incorrect because a currency swap is executed by two parties making a series of interest rate payments to each other in different currencies, as opposed to the same currency.

34. A is correct. The primary commodity derivatives are futures, but forwards, swaps, and options are also used.

B is incorrect because the commodity market is extremely large and subject to an almost unimaginable array of risks.

C is incorrect because commodity and financial traders have become relatively homogeneous since the creation of financial futures. Historically, commodity traders and financial traders were quite different groups, and there used to be a tendency to think of the commodity world as somewhat separate from the financial world.

35. A is correct. Derivative markets typically have greater liquidity than the underlying spot market as a result of the lower capital required to trade derivatives compared with the underlying. Derivatives also have lower transaction costs and lower capital requirements than the underlying.

     B is incorrect because transaction costs for derivatives are lower than the underlying spot market. C is incorrect because derivatives markets have lower capital requirements than the underlying spot market.

36. B is correct. One of the benefits of derivative markets is that derivatives create trading strategies not otherwise possible in the underlying spot market, thus providing opportunities for more effective risk management than simply replicating the payoff of the underlying.

     A is incorrect because effective risk management is one of the primary purposes associated with derivative markets. C is incorrect because one of the operational advantages associated with derivatives is that it is easier to go short compared to the underlying spot market.

37. C is correct. The futures market reveals the price that the holder of an asset could take and avoid the risk of uncertainty.

     A is incorrect because although the futures price is sometimes thought of as predictive, it provides only a little more information than does a spot price and is not really a forecast of the futures spot price.

     B is incorrect because by virtue of the fact that the futures market requires less capital, information can flow into the futures market before it gets into the spot market.

38. C is correct. When prices deviate from fundamental values, derivative markets offer a less costly way to exploit mispricing in comparison to other free and competitive financial markets.

     A is incorrect because derivative markets tend to transfer liquidity to (not from) the broader financial markets, because investors are far more willing to trade if they can more easily manage their risk, trade at lower cost and with less capital, and go short more easily. An increased willingness to trade leads to a more liquid market.

     B is incorrect because it is likely (not unlikely) that fundamental value will be reflected in the derivative markets both before and after it is restored in the underlying market owing to lower capital requirements and transaction costs in the derivative markets.

39. B is correct. Opponents of derivatives claim that excessive speculative trading brings instability to the markets. Defaults by speculators can lead to defaults by their creditors, their creditors' creditors, and so on.

     A is incorrect because derivatives are one of many mechanisms through which excessive risk can be taken. There are many ways to take on leverage that look far less harmful but can be just as risky.

     C is incorrect because responses to crashes and crises typically call for more rules and regulations restricting the use of derivatives, such as requiring more collateral and credit mitigation measures. Such rules and regulations are generally implemented after a crash and are directed at limiting government bailouts of the costs from derivatives risks.

40. C is correct. Derivatives trading brings extensive benefits to financial markets (low costs, low capital requirements, ease of going short, etc.) and thus benefits society as a whole. Gambling, on the other hand, typically benefits only a limited number of participants.

    A is incorrect because the general image of speculators is not a good one. Speculators are often thought to be short-term traders who attempt to exploit temporary inefficiencies, caring little about long-term fundamental values.

    B is incorrect because speculation and gambling are both forms of financial risk taking.

41. C is correct. Opponents argue that speculators use large amounts of leverage, thereby subjecting themselves and their creditors to substantial risk if markets do not move in their hoped-for direction. Defaults by speculators can then lead to defaults by their creditors, their creditors' creditors, and so on. These effects can, therefore, be systemic and reflect an epidemic contagion whereby instability can spread throughout markets and an economy, if not the entire world.

    A is incorrect because central clearing of OTC derivatives, similar to how exchange-traded derivatives are cleared, is intended to lessen the risk of contagion.

    B is incorrect because it is derivatives' low cost and low capital requirements, not high cost and high capital requirements, that opponents point to as contributing to an excessive amount of speculative trading that brings instability to the markets.

42. C is correct. Many derivatives are extremely complex and require a high-level understanding of mathematics. As a result, the financial industry employs many mathematicians, physicists, and computer scientists.

    A is incorrect because scientists create models of markets by using scientific principles that often fail. For example, to a physicist modeling the movements of celestial bodies, the science is reliable and the physicist is unlikely to misapply the science. The same science applied to financial markets is far less reliable. Financial markets are driven by the actions of people who are not as consistent as the movements of celestial bodies.

    B is incorrect because the complex nature of derivatives has made many distrust, as opposed to trust, derivatives, the people who work with them, and the scientific methods they use.

43. A is correct. The benefits of derivatives, such as low transaction costs, low capital requirements, use of leverage, and the ease in which participants can go short, also can result in excessive speculative trading. These activities can lead to defaults on the part of speculators and creditors.

    B is incorrect because arbitrage activities tend to bring about a convergence of prices to intrinsic value. C is incorrect because asymmetric performance is not itself destabilizing.

44. C is correct. The law of one price occurs when market participants engage in arbitrage activities so that identical assets sell for the same price in different markets.

    A is incorrect because the law of one price refers to identical assets. B is incorrect because it refers to arbitrage not the law of one price.

45. A is correct. Arbitrage opportunities exist when the same asset or two equivalent combinations of assets that produce the same results sell for different prices. When this situation occurs, market participants would buy the asset in the cheaper market and simultaneously sell it in the more expensive market, thus earning a riskless arbitrage profit without committing any capital.

    B is incorrect because it is not the definition of an arbitrage opportunity. C is incorrect because it is not the definition of an arbitrage opportunity.

46. B is correct. $C_T = Max(0, S_T - X) = Max(0, 55 - 50) = 5$
    $\Pi = C_T - C_0 = 5 - 4 = 1$
47. A is correct. $C_T = Max(0, S_T - X) = Max(0, 48 - 50) = 0$
    $\Pi = C_T - C_0 = 0 - 4 = -4$
48. A is correct. $-C_T = -Max(0, S_T - X) = -Max(0, 49 - 50) = 0$
    $\Pi = -C_T + C_0 = -0 + 4 = 4$
49. C is correct. $-C_T = -Max(0, S_T - X) = -Max(0, 52 - 50) = -2$
    $\Pi = -C_T + C_0 = -2 + 4 = 2$
50. C is correct. $C_T = Max(0, S_T - X) = Max(0, 99 - 105) = 0$
    $\Pi = C_T - C_0 = 0 - 7 = -7$
51. B is correct. $C_T = Max(0, S_T - X) = Max(0, 112 - 105) = 7$
    $\Pi = C_T - C_0 = 7 - 7 = 0$
    Note: \$112 is the breakeven price
52. B is correct. $C_T = Max(0, S_T - X) = Max(0, 115 - 105) = 10$
    $\Pi = C_T - C_0 = 10 - 7 = 3$
53. C is correct. $P_T = Max(0, X - S_T) = Max(0, 95 - 100) = 0$
    $\Pi = P_T - P_0 = 0 - 5 = -5$
54. C is correct. $P_T = Max(0, X - S_T) = Max(0, 95 - 95) = 0$
    $\Pi = P_T - P_0 = 0 - 5 = -5$
55. B is correct. $P_T = Max(0, X - S_T) = Max(0, 95 - 85) = 10$
    $\Pi = P_T - P_0 = 10 - 5 = 5$

CHAPTER 2

BASICS OF DERIVATIVE PRICING AND VALUATION

SOLUTIONS

1. C is correct. An asset's current price, S_0, is determined by discounting the expected future price of the asset by r (the risk-free rate) plus λ (the risk premium) over the period from 0 to T, as illustrated in the following equation:

$$S_0 = \frac{E(S_T)}{(1 + r + \lambda)^T}.$$

   Thus, an asset's current price inversely relates to its level of risk via the related risk premium, λ.

   A is incorrect because an asset's current price in spot markets is calculated using the risk-free rate plus a risk premium.

   B is incorrect because an asset's current price in spot markets is inversely related, not directly related, to its level of risk.

2. A is correct. An illiquid position is a limit to arbitrage because it may be difficult to realize gains of an illiquid offsetting position. A significant opportunity arises from a sufficiently large price differential or a small price differential that can be employed on a very large scale.

3. A is correct. Some arbitrage opportunities represent such small price discrepancies that they are only worth exploiting if the transaction costs are low. An arbitrage opportunity may require short-selling assets at costs that eliminate any profit potential. If the law of one price holds, there is no arbitrage opportunity.

4. C is correct. Arbitrage is a type of transaction undertaken when two assets or portfolios produce identical results but sell for different prices. A trader buys the asset or portfolio with the lower price and sells the asset or portfolio with the higher price, generating a net inflow of funds at the start of the holding period. Because the two assets or portfolios produce identical results, a long position in one and short position in the other means that at

the end of the holding period, the payoffs offset. Therefore, there is no money gained or lost at the end of the holding period, so there is no risk.

5. B is correct. A long asset and a short risk-free asset (meaning to borrow at the risk-free rate) can be combined to produce a long derivative position.

   A is incorrect because a short derivative and a long asset combine to produce a position equivalent to a long risk-free bond, not a long derivative.

   C is incorrect because a short derivative and a short risk-free bond combine to produce a position equivalent to a short asset, not a long derivative.

6. B is correct. Virtually all derivative pricing models discount the expected payoff of the derivative at the risk-free rate.

   A is incorrect because derivatives are priced by assuming that the market is free of arbitrage opportunities via the principle of no arbitrage, not by assuming that the market offers them.

   C is incorrect because the application of a risk premium to the expected payoff of the derivative and its risk is not appropriate in the pricing of derivatives. An investor's risk premium is not relevant to pricing a derivative.

7. B is correct. The forward price is agreed upon at the start of the contract and is the fixed price at which the underlying will be purchased (or sold) at expiration. Payment is made at expiration. The value of the forward contract may change over time, but the forward price does not change.

8. C is correct. The price of a forward contract is a contractually fixed price, established at initiation, at which the underlying will be purchased (or sold) at expiration. The value of a forward contract at initiation is zero; therefore, the forward price is greater than the value of the forward contract at initiation.

9. B is correct. The value of the forward contract, unlike its price, will adjust as market conditions change. The forward price is fixed at initiation.

10. A is correct. When a forward contract expires, if the spot price is higher than the forward price, the long party profits from paying the lower forward price for the underlying. Therefore, the forward contract has a positive value to the long party and a negative value to the short party. However, if the forward price is higher than the spot price, the short party profits from receiving the higher forward price (the contract value is positive to the short party and negative to the long party).

11. B is correct. At initiation, the forward price is the future value of the spot price (spot price compounded at the risk-free rate over the life of the contract). If the forward price were set to the spot price or the present value of the spot price, it would be possible for one side to earn an arbitrage profit by selling the asset and investing the proceeds until contract expiration.

12. A is correct. The forward price of each stock is found by compounding the spot price by the risk-free rate for the period and then subtracting the future value of any benefits and adding the future value of any costs. In the absence of any benefits or costs, the one-year forward prices of BWQ and ZER should be equal. After subtracting the benefits related to BWQ, the one-year forward price of BWQ is lower than the one-year forward price of ZER.

13. A is correct. An asset's forward price is increased by the future value of any costs and decreased by the future value of any benefits: $F_0(T) = S_0(1 + r)^T - (\gamma - \theta)(1 + r)^T$. If the net cost of carry (benefits less costs) is positive, the forward price is lower than if the net cost of carry was zero.

14. C is correct. When a commodity's storage costs exceed its convenience yield benefits, the net cost of carry (benefits less costs) is negative. Subtracting this negative amount from the spot price compounded at the risk-free rate results in an addition to the compounded spot price. The result is a commodity forward price that is higher than the spot price compounded. The commodity's forward price is less than the spot price compounded when the convenience yield benefits exceed the storage costs and the commodity's forward price is the same as the spot price compounded when the costs equal the benefits.

15. C is correct. The convenience yield is a benefit of holding the asset and generally exists when a commodity is in short supply. The future value of the convenience yield is subtracted from the compounded spot price and reduces the commodity's forward price relative to its spot price. The opportunity cost is the risk-free rate. In the absence of carry costs, the forward price is the spot price compounded at the risk-free rate and will exceed the spot price. Dividends are benefits that reduce the forward price but the lack of dividends has no effect on the spot price relative to the forward price of a commodity in short supply.

16. B is correct. When interest rates are constant, forwards and futures will likely have the same prices. The price differential will vary with the volatility of interest rates. In addition, if futures prices and interest rates are uncorrelated, forward and futures prices will be the same. If futures prices are positively correlated with interest rates, futures contracts are more desirable to holders of long positions than are forwards. This is because rising prices lead to future profits that are reinvested in periods of rising interest rates, and falling prices lead to losses that occur in periods of falling interest rates. If futures prices are negatively correlated with interest rates, futures contracts are less desirable to holders of long positions than are forwards. The more desirable contract will tend to have the higher price.

17. C is correct. Futures contracts are marked-to-market on a daily basis. The accumulated gains and losses from the previous day's trading session are deducted from the accounts of those holding losing positions and transferred to the accounts of those holding winning positions. Futures contracts trade on an exchange; forward contracts are over-the-counter transactions. Typically both forward and futures contracts are initiated at a zero value.

18. A is correct. If futures prices and interest rates are negatively correlated, forwards are more desirable to holders of long positions than are futures. This is because rising prices lead to futures profits that are reinvested in periods of falling interest rates. It is better to receive all of the cash at expiration under such conditions. If futures prices and interest rates are uncorrelated, forward and futures prices will be the same. If futures prices are positively correlated with interest rates, futures contracts are more desirable to holders of long positions than are forwards.

19. B is correct. Valuation of the swap during its life appeals to replication and the principle of arbitrage. Valuation consists of reproducing the remaining payments on the swap with other transactions. The value of that replication strategy is the value of the swap. The swap price is typically set such that the swap contract has a value of zero at initiation. The value of a swap contract will change during the life of the contract as the value of the underlying changes in value.

20. C is correct. Replication is the key to pricing a swap. The swap price is determined at initiation by replication. The value (not the price) of the swap is typically zero at initiation and the fixed swap price is typically determined such that the value of the swap will be zero at initiation.

21. B is correct. The principal of replication articulates that the valuation of a swap is the present value of all the net cash flow payments from the swap, not simply the present

value of the fixed payments of the swap or the present value of the underlying at the end of the contract.

22. B is correct. When two parties engage in a series of forward contracts and initially agree on a price of $FS_0(T)$, some of the forward contracts have positive values and some have negative values, but their combined value equals zero.

A is incorrect because for a swap, all payments are fixed and equal, not variable.

C is incorrect because forward prices are determined by the spot price and the net cost of carry, meaning that forward contracts expiring at different times will have different prices, not the same price.

23. C is correct. On each payment date, the swap owner receives a payment based on the value of the underlying at the time of each respective payment.

A is incorrect because in a swap involving a series of fixed payments exchanged for a series of floating payments, each floating payment reflects the value of the underlying at the time of payment, not a designated value at contract initiation.

B is incorrect because in a swap involving a series of fixed payments exchanged for a series of floating payments, each floating payment is based on the value of the underlying at the time of each respective payment, not on the market value at the end of the swap.

24. B is correct. If the underlying has a value equal to the exercise price at expiration, both options will have zero value since they both have the same exercise price. For example, if the exercise price is $25 and at expiration the underlying price is $25, both the call option and the put option will have a value of zero. The value of an option cannot fall below zero. The holder of an option is not obligated to exercise the option; therefore, the options each have a minimum value of zero. If the call has a positive value, the put, by definition, must have a zero value and vice versa. Both cannot have a positive value.

25. C is correct. A European put option will be valuable at expiration if the exercise price is greater than the underlying price. The holder can put (deliver) the underlying and receive the exercise price, which is higher than the spot price. A European put option would be worthless if the exercise price was equal to or less than the underlying price.

26. B is correct. The value of a European call option at expiration is the greater of zero or the value of the underlying minus the exercise price.

27. B is correct. A European call option with two months until expiration will typically have positive time value, where time value reflects the value of the uncertainty that arises from the volatility in the underlying. The call option has a zero exercise value if the spot price is below the exercise price. The exercise value of a European call option is $\text{Max}(0, S_t - X)$, where S_t is the current spot price at time t and X is the exercise price.

28. A is correct. When the price of the underlying is below the exercise price for a put, the option is said to be in-the-money. If the price of the underlying is the same as the exercise price, the put is at-the-money and if it is above the exercise price, the put is out-of-the-money.

29. A is correct. An in-the-money European put option decreases in value with an increase in the risk-free rate. A higher risk-free rate reduces the present value of any proceeds received on exercise.

30. A is correct. The value of a European call option is inversely related to the exercise price. A lower exercise price means there are more potential outcomes at which the call expires in-the-money. The option value will be greater the lower the exercise price. For a higher exercise price, the opposite is true. Both the time to expiration and the volatility of the underlying are directly (positively) related to the value of a European call option.

31. B is correct. The value of a European call option is inversely related to the exercise price and directly related to the time to expiration. Option 1 and Option 2 have the same exercise price; however, Option 2 has a longer time to expiration. Consequently, Option 2 would likely have a higher value than Option 1. Option 2 and Option 3 have the same time to expiration; however, Option 2 has a lower exercise price. Thus, Option 2 would likely have a higher value than Option 3.

32. B is correct. The value of a European put option can be either directly or indirectly related to time to expiration. The direct effect is more common, but the inverse effect can prevail the longer the time to expiration, the higher the risk-free rate, and the deeper in-the-money is the put. The value of a European put option is directly related to the exercise price and the volatility of the underlying.

33. B is correct. Prior to expiration, the lowest value of a European put is the greater of zero or the present value of the exercise price minus the value of the underlying.

34. C is correct. Payments, such as dividends, reduce the value of the underlying, which increases the value of a European put option. Carrying costs reduce the value of a European put option. An increase in the risk-free interest rate may decrease the value of a European put option.

35. A is correct. A long bond can be synthetically created by combining a long asset, a long put, and a short call. A fiduciary call is created by combining a long call with a risk-free bond. A protective put is created by combining a long asset with a long put.

36. B is correct. According to put–call parity, a synthetic call can be constructed by combining a long asset, long put, and short bond positions.

37. C is correct. The actual probabilities of the up and down moves in the underlying do not appear in the binomial option pricing model, only the pseudo or "risk-neutral" probabilities. Both the spot price of the underlying and two possible prices one period later are required by the binomial option pricing model.

38. C is correct. Pricing an option relies on the facts that a perfectly hedged investment earns the risk-free rate and that, based on the binomial option pricing model, the size of the two possible changes in the option price (meaning the potential step up or step down in the option value) after one period are equivalent.

39. B is correct. When the volatility of the underlying decreases, the value of the option also decreases, meaning that the upper payoff value of the hedge portfolio combining them declines. However, the lower payoff value remains at zero.

40. B is correct. The binomial model does not consider the actual probabilities of upward and downward movements in determining the option value. Thus, a change in this probability has no effect on the calculated option price.

41. C is correct. If an option is trading above the value predicted by the binomial model, investors can engage in arbitrage by selling a call, buying shares of the underlying, and funding the transaction by borrowing at the risk-free rate. This will earn a return in excess of the risk-free rate.

42. C is correct. Prior to expiration, an American call option will typically have a value in the market that is greater than its exercise value. Although the American option is at-the-money and therefore has an exercise value of zero, the time value of the call option would likely lead to the option having a positive market value.

43. B is correct. At expiration, the values of American and European call options are effectively the same; both are worth the greater of zero and the exercise value.

44. A is correct. When a dividend is declared, an American call option will have a higher value than a European call option because an American call option holder can exercise early to

capture the value of the dividend. At expiration, both types of call options are worth the greater of zero and the exercise value. A change in the risk-free rate does not affect the relative values of American and European call options.

45. A is correct. Put–call forward parity demonstrates that the outcome of a protective put with a forward contract (long put, long risk-free bond, long forward contract) equals the outcome of a fiduciary call (long call, long risk-free bond). The outcome of a protective put with a forward contract is also equal to the outcome of a protective put with asset (long put, long asset).

46. A is correct. Under put–call parity, initiating a fiduciary call (buying a call option on an asset that expires at time T together with a risk-free zero-coupon bond that also expires at time T) is equivalent to holding the same asset and initiating a protective put on it (buying a put option with an exercise price of X that can be used to sell the asset for X at time T).

47. B is correct. On the one hand, buying a call option on an asset and a risk-free bond with the same maturity is known as a fiduciary call. If the fiduciary call expires in the money (meaning that the value of the call, $S_T - X$, is greater than the risk-free bond's price at expiration, X), then the total value of the fiduciary call is $(S_T - X) + X$, or S_T. On the other hand, holding an underlying asset, S_T, and buying a put on that asset is known as a protective put. If the put expires out of the money, meaning that the value of the asset, S_T, is greater than the put's value at expiration, 0, then the total value of the protective put is $S_T - 0$, or S_T. A protective put and a fiduciary call produce the same result.

48. A is correct. One can synthetically create a long asset position by buying a call, shorting a put, and buying a bond.

   B is incorrect because combining a short call and a short bond with the right to sell (not buy) another asset via a long put could not result in a new synthetic long asset position.

   C is incorrect because combining a long call, a short asset, and a long bond creates a long put, not a synthetic long asset.

49. A is correct. Put–call–forward parity is based on the assumption that no arbitrage is possible within the spot, forward, and option markets.

   B is incorrect because the value of a European put at expiration is the greater of either zero or the exercise price minus the value of the underlying, not the greater of zero or the underlying value minus the exercise price. In addition, put–call–forward parity is related to the equality of a fiduciary call and a synthetic protective put or to a protective put and a synthetic fiduciary call, not specifically to the value of a put at expiration.

   C is incorrect because the value of a European call at expiration is the greater of either zero or the underlying value minus the exercise price, not the greater of zero or the exercise price minus the value of the underlying. In addition, put–call–forward parity is related to the equality of a fiduciary call and a synthetic protective put or to a protective put and a synthetic fiduciary call, not specifically to the value of a call at expiration.

50. A is correct. Purchasing a long forward contract and a risk-free bond creates a synthetic asset. Combining a long synthetic asset, a long put, and a short call is risk free because its payoffs produce a known cash flow of the value of the exercise price.

CHAPTER 3

PRICING AND VALUATION OF FORWARD COMMITMENTS

SOLUTIONS

1. B is correct.

   The no-arbitrage futures price is equal to the following:

   $$F_0 = FV[B_0 + AI_0 - PVCI]$$
   $$F_0 = (1 + 0.003)^{0.25}(112.00 + 0.08 - 0) = 112.1640.$$

   The adjusted price of the futures contract is equal to the conversion factor multiplied by the quoted futures price:

   $$F_0 = CF \times Q_0$$
   $$F_0 = (0.90)(125) = 112.50.$$

   Adding the accrued interest of 0.20 in three months (futures contract expiration) to the adjusted price of the futures contract gives a total price of 112.70.

   This difference means that the futures contract is overpriced by $112.70 - 112.1640 = 0.5360$. The available arbitrage profit is the present value of this difference: $0.5360/(1.003)^{0.25} = 0.5356$.

2. B is correct. The no-arbitrage futures price is

   $$F_0 = S_0 \exp^{(r_c + CC - CB)T}$$
   $$F_0 = 16,080\exp^{(0.002996 + 0 - 0.011)(3/12)} = 16,047.86.$$

3. A is correct. The carry arbitrage model price of the forward contract is

   $$FV(S_0) = S_0(1 + r)^T = \$250(1 + 0.003)^{0.75} = \$250.562289.$$

The market price of the TSI forward contract is \$250.562289. A carry or reverse carry arbitrage opportunity does not exist because the market price of the forward contract is equal to the carry arbitrage model price.

4. B is correct. From the perspective of the long position, the forward value is equal to the present value of the difference in forward prices:

$$V_t = PV[F_t - F_0],$$

where

$$F_t = FV(S_t + CC_t - CB_t).$$

All else equal, an increase in the risk-free rate before contract expiration would cause the forward price, F_t, to increase. This increase in the forward price would cause the value of the TSI forward contract, from the perspective of the short, to decrease. Therefore, an increase in the risk-free rate would lead to a loss on the short position in the TSI forward contract.

5. C is correct. The no-arbitrage price of the forward contract, three months after contract initiation, is

$$F_{0.25} = FV_{0.25}(S_{0.25} + CC_{0.25} - CB_{0.25})$$
$$F_{0.25} = [\$245 + 0 - \$1.50/(1 + 0.00325)^{(0.5 - 0.25)}](1 + 0.00325)^{(0.75 - 0.25)} = \$243.8966.$$

Therefore, from the perspective of the long, the value of the TSI forward contract is

$$V_{0.25} = PV_{0.25}[F_{0.25} - F_0]$$
$$V_{0.25} = (\$243.8966 - \$250.562289)/(1 + 0.00325)^{0.75 - 0.25} = -\$6.6549.$$

Because Troubadour is short the TSI forward contract, the value of his position is a gain of \$6.6549.

6. C is correct. The swap pricing equation is

$$r_{FIX} = \frac{1 - PV_n(1)}{\sum_{i=1}^{n} PV_i(1)}.$$

That is, the fixed swap rate is equal to 1 minus the final present value factor (in this case, Year 3) divided by the sum of the present values (in this case, the sum of Years 1, 2, and 3). The sum of present values for Years 1, 2, and 3 is calculated as

$$\sum_{i=1}^{n} PV_i(1) = 0.990099 + 0.977876 + 0.965136 = 2.933111.$$

Thus, the fixed-swap rate is calculated as

$$r_{FIX} = \frac{1 - 0.965136}{2.933111} = 0.01189 \text{ or } 1.19\%.$$

7. B is correct. The value of a swap from the perspective of the receive-fixed (pay-floating) party is calculated as

$$V = NA \times (FS_0 - FS_t) \times \sum_{i=1}^{n} PV_i.$$

The swap has two years remaining until expiration. The sum of the present values for Years 1 and 2 is

$$\sum_{i=1}^{n} PV_i = 0.990099 + 0.977876 = 1.967975.$$

Given the current equilibrium two-year swap rate of 1.12% and the fixed swap rate at initiation of 3.00%, the swap value per dollar notional is calculated as

$$V = 1 \times (0.03 - 0.0112) \times 1.967975 = 0.036998.$$

The current value of the swap, from the perspective of the receive-fixed party, is $50,000,000 \times 0.036998 = \$1,849,897$.

From the perspective of the bank, as the pay-fixed party, the value of the swap is −$1,849,897.

8. C is correct. The equilibrium swap fixed rate for yen is calculated as

$$r_{JPY} = \frac{1 - PV_{n,JPY}(1)}{\sum_{i=1}^{4} PV_{i,JPY}(1)}.$$

The yen present value factors are calculated as

$$PV(1)_{i,JPY} = \frac{1}{1 + Rspo\, t_{i,JPY}\left(\dfrac{NAD_i}{NTD}\right)},$$

where

90-day PV factor = $1/[1 + 0.0005(90/360)] = 0.999875$
180-day PV factor = $1/[1 + 0.0010(180/360)] = 0.999500$
270-day PV factor = $1/[1 + 0.0015(270/360)] = 0.998876$
360-day PV factor = $1/[1 + 0.0025(360/360)] = 0.997506$

Sum of present value factors = 3.995757
Therefore, the yen periodic rate is calculated as

$$r_{JPY} = \frac{1 - PV_n(1)}{\sum_{i=1}^{4} PV_i(1)} = \frac{1 - 0.997506}{3.995757} = 0.000624 = 0.0624\%.$$

The annualized rate is (360/90) times the periodic rate of 0.0624%, or 0.2496%.

9. B is correct. The value of an equity swap at time t is calculated as

$$V_{EQ,t} = V_{FIX}(C_0) - (S_t/S_{t-1})NA_E - PV(Par - NA_E).$$

The swap was initiated six months ago, so the first reset has not yet passed; thus, there are five remaining cash flows for this equity swap. The fair value of the swap is determined by comparing the present value of the implied fixed-rate bond with the return on the equity index. The fixed swap rate of 2.00%, the swap notional amount of $20,000,000, and the present value factors in Exhibit 5 result in a present value of the implied fixed-rate bond's cash flows of $19,818,678:

Date (in years)	PV Factors	Fixed Cash Flow	PV (fixed cash flow)
0.5	0.998004 or 1/[1 + 0.0040(180/360)]	$400,000	$399,202
1.5	0.985222 or 1/[1 + 0.0100(540/360)]	$400,000	$394,089
2.5	0.970874 or 1/[1 + 0.0120(900/360)]	$400,000	$388,350
3.5	0.934579 or 1/[1 + 0.0200(1,260/360)]	$400,000	$373,832
4.5	0.895255 or 1/[1 + 0.0260(1,620/360)]	$20,400,000	$18,263,205
Total			$19,818,678

The value of the equity leg of the swap is calculated as $(103/100)(\$20,000,000) = \$20,600,000$.

Note the swap's notional amount and the implied fixed-rate bond's par value are both $20,000,000; therefore, the term $-\text{PV}(\text{Par} - \text{NA}_E)$ reduces to zero.

The swap was designed to profit if rates fell or equities declined. Neither happened, so the swap value will be negative for the bank. The fair value of the equity swap, from the perspective of the bank (receive-fixed, pay-equity party) is calculated as

$$V_{EQ} = \$19,818,678 - \$20,600,000 = -\$781,322.$$

10. B is correct. The equity index level at which the swap's fair value would be zero can be calculated by setting the swap valuation formula equal to zero and solving for S_t:

$$V_{EQ,t} = V_{FIX}(C_0) - (S_t/S_{t-1})\text{NA}_E = 0.$$

The value of the fixed leg of the swap has a present value of $19,818,678, or 99.0934% of par value:

Date (years)	PV Factors	Fixed Cash Flow	PV (fixed cash flow)
0.5	0.998004	$400,000	$399,202
1.5	0.985222	$400,000	$394,089
2.5	0.970874	$400,000	$388,350
3.5	0.934579	$400,000	$373,832
4.5	0.895255	$20,400,000	$18,263,205
Total			$19,818,678

Treating the swap notional value as par value and substituting the present value of the fixed leg and S_0 into the equation yields

$$0 = 99.0934 - \left(\frac{S_t}{100}\right)100$$

Solving for S_t yields

$$S_t = 99.0934.$$

11. A is correct. The current value of the 6×9 FRA is calculated as

$$V_g = NA \times \{[FRA_g - FRA_0]t_m\}/[1 + D_{(T-g)} \, t_{(T-g)}].$$

The 6×9 FRA expires six months after initiation. The bank entered into the FRA 90 days ago; thus, the FRA will expire in 90 days. To value the FRA, the first step is to compute the new FRA rate, which is the rate on Day 90 of an FRA that expires in 90 days in which the underlying is the 90-day Libor:

$$FRA_g = \{[1 + L_T t_T]/[1 + L_h t_h] - 1\}/t_m$$
$$FRA_g = \{[1 + L_{180}(180/360)]/[1 + L_{90} \, (90/360)] - 1\}/(90/360)$$

Exhibit 7 indicates that $L_{90} = 0.90\%$ and $L_{180} = 0.95\%$, so

$$FRA_g = \{[1 + 0.0095(180/360)]/[1 + 0.0090(90/360)] - 1\}/(90/360)$$
$$FRA_g = \{[1.00475/1.00225] - 1]\} \times 4 = 0.009978, \text{ or } 0.9978\%.$$

Therefore, given the FRA rate at initiation of 0.70% and notional principal of $20 million from Exhibit 1, the current value of the forward contract is calculated as

$$V_g = \$20,000,000 \times [(0.009978 - 0.0070)(90/360)]/[1 + 0.0095(180/360)].$$
$$= \$14,890.00/1.00475 = \$14,819.61.$$

12. C is correct. The no-arbitrage fixed rate on the 1×4 FRA is calculated as

$$FRA_0 = \{[1 + L_T t_T]/[1 + L_h t_h] - 1\}/t_m.$$

For a 1×4 FRA, the two rates needed to compute the no-arbitrage FRA fixed rate are $L_{30} = 0.75\%$ and $L_{120} = 0.92\%$. Therefore, the no-arbitrage fixed rate on the 1×4 FRA rate is calculated as

$$FRA_0 = \{[1 + 0.0092(120/360)]/[1 + 0.0075(30/360)] - 1\}/(90/360).$$
$$FRA_0 = \{[1.003066/1.000625] - 1\} \times 4 = 0.009761, \text{ or } 0.98\% \text{ rounded.}$$

13. B is correct. The fixed rate on the 2×5 FRA is calculated as

$$FRA_0 = \{[1 + L_T t_T]/[1 + L_h t_h] - 1\}/t_m.$$

For a 2 × 5 FRA, the two rates needed to compute the no-arbitrage FRA fixed rate are $L_{60} = 0.82\%$ and $L_{150} = 0.94\%$. Therefore, the no-arbitrage fixed rate on the 2 × 5 FRA rate is calculated as

$$FRA_0 = \{[1 + 0.0094(150/360)]/[1 + 0.0082(60/360)] - 1\}/(90/360)$$
$$FRA_0 = \{[(1.003917/1.001367) - 1\} \times 4 = 0.010186, \text{ or } 1.02\% \text{ rounded.}$$

14. A is correct. Given a three-month US dollar Libor of 1.10% at expiration, the settlement amount for the bank as the pay-fixed (receive-floating) party is calculated as

Settlement amount pay-fixed (receive floating) = $NA \times \{[L_m - FRA_0]t_m\}/[1 + D_m t_m]\}$.

Settlement amount pay-fixed (receive floating) = $\$20,000,000 \times \{[0.011 - 0.0070] \times (90/360)]/[1 + 0.011(90/360)]\}$.

Settlement amount pay-fixed (receive floating) = $\$20,000,000 \times (0.001)/1.00275 = \$19,945.15$.

Therefore, the bank will receive $19,945 (rounded) as the receive-floating party.

15. C is correct. Doyle's first statement is correct. Unless the Eurodollar futures contract's quoted price is equal to the no-arbitrage futures price, there is an arbitrage opportunity. Moreover, if the quoted futures price is less than the no-arbitrage futures price, then to take advantage of the arbitrage opportunity, the Eurodollar futures contract should be purchased and the underlying Eurodollar bond should be sold short. Doyle would then lend the short sale proceeds at the risk-free rate. The strategy that comprises those transactions is known as reverse carry arbitrage.

Doyle's second statement is also correct. Based on the cost of carry model, the futures price is calculated as the future value of the sum of the underlying plus the underlying carry costs minus the future value of any ownership benefits. If the Eurodollar bond's interest payment was expected in five months instead of two, the benefit of the cash flow would occur three months later, so the future value of the benefits term would be slightly lower. Therefore, the Eurodollar futures contract price would be slightly higher if the Eurodollar bond's interest payment was expected in five months instead of two months.

A is incorrect because Doyle's Statement 2 is correct (not incorrect). Based on the cost of carry model, the futures price would be higher if the underlying Eurodollar bond's interest payment took place in five months instead of two months.

B is incorrect because Doyle's Statement 1 is correct (not incorrect). If the Eurodollar's futures contract price is less than the price suggested by the carry arbitrage model, the futures contract should be purchased.

16. B is correct. The full spot price of the three-year Treasury note is calculated as

$$S_0 = \text{Quoted bond price} + \text{Accrued interest} = B_0 + AI_0.$$

Accrued interest $(AI) = \text{Accrual period} \times \text{Periodic coupon amount} = \left(\dfrac{NAD}{NTD}\right) \times \left(\dfrac{C}{n}\right)$.

$$AI = (60/180) \times (0.015/2) = 0.25.$$
$$S_0 = 101 + 0.25 = 101.25.$$

A is incorrect because 101 is the quoted clean (not the full spot) price of the three-year Treasury note. The clean price excludes accrued interest; the full price, also referred to as the dirty price, includes accrued interest.

C is incorrect because the number of days until the next coupon payment (instead of the accrual period) is incorrectly used to compute accrued interest:

$$AI = (120/180) \times (0.015/2) = 0.50.$$
$$S_0 = 101 + 0.50 = 101.50.$$

17. A is correct. The equilibrium 10-year quoted futures contract price based on the carry arbitrage model is calculated as

$$Q_0 = (1/CF) \times [FV(B_0 + AI_0) - AI_T - FVCI].$$
$$CF = 0.7025.$$
$$B_0 = 104.00.$$
$$AI_0 = 0.17.$$
$$AI_T = (120/180 \times 0.02/2) = 0.67.$$
$$FVCI = 0.$$
$$Q_0 = (1/0.7025) \times \left[(1 + 0.0165)^{3/12}(104.17) - 0.67 - 0\right] = 147.94.$$

B is incorrect because accrued interest at expiration is not subtracted in the equilibrium quoted futures contract price formula:

$$Q_0 = (1/0.7025) \times \left[(1 + 0.0165)^{3/12}(104.17) - 0\right] = 148.89.$$

C is incorrect because the future value is incorrectly calculated (the exponent of 3/12 is omitted):

$$Q_0 = (1/0.7025) \times \left[(1 + 0.0165)(104.17) - 0.67 - 0\right] = 149.78.$$

18. B is correct. The value of the JGB forward position is calculated as

$$V_t = PV[F_t - F_0] = (155 - 153)/(1 + 0.0012)^{\frac{6}{12}} = 1.9988.$$

Therefore, the value of the long forward position is 1.9988 per JPY100 par value.

For the long position in eight contracts with each contract having a par value of 100 million yen, the value of the position is calculated as

$$0.019988 \times (JPY100,000,000) \times 8 = JPY15,990,409.$$

A is incorrect because the present value of the difference between the price when the contracts were purchased and the current price of the contracts was incorrectly computed (the exponent of 6/12 is omitted):

$$V_t = F_t - F_0 = (155 - 153)/(1 + 0.0012) = 1.9980.$$
$$0.019980 \times (JPY100,000,000) \times 8 = JPY15,980,823.$$

C is incorrect because the absolute difference (not the present value of the difference) between the price when the contracts were purchased and the current price of the contracts was computed:

$$V_t = F_t - F_0 = (155 - 153) = 2.$$
$$0.02 \times (\text{JPY}100{,}000{,}000) \times 8 = \text{JPY}16{,}000{,}000.$$

19. B is correct. The swap's fixed rate is calculated as

$$r_{FIX} = [1 - \text{PV}_n(1)]/\sum_{i=1}^{n} \text{PV}_i(1).$$
$$\text{PV}_i(1) = 1/[1 + \text{Rspot}_i\,(\text{NAD}_i/\text{NTD})].$$
$$90 - \text{day PV factor} = 1/[1 + 0.019 \times (90/360)] = 0.9953.$$
$$180 - \text{day PV factor} = 1/[1 + 0.020 \times (180/360)] = 0.9901.$$
$$270 - \text{day PV factor} = 1/[1 + 0.021 \times (270/360)] = 0.9845.$$
$$360 - \text{day PV factor} = 1/[1 + 0.022 \times (360/360)] = 0.9785.$$
$$\sum_{i=1}^{4} \text{PV}_i(1) = 0.9953 + 0.9901 + 0.9845 + 0.9785 = 3.9483.$$
$$r_{FIX} = (1 - 0.9785)/3.9483 = 0.0055 = 0.55\%.$$

A is incorrect because the 90-day PV factor is incorrectly used in the numerator of the swap pricing equation instead of the final present value term:

$$r_{FIX} = [1 - \text{PV}_n(1)]/\sum_{i=1}^{n} \text{PV}_i(1).$$
$$r_{FIX} = (1 - 0.9953)/3.9483 = 0.0012 = 0.12\%.$$

C is incorrect because the sum of the present value terms excludes the final present value term:

$$\sum_{i=1}^{3} \text{PV}_i(1) = 0.9953 + 0.9901 + 0.9845 = 2.9699.$$
$$r_{FIX} = [1 - \text{PV}_n(1)]/\sum_{i=1}^{n} \text{PV}_i(1).$$
$$r_{FIX} = (1 - 0.9785)/2.9699 = 0.0072 = 0.72\%.$$

20. B is correct. The value of the pay-fixed interest rate swap is calculated as

$$-V_{SWAP,t} = \text{NA} \times (\text{FS}_t - \text{FS}_0) \times \sum_{i=1}^{n} \text{PV}_i.$$
$$\text{FS}_t = r_{FIX} = [1 - \text{PV}_n(1)]/\sum_{i=1}^{3} \text{PV}_i(1) = (1 - 0.9976)/2.9961 = 0.000801 = 0.08\%.$$
$$-V_{SWAP,t} = \text{NA} \times (\text{FS}_t - \text{FS}_0) \times \sum_{i=1}^{3} \text{PV}_i$$
$$= \text{JPY5billion} \times (0.000801 - 0.001) \times 2.9961$$
$$= -\text{JPY}2{,}980{,}500.$$

Given that rates have declined since the inception of the swap, the value of the pay-fixed, receive-floating position is currently a loss of JPY2,980,500.

A is incorrect because the arithmetic average of the yen spot rates (instead of the current fixed swap rate) was incorrectly used to calculate the value of the pay-fixed swap:

Arithmetic average of yen spot rates = $(0.0003 + 0.0006 + 0.0008)/3 = 0.0006$.

$$-V_{SWAP,t} = NA \times (FS_t - FS_0) \times \sum_{i=1}^{3} PV_i$$
$$= JPY5billion \times (0.0006 - 0.001) \times 2.9961$$
$$= -JPY6,491,550.$$

C is incorrect because the product of the notional amount and the difference between the initial swap fixed rate and the current swap fixed rate was not multiplied by the sum of the present values:

$$-V_{SWAP,t} = NA \times (FS_t - FS_0) = JPY5billion \times (0.0008 - 0.001) = -JPY994,793.$$

CHAPTER 4

VALUATION OF CONTINGENT CLAIMS

SOLUTIONS

1. A is correct. The hedge ratio requires the underlying stock and call option values for the up move and down move. $S^+ = 56$, and $S^- = 46$. $c^+ = \text{Max}(0, S^+ - X) = \text{Max}(0, 56 - 50) = 6$, and $c^- = \text{Max}(0, S^- - X) = \text{Max}(0, 46 - 50) = 0$. The hedge ratio is

$$h = \frac{c^+ - c^-}{S^+ - S^-} = \frac{6 - 0}{56 - 46} = \frac{6}{10} = 0.60$$

2. C is correct. For this approach, the risk-free rate is $r = 0.05$, the up factor is $u = S^+/S = 56/50 = 1.12$, and the down factor is $d = S^-/S = 46/50 = 0.92$. The risk-neutral probability of an up move is

$$\pi = [\text{FV}(1) - d]/(u - d) = (1 + r - d)/(u - d)$$
$$\pi = (1 + 0.05 - 0.92)/(1.12 - 0.92) = 0.13/0.20 = 0.65$$

3. A is correct. The call option can be estimated using the no-arbitrage approach or the expectations approach. With the no-arbitrage approach, the value of the call option is

$$c = hS + \text{PV}(-hS^- + c^-).$$
$$h = (c^+ - c^-)/(S^+ - S^-) = (6 - 0)/(56 - 46) = 0.60.$$
$$c = (0.60 \times 50) + (1/1.05) \times [(-0.60 \times 46) + 0].$$
$$c = 30 - [(1/1.05) \times 27.6] = 30 - 26.286 = 3.714.$$

Using the expectations approach, the risk-free rate is $r = 0.05$, the up factor is $u = S^+/S = 56/50 = 1.12$, and the down factor is $d = S^-/S = 46/50 = 0.92$. The value of the call option is

$$c = PV \times [\pi c^+ + (1 - \pi)c^-].$$
$$\pi = [FV(1) - d]/(u - d) = (1.05 - 0.92)/(1.12 - 0.92) = 0.65.$$
$$c = (1/1.05) \times [0.65(6) + (1 - 0.65)(0)] = (1/1.05)(3.9) = 3.714.$$

Both approaches are logically consistent and yield identical values.

4. B is correct. You should sell (write) the overpriced call option and then go long (buy) the replicating portfolio for a call option. The replicating portfolio for a call option is to buy h shares of the stock and borrow the present value of $(hS^- - c^-)$.

$$c = hS + PV(-hS^- + c^-).$$
$$h = (c^+ - c^-)/(S^+ - S^-) = (6 - 0)/(56 - 46) = 0.60.$$

For the example in this case, the value of the call option is 3.714. If the option is overpriced at, say, 4.50, you short the option and have a cash flow at Time 0 of +4.50. You buy the replicating portfolio of 0.60 shares at 50 per share (giving you a cash flow of −30) and borrow $(1/1.05) \times [(0.60 \times 46) - 0] = (1/1.05) \times 27.6 = 26.287$. Your cash flow for buying the replicating portfolio is $-30 + 26.287 = -3.713$. Your net cash flow at Time 0 is $+ 4.50 - 3.713 = 0.787$. Your net cash flow at Time 1 for either the up move or down move is zero. You have made an arbitrage profit of 0.787.

In tabular form, the cash flows are as follows:

Transaction	Time Step 0	Time Step 1 Down Occurs	Time Step 1 Up Occurs
Sell the call option	4.50	0	−6.00
Buy h shares	$-0.6 \times 50 = -30$	$0.6 \times 46 = 27.6$	$0.6 \times 56 = 33.6$
Borrow $-PV(-hS^- + c^-)$	$-(1/1.05) \times [(-0.6 \times 46) + 0] = 26.287$	$-0.6 \times 46 = -27.6$	$-0.6 \times 46 = -27.6$
Net cash flow	0.787	0	0

5. A is correct. Using the expectations approach, the risk-neutral probability of an up move is

$$\pi = [FV(1) - d]/(u - d) = (1.03 - 0.800)/(1.300 - 0.800) = 0.46.$$

The terminal value calculations for the exercise values at Time Step 2 are

$$c^{++} = Max(0, u^2 S - X) = Max[0, 1.30^2(38) - 40] = Max(0, 24.22) = 24.22.$$
$$c^{-+} = Max(0, udS - X) = Max[0, 1.30(0.80)(38) - 40] = Max(0, -0.48) = 0.$$
$$c^{--} = Max(0, d^2 S - X) = Max[0, 0.80^2(38) - 40] = Max(0, -15.68) = 0.$$

Discounting back for two years, the value of the call option at Time Step 0 is

$$c = PV[\pi^2 c^{++} + 2\pi(1 - \pi)c^{-+} + (1 - \pi)^2 c^{--}].$$
$$c = [1/(1.03)]^2[0.46^2(24.22) + 2(0.46)(0.54)(0) + 0.54^2(0)].$$
$$c = [1/(1.03)]^2[5.1250] = 4.8308.$$

6. A is correct. Using the expectations approach, the risk-neutral probability of an up move is

$$\pi = [\text{FV}(1) - d]/(u - d) = (1.03 - 0.800)/(1.300 - 0.800) = 0.46.$$

An American-style put can be exercised early. At Time Step 1, for the up move, p^+ is 0.2517 and the put is out of the money and should not be exercised early ($X < S$, $40 < 49.4$). However, at Time Step 1, p^- is 8.4350 and the put is in the money by 9.60 ($X - S = 40 - 30.40$). So, the put is exercised early, and the value of early exercise (9.60) replaces the value of not exercising early (8.4350) in the binomial tree. The value of the put at Time Step 0 is now

$$p = \text{PV}[\pi p^+ + (1 - \pi)p^-] = [1/(1.03)][0.46(0.2517) + 0.54(9.60)] = 5.1454.$$

Following is a supplementary note regarding Exhibit 1.

The values in Exhibit 1 are calculated as follows.

At Time Step 2:

$$p^{++} = \text{Max}(0, X - u^2S) = \text{Max}[0,40 - 1.300^2(38)] = \text{Max}(0,40 - 64.22) = 0.$$
$$p^{-+} = \text{Max}(0, X - udS) = \text{Max}[0,40 - 1.300(0.800)(38)] = \text{Max}(0,40 - 39.52) = 0.48.$$
$$p^{--} = \text{Max}(0, X - d^2S) = \text{Max}[0,40 - 0.800^2(38)] = \text{Max}(0,40 - 24.32) = 15.68.$$

At Time Step 1:

$$p^+ = \text{PV}[\pi p^{++} + (1 - \pi)p^{-+}] = [1/(1.03)][0.46(0) + 0.54(0.48)] = 0.2517.$$
$$p^- = \text{PV}[\pi p^{-+} + (1 - \pi)p^{--}] = [1/(1.03)][0.46(0.48) + 0.54(15.68)] = 8.4350.$$

At Time Step 0:

$$p = \text{PV}[\pi p^+ + (1 - \pi)p^-] = [1/(1.03)][0.46(0.2517) + 0.54(8.4350)] = 4.5346.$$

7. C is correct. Both statements are correct. The expected future payoff is calculated using risk-neutral probabilities, and the expected payoff is discounted at the risk-free rate.
8. C is correct. Using the expectations approach, per 1 of notional value, the values of the call option at Time Step 2 are

$$c^{++} = \text{Max}(0, S^{++} - X) = \text{Max}(0,0.050 - 0.0275) = 0.0225.$$
$$c^{+-} = \text{Max}(0, S^{+-} - X) = \text{Max}(0,0.030 - 0.0275) = 0.0025.$$
$$c^{--} = \text{Max}(0, S^{--} - X) = \text{Max}(0,0.010 - 0.0275) = 0.$$

At Time Step 1, the call values are

$$c^+ = \text{PV}[\pi c^{++} + (1 - \pi)c^{+-}].$$
$$c^+ = 0.961538[0.50(0.0225) + (1 - 0.50)(0.0025)] = 0.012019.$$
$$c^- = \text{PV}[\pi c^{+-} + (1 - \pi)c^{--}].$$
$$c^- = 0.980392[0.50(0.0025) + (1 - 0.50)(0)] = 0.001225.$$

At Time Step 0, the call option value is

$$c = \text{PV}[\pi c^+ + (1 - \pi)c^-].$$
$$c = 0.970874[0.50(0.012019) + (1 - 0.50)(0.001225)] = 0.006429.$$

The value of the call option is this amount multiplied by the notional value, or $0.006429 \times 1{,}000{,}000 = 6{,}429$.

9. A is correct. Reason 1 is correct: A higher exercise price does lower the exercise value (payoff) at Time 2. Reason 2 is not correct because the risk-neutral probabilities are based on the paths that interest rates take, which are determined by the market and not the details of a particular option contract.

10. C is correct. The no-arbitrage approach to creating a call option involves buying Delta $= N(d_1) = 0.6217$ shares of the underlying stock and financing with $-N(d_2) = -0.5596$ shares of a risk-free bond priced at $\exp(-rt)(X) = \exp(-0.0022 \times 0.25)(55) = \$54.97$ per bond. Note that the value of this replicating portfolio is $n_S S + n_B B = 0.6217(57.03) - 0.5596(54.97) = \$4.6943$ (the value of the call option with slight rounding error).

11. B is correct. The formula for the BSM price of a put option is $p = e^{-rt}XN(-d_2) - SN(-d_1)$. $N(-d_1) = 1 - N(d_1) = 1 - 0.6217 = 0.3783$, and $N(-d_2) = 1 - N(d_2) = 1 - 0.5596 = 0.4404$.

    Note that the BSM model can be represented as a portfolio of the stock ($n_S S$) and zero-coupon bonds ($n_B B$). For a put, the number of shares is $n_S = -N(-d_1) < 0$ and the number of bonds is $n_B = -N(-d_2) > 0$. The value of the replicating portfolio is $n_S S + n_B B = -0.3783(57.03) + 0.4404(54.97) = \$2.6343$ (the value of the put option with slight rounding error). B is a risk-free bond priced at $\exp(-rt)(X) = \exp(-0.0022 \times 0.25)(55) = \$54.97$.

12. A is correct. Black's model to value a call option on a futures contract is $c = e^{-rT}[F_0(T) N(d_1) - XN(d_2)]$. The underlying F_0 is the futures price (186.73). The correct discount rate is the risk-free rate, $r = 0.39\%$.

13. B is correct. Lee is pointing out the option price's sensitivity to small changes in time. In the BSM approach, option price sensitivity to changes in time is given by the option Greek theta.

14. A is correct. The put is priced at $7.4890 by the BSM model when using the historical volatility input of 24%. The market price is $7.20. The BSM model overpricing suggests the implied volatility of the put must be lower than 24%.

15. C is correct. Solomon's forecast is for the three-month Libor to exceed 0.85% in six months. The correct option valuation inputs use the six-month FRA rate as the underlying, which currently has a rate of 0.75%.

16. B is correct because selling call options creates a short position in the ETF that would hedge his current long position in the ETF.

    Exhibit 2 could also be used to answer the question. Solomon owns 10,000 shares of the GPX, each with a delta of +1; by definition, his portfolio delta is +10,000. A delta hedge could be implemented by selling enough calls to make the portfolio delta neutral:

$$N_H = -\frac{\text{Portfolio delta}}{\text{Delta}_H} = -\frac{+10{,}000}{+0.6232} = -16{,}046 \text{ calls.}$$

17. C is correct. Because the gamma of the stock position is 0 and the put gamma is always non-negative, adding a long position in put options would most likely result in a positive portfolio gamma.

    Gamma is the change in delta from a small change in the stock's value. A stock position always has a delta of +1. Because the delta does not change, gamma equals 0.

    The gamma of a call equals the gamma of a similar put, which can be proven using put–call parity.

CHAPTER 5

CREDIT DEFAULT SWAPS

SOLUTIONS

1. A is correct. Deem Advisors would prefer a cash settlement. Deem Advisors owns Bond 2 (trading at 50% of par), which is worth more than the cheapest-to-deliver obligation (Bond 1, also a senior secured bond, trading at 40% of par). Based on the price of this cheapest-to-deliver security, the estimated recovery rate is 40%. Thus, Deem Advisors can cash settle for $6 million [= (1 − 40%) × $10 million] on its CDS contract and sell the bond it owns, Bond 2, for $5 million, for total proceeds of $11 million. If Deem Advisors were to physically settle the contract, only $10 million would be received, the face amount of the bonds, and it would deliver Bond 2.

   B is incorrect because if Deem Advisors were to physically settle the contract, it would receive only $10 million, which is less than the $11 million that could be obtained from a cash settlement. C is incorrect because Deem Advisors would not be indifferent between settlement protocols as the firm would receive $1 million more with a cash settlement in comparison to a physical settlement.

2. C is correct. A downward-sloping credit curve implies a greater probability of default in the earlier years than in the later years. Downward-sloping curves are less common and often are the result of severe near-term stress in the financial markets.

   A is incorrect because a flat credit curve implies a constant hazard rate (conditional probability of default). B is incorrect because an upward-sloping credit curve implies a greater probability of default in later years.

3. A is correct. UNAB experienced a credit event when it failed to make the scheduled coupon payment on the outstanding subordinated unsecured obligation. Failure to pay, a credit event, occurs when a borrower does not make a scheduled payment of principal or interest on outstanding obligations after a grace period, even without a formal bankruptcy filing.

   B is incorrect because a credit event can occur without filing for bankruptcy. The three most common credit events are bankruptcy, failure to pay, and restructuring.

C is incorrect because a credit event (failure to pay) occurs when a borrower does not make a scheduled payment of principal or interest on *any* outstanding obligations after a grace period, even without a formal bankruptcy filing.

4. C is correct. An approximation for the upfront premium is (Credit spread – Fixed coupon rate) × Duration of the CDS. To buy 10-year CDS protection, Deem Advisors would have to pay an approximate upfront premium of 1,400 bps [(700 – 500) × 7], or 14% of the notional.

   A is incorrect because 200 bps, or 2%, is derived by taking the simple difference between the credit spread and the fixed coupon rate (700 – 500), ignoring the duration component of the calculation. B is incorrect because 980 bps, or 9.8%, is the result of dividing the credit spread by the fixed coupon rate and multiplying by the duration of the CDS [(700/500) × 7].

5. B is correct. Deem Advisors purchased protection and therefore is economically short and benefits from an increase in the company's spread. Since putting on the protection, the credit spread increased by 200 bps, and Deem Advisors realizes the profit by entering into a new, offsetting contract (sells protection to another party at a higher premium).

   A is incorrect because a decrease (not increase) in the spread would result in a loss for the credit protection buyer. C is incorrect because Deem Advisors, the credit protection buyer, would profit from an increase in the company's credit spread, not break even.

6. A is correct. A difference in credit spreads in the bond market and CDS market is the foundation of the basis trade strategy. If the spread is higher in the bond market than in the CDS market, it is said to be a negative basis. In this case, the bond credit spread is currently 4.50% (bond yield minus Libor) and the comparable CDS contract has a credit spread of 4.25%. The credit risk is cheap in the CDS market relative to the bond market. Since the protection and the bond were both purchased, if convergence occurs, the trade will capture the 0.25% differential in the two markets (4.50% – 4.25%).

   B is incorrect because the bond market implies a 4.50% credit risk premium (bond yield minus the market reference rate) and the CDS market implies a 4.25% credit risk premium. Convergence of the bond market credit risk premium and the CDS credit risk premium would result in capturing the differential, 0.25%. The 1.75% is derived by incorrectly subtracting Libor from the credit spread on the CDS (= 4.25% – 2.50%).

   C is incorrect because convergence of the bond market credit risk premium and the CDS credit risk premium would result in capturing the differential, 0.25%. The 2.75% is derived incorrectly by subtracting the credit spread on the CDS from the current bond yield (= 7.00% – 4.25%).

7. C is correct. Parties to CDS contracts generally agree that their contracts will conform to ISDA specifications. These terms are specified in the ISDA master agreement, which the parties to a CDS sign before any transactions are made. Therefore, to satisfy the compliance requirements referenced by Chan, the sovereign wealth fund must sign an ISDA master agreement with SGS.

8. A is correct. A CDS index (e.g., CDX and iTraxx) would allow the Fund to simultaneously fully hedge multiple fixed-income exposures. A tranche CDS will also hedge multiple exposures, but it would only partially hedge those exposures.

9. A is correct. Based on Exhibit 1, the probability of survival for the first year is 99.78% (100% minus the 0.22% hazard rate). Similarly, the probability of survival for the second and third years is 99.65% (100% minus the 0.35% hazard rate) and 99.50% (100% minus the 0.50% hazard rate), respectively. Therefore, the probability of survival of the Orion

bond through the first three years is equal to $0.9978 \times 0.9965 \times 0.9950 = 0.9893$, and the probability of default sometime during the first three years is $1 - 0.9893$, or 1.07%.

10. B is correct. The trade assumes that £6 million of five-year CDS protection on Orion is initially sold, so the Fund received the premium. Because the credit spread of the Orion CDS narrowed from 150 bps to 100 bps, the CDS position will realize a financial gain. This financial gain is equal to the difference between the upfront premium received on the original CDS position and the upfront premium to be paid on a new, offsetting CDS position. To close the position and monetize this gain, the Fund should unwind the position by buying protection for a lower premium (relative to the original premium collected).

11. B is correct. The gain on the hypothetical Orion trade is £117,000, calculated as follows.
    Approximate profit = Change in credit spread (in bps) × Duration × Notional amount.
    Approximate profit = (150 bps − 100 bps) × 3.9 × £6 million.
    Approximate profit = 0.005 × 3.9 × £6 million.
    $$= £117,000.$$
    The Fund gains because it sold protection at a spread of 150 bps and closed out the position by buying protection at a lower spread of 100 bps.

12. B is correct. Based on Outlook 1, Chan and Smith anticipate that Europe's economy will weaken. In order to profit from this forecast, one would buy protection using a high-yield CDS index (e.g., iTraxx Crossover) and sell protection using an investment-grade CDS index (e.g., iTraxx Main).

13. B is correct. To take advantage of Chan's view of the US credit curve steepening in the short term, a curve trade will entail shorting (buying protection using) a long-term (20-year) CDX and going long (selling protection using) a short-term (2-year) CDX. A steeper curve means that long-term credit risk increases relative to short-term credit risk.

14. B is correct. The shares of Zega can be sold at a higher price as a result of the unsolicited bid in the market. If Delta Corporation issues significantly more debt, there is a higher probability that it may default. If the Fund sells protection on Delta now, the trade will realize a profit as credit spreads widen. An equity-versus-credit trade would be to go long (buy) the Zega shares and buy protection on Delta.

CHAPTER 6

INTRODUCTION TO COMMODITIES AND COMMODITY DERIVATIVES

SOLUTIONS

1. C is correct. Commodity arbitrage involves an ability to inventory physical commodities and the attempt to capitalize on mispricing between the commodity (along with related storage and financing costs) and the futures price. The Apex Fund has access to storage facilities and uses these facilities in the attempt to capitalize on mispricing opportunities.

2. C is correct. Government actions can affect the supply or demand of all four sectors of the Apex Fund. With respect to energy, environmental mandates imposed by governments have tightened pollution standards, which have led to increasing processing costs that negatively affect demand. The supply of livestock, such as hogs and cattle, is affected by government-permitted use of drugs and growth hormones. Softs, or cash crops, can be affected by government actions, such as the attempt to maintain strategic stockpiles to control domestic prices. The level of demand and relative value of a precious metal, such as gold, is directly linked to government actions associated with managing to inflation targets.

3. C is correct. Expected future cash flows affect the valuation of financial assets, such as stocks and bonds, but do not affect the valuation of commodities. Financial assets (stocks and bonds) are valued based on expected future cash flows. In contrast, the valuation of a commodity is based on a discounted forecast of a future commodity price, which incorporates storage and transportation costs.

4. C is correct. When the near-term (i.e., closer to expiration) futures contract price is higher than the longer-term futures contract price, the futures market for the commodity is in backwardation. Because gasoline is the only one of the three futures markets in Exhibit 2 in which the near-term futures contract price ($2.2701) is higher than the longer-term contract price ($2.0307), the gasoline futures market is the only one in backwardation.

5. B is correct. The theory of storage focuses on the level of commodity inventories and the state of supply and demand. A commodity that is regularly stored should have a higher price in the future (contango) to account for those storage costs. Because coffee is a commodity that requires storage, its higher future price is consistent with the theory of storage.

6. C is correct. Roll returns are generally positive (negative) when the futures market is in backwardation (contango) and zero when the futures market is flat. Because the gasoline market is in backwardation, its roll returns will most likely be positive.

7. A is correct. The total return on the trade represents the sum of three components: price return, roll return, and collateral return.

   Price return = (Current price − Previous price)/Previous price = (877.0 − 865.0)/865.0
   = 1.387%.

   Roll return = [(Near-term futures contract closing price − Farther-term futures contract closing price)/Near-term futures contract closing price] × Percentage of the position in the futures contract being rolled.

   Because the entire position is being rolled, the percentage of the position in the futures contract being rolled is equal to 100%. So:

   Roll return = [(877.0 − 883.0)/877.0] × 100% = −0.684%.
   Collateral return = [3 months/12 months] × 0.60% = 0.15%.
   Total return = 1.387% − 0.684% + 0.15% = 0.853%.

8. A is correct. The total return swap involves a monthly cash settlement (reset) based on the performance of the underlying reference asset (S&P GSCI) given a notional amount of $25 million. If the level of the index increases between the two valuation dates (in this case, May and June), the long position (the swap buyer) receives payment. If the level of the index decreases between the two valuation dates, the swap seller receives payment.

   The return on the reference index for the month of June is [(2,525.21 − 2,582.23)/ 2,582.23], which is equivalent to −2.2082%. Therefore, the swap buyer (long position) must pay the swap seller a cash settlement for the month of June. The June payment calculation is equal to $25,000,000 × −2.2082%, or −$552,042.23.

9. B is correct. The most common way to invest in commodities is via derivatives, and commodities do not generate future cash flows beyond what can be realized through their purchase and sale. Also, storage costs are positively related to futures prices. Physical assets have to be stored, and storage incurs costs (rent, insurance, spoilage, etc.). Therefore, a commodity that is regularly stored should have a higher price in the future to account for those storage costs.

10. B is correct. The Brent crude oil futures market is in a state of backwardation. Commodity futures markets are in a state of backwardation when the spot price is greater than the price of near-term (i.e., nearest-to-expiration) futures contracts and, correspondingly, the price of near-term futures contracts is greater than that of longer-term contracts. The calendar spread is the difference between the near-term futures contract price and the longer-term futures contract price, which is $73.64 − $73.59 = $0.05. The basis for the near-term Brent crude oil futures contract is the difference between the spot price and the near-term futures price: $77.56 − $73.59 = $3.97.

11. B is correct. The Brent crude oil futures market is in a state of backwardation: The spot price is greater than the price of near-term (i.e., nearest-to-expiration) futures contracts. Commodities (in this case, Brent crude oil) are physical assets, not virtual assets, such as stocks and bonds. Physical assets have to be stored, and storage incurs costs (rent, insurance, inspections, spoilage, etc.). According to the theory of storage, a commodity that is consumed along a value chain that allows for just-in-time delivery and use (i.e., minimal inventories and storage) can avoid these costs. Yamata's research concluded that energy is consumed on a real-time basis and requires minimal storage. In this situation, demand dominates supply, and current prices are higher than futures prices (state of backwardation).

12. C is correct. The contract was held for one year, so the price return of −12% is an annualized figure. Additionally, the −24% roll return is also annualized. Nabli's collateral return equals 1.2% per year × 100% initial collateral investment = 1.2%. Therefore, the total return (annualized) is calculated as follows:

Total return = Price return + Roll return + Collateral return.
Total return = −12% + (−24%) + 1.2% = −34.8%.

13. C is correct. Roll returns are generally negative (positive) when the futures market is in contango (backwardation) and zero when the futures market is flat.

14. C is correct. Index B is likely to have higher performance than Index A in a market that is trending upward. Indexes that (perhaps inadvertently) contain contracts that more commonly trade in backwardation may improve forward-looking performance because this generates a positive roll return. Similarly, indexes that contain contracts that more commonly trade in contango may hurt performance for the same reason (i.e., negative roll return).

15. A is correct. Nabli expects the price of Brent crude oil to increase more than that of heavy crude oil, and Nabli can take advantage of this prediction by entering into a basis swap that is long Brent crude oil and short heavy crude oil. Nabli should take a short (not long) position in a volatility swap to take advantage of his prediction that Brent crude oil's price volatility will be lower than its expected volatility. Nabli should take a long (not short) position in an excess return swap to take advantage of his expectation that the level of the ICE Brent Index will increase faster than leading oil benchmarks.

16. B is correct. Hedgers trade in the futures markets to hedge their exposures related to the commodity, as stated in Farmhouse's risk management policy.

17. C is correct. The life cycle of livestock does vary widely by product. Grains have uniform, well-defined seasons and growth cycles specific to geographic regions. Therefore, both statements are correct.

18. C is correct. Commodity prices are affected by supply and demand, and improvements in freezing technology can improve the firm's ability to store its products for longer periods and manage the volatility of supply and demand. For example, during times of excess supply, a livestock producer, such as Farmhouse, can freeze its products and offer them during better market supply conditions.

19. B is correct. The futures market for soybeans is in a state of contango because the spot price is lower than the futures price.

20. C is correct. In Exhibit 1, the spot price of soybeans is less than the futures price. This observation can be explained only by the hedging pressure hypothesis. According to this hypothesis, hedging pressure occurs when both producers and consumers seek to protect themselves from commodity market price volatility by entering into price hedges to

stabilize their projected profits and cash flows. If consumers are more interested in hedging than producers are, the futures price will exceed the spot price.

In contrast, the insurance theory predicts that the futures price has to be lower than the current spot price as a form of payment or remuneration to the speculator who takes on the price risk and provides price insurance to the commodity seller. Similarly, the theory of storage also predicts that when a commodity's convenience yield is greater than its direct storage costs, the futures price will be lower than the spot price.

21. A is correct. The total return for a fully collateralized position is the sum of the price return, the roll return, and the collateral return:

$$\text{Price return} = (\text{Current price} - \text{Previous price})/\text{Previous price}$$
$$= (2.99 - 2.93)/2.93$$
$$= 2.05\%.$$

$$\text{Roll return} = (\text{Near-term futures closing price} - \text{Farther-term futures closing price})/$$
$$\text{Near-term futures closing price} \times \text{Percentage of position in futures}$$
$$\text{contract being rolled}$$
$$= [(2.99 - 3.03)/2.99] \times 100\%$$
$$= -1.34\%.$$

$$\text{Collateral return} = \text{Annual rate} \times \text{Period length as a fraction of the year}$$
$$= 3\% \times 0.25$$
$$= 0.75\%.$$

Therefore, the total return for three months = $2.05\% - 1.34\% + 0.75\% = 1.46\%$.

22. C is correct. Investment positions are evaluated on the basis of total return, and the roll return is part of the total return. Even though negative roll return negatively affects the total return, this effect could be more than offset by positive price and collateral returns. Therefore, it is possible that positions with negative roll returns outperform positions with positive roll returns, depending on the price and collateral returns.

CHAPTER 7

CURRENCY MANAGEMENT: AN INTRODUCTION

SOLUTIONS

1.

Template for Question 1

Asset	Foreign-Currency Portfolio Return	USD Relative to Foreign-Currency (circle one)
Portfolio A	15%	Appreciated
		Depreciated

Justification

The 19.5% domestic-currency return for Portfolio A is higher than the 15% foreign-currency portfolio return in GBP; therefore, the USD necessarily depreciated relative to the GBP.

The domestic-currency return on a foreign portfolio will reflect both the foreign-currency return on the portfolio and the percentage movements in the spot exchange rate between the domestic and foreign currency. The domestic-currency return is multiplicative with respect to these two factors:

$$R_{DC} = (1 + R_{FC})(1 + R_{FX}) - 1$$

where R_{DC} is the domestic-currency return (in percent), R_{FC} is the foreign-currency return of the asset (portfolio), and R_{FX} is the percentage change of the foreign currency against the domestic currency. (Note that in the R_{FX} expression the domestic currency—the USD in this case—is the price currency.)

Solving for R_{FX}: $(1 + 15\%)(1 + R_{FX}) - 1 = 19.50\%$; $R_{FX} = 3.91\%$

Thus, the USD depreciated relative to the GBP. That is, the GBP appreciated against the USD because R_{FX} is quoted in terms of USD/GBP, with the USD as the price currency and GBP as the base currency, and in this example R_{FX} is a positive number (3.91%).

2.

Template for Question 2

Asset	Percentage Movement in the Spot Exchange Rate	Foreign-Currency Portfolio Return (circle one)
Portfolio B	EUR appreciated 5% against the USD	Positive
		Negative

Justification

The domestic-currency return for Portfolio B is 0%, and the EUR appreciated 5% against the USD; therefore, the foreign-currency return for Portfolio B is necessarily negative.

The domestic-currency return on a foreign portfolio will reflect both the foreign-currency return on the portfolio and the percentage movements in the spot exchange rate between the domestic and foreign currency. The domestic-currency return is multiplicative with respect to these two factors:

$$R_{DC} = (1 + R_{FC})(1 + R_{FX}) - 1$$

where R_{DC} is the domestic-currency return (in percent), R_{FC} is the foreign-currency return of the asset (portfolio), and R_{FX} is the percentage change of the foreign currency against the domestic currency. (Note that once again, the domestic currency—the USD—is the price currency in the USD/EUR quote for R_{FX}.)

Solving for R_{FC}: $(1 + R_{FC})(1 + 5\%) - 1 = 0\%$; $R_{FC} = -4.76\%$

3. Any *two* of the following four points is acceptable:
   - Trading requires dealing on the bid/offer spread offered by dealers. Dealer profit margin is based on these spreads. Maintaining a 100% hedge will require frequent rebalancing of minor changes in currency movements and could prove to be expensive. "Churning" the hedge portfolio would progressively add to hedging costs and reduce the hedge's benefits.
   - A long position in currency options involves an upfront payment. If the options expire out-of-the-money, this is an unrecoverable cost.
   - Forward contracts have a maturity date and need to be "rolled" forward with an FX swap transaction to maintain the hedge. Rolling hedges typically generate cash inflows and outflows, based on movements in the spot rate as well as roll yield. Cash may have to be raised to settle the hedging transactions (increases the volatility in the organization's cash accounts). The management of these cash flow costs can accumulate and become a large portion of the portfolio's value, and they become more expensive for cash outflows as interest rates increase.
   - Hedging requires maintaining the necessary administrative infrastructure for trading (personnel and technology systems). These overhead costs can become a significant portion of the overall costs of currency trading.

4. Optimal hedging decisions require balancing the benefits of hedging against the costs of hedging. Hedging costs come mainly in two forms: trading costs and opportunity costs. Gupta is referring to the opportunity cost of the 100% hedge strategy. The opportunity cost of the 100% hedge strategy for Portfolio B is the forgone opportunity of benefiting from favorable currency rate movements. Gupta is implying that accepting some currency risk has the potential to enhance portfolio return. A complete hedge eliminates this possibility.

5. A solution is to put in place a currency overlay program for active currency management. Because internal resources for active management are lacking, the fund manager would outsource currency exposure management to a sub-advisor that specializes in foreign exchange management. This approach would allow the fund manager of Portfolio A to separate the currency hedging function (currency beta), which can be done effectively internally, and the active currency management function (currency alpha), which can be managed externally by a foreign currency specialist.

6.

Template for Question 6

Gupta's Statements	Active Currency Approach (circle one)	Justification
"Many traders believe that it is not necessary to examine factors like the current account deficit, inflation, and interest rates because current exchange rates already reflect the market view on how these factors will affect future exchange rates."	Carry trade ——— Technical analysis ——— Economic fundamental	Gupta is describing active currency management based on market technicals. Market technicians believe that in a liquid, freely-traded market the historical price data already incorporates all relevant information on future price movements. Technicians believe that it is not necessary to look outside the market at data like the current account deficit, inflation, and interest rates because current exchange rates already reflect the market consensus view on how these factors will affect future exchange rates.
"The six-month interest rate in India is 8% compared to 1% in the United States. This presents a yield pick-up opportunity."	Carry trade ——— Technical analysis ——— Economic fundamental	Gupta is describing active currency management based on the carry trade. This strategy is implemented by borrowing in low-yield currencies (USD at 1%) and investing in high-yield currencies (INR at 8%).
"The currency overlay manager will estimate the fair value of the currencies with the expectation that observed spot rates will converge to long-run equilibrium values described by parity conditions."	Carry trade ——— Technical analysis ——— Economic fundamental	Gupta is describing active currency management based on economic fundamentals. This approach assumes that, in free markets, exchange rates are determined by logical economic relationships that can be modeled. A fundamentals-based approach estimates the "fair value" of the currency, with the expectation that observed spot rates will converge to long-run equilibrium values described by parity conditions.

7. Statements 1 and 2 compare differences between speculative volatility traders and hedgers of volatility. Statement 1 best explains the view of a speculative volatility trader. Speculative volatility traders often want to be net-short volatility, if they believe that market conditions will remains stable. The reason for this is that most options expire out-of-the-money, and the option writer can then keep the option premium as a payment earned for accepting volatility risk. (Speculative volatility traders would want to be long volatility if they thought volatility was likely to increase.) Statement 2 best describes the view of a hedger of volatility. Most hedgers are net-long volatility since they want to buy protection from unanticipated price volatility. Buying currency risk protection generally means a long option position. This can be thought of as paying an insurance premium for protection against exchange rate volatility.

8. In practice, matching the *current* market value of the foreign-currency exposure in the portfolio with an equal and offsetting position in a forward contract is likely to be ineffective over time because the market value of foreign-currency assets will change with market conditions. A static hedge (i.e., an unchanging hedge) will tend to accumulate unwanted currency exposures as the value of the foreign-currency assets change. This will result in a mismatch between the market value of the foreign-currency asset portfolio and the nominal size of the forward contract used for the currency hedge (resulting in currency risk). For this reason, the portfolio manager will generally need to implement a dynamic hedge by rebalancing the portfolio periodically.

9. The fund manager should implement a dynamic hedging approach. Dynamic hedging requires rebalancing the portfolio periodically. The rebalancing would require adjusting some combination of the size, number, and maturities of the foreign-currency contracts.

    Although rebalancing a dynamic hedge will keep the actual hedge ratio close to the target hedge ratio, it has the disadvantage of increased transaction costs compared to a static hedge.

10. C is correct. The domestic-currency return is a function of the foreign-currency return and the percentage change of the foreign currency against the domestic currency. Mathematically, the domestic-currency return is expressed as:

$$R_{DC} = (1 + R_{FC})(1 + R_{FX}) - 1$$

where R_{DC} is the domestic-currency return (in percent), R_{FC} is the foreign-currency return, and R_{FX} is the percentage change of the foreign currency against the domestic currency. Note that this R_{FX} expression is calculated using the investor's domestic currency (the EUR in this case) as the *price* currency in the P/B quote. This is different than the market-standard currency quotes in Exhibit 1, where the EUR is the *base* currency in each of these quotes. Therefore, for the foreign currency (USD, GBP, or CHF) to *appreciate* against the EUR, the market-standard quote (USD/EUR, GBP/EUR, or CHF/EUR, respectively) must *decrease*; that is, the EUR must depreciate.

The Euro-Swiss (CHF/EUR) is the only spot rate with a negative change (from 1.2175 to 1.2080), meaning the EUR depreciated against the CHF (the CHF/EUR rate decreased). Or put differently, the CHF appreciated against the EUR, adding to the EUR-denominated return for the German investor holding CHF-denominated assets. This would result in a higher domestic-currency return (R_{DC}), for the German investor, relative to the foreign-currency return (R_{FC}) for the CHF-denominated assets. Both the Euro-dollar (USD/EUR) and Euro-sterling (GBP/EUR) experienced a positive change in the spot rate, meaning the EUR appreciated against these two currencies (the USD/EUR rate and the GBP/EUR rate both increased). This would result in a lower domestic-currency return (R_{DC}) for the German investor relative to the foreign-currency return (R_{FC}) for the USD- and GBP-denominated assets.

A is incorrect because the Euro-dollar (USD/EUR) experienced a positive change in the spot rate, meaning the EUR appreciated against the USD (the USD/EUR rate increased). This would result in a lower domestic-currency (i.e., EUR-denominated) return relative to the foreign-currency return for the USD-denominated assets, since the USD has depreciated against the EUR.

B is incorrect because the Euro-sterling (GBP/EUR) experienced a positive change in the spot rate, meaning the EUR appreciated against the GPB (the GBP/EUR rate increased). This would result in a lower domestic-currency (i.e., EUR-denominated) return relative to the foreign-currency return for the GBP-denominated assets, since the GBP has depreciated against the EUR.

11. C is correct. An increase in the expected correlation between movements in the foreign-currency asset returns and movements in the spot exchange rates from 0.50 to 0.80 would increase the domestic-currency return *risk* but would not change the *level* of expected domestic-currency return. The domestic-currency return risk is a function of the foreign-currency return risk [$\sigma(R_{FC})$], the exchange rate risk [$\sigma(R_{FX})$], and the correlation between the foreign-currency returns and exchange rate movements. Mathematically, this is expressed as:

$$\sigma^2(R_{DC}) \approx \sigma^2(R_{FC}) + \sigma^2(R_{FX}) + 2\sigma(R_{FC})\sigma(R_{FX})\rho(R_{FC}R_{FX})$$

If the correlation increases from +0.50 to +0.80, then the *variance* of the expected domestic-currency return will increase—but this will not affect the *level* of the expected domestic-currency return (R_{DC}). Refer to the equation shown for the answer in Question 1 and note that Ostermann's expected R_{FC} has not changed. (Once again, note as well that R_{FX} is defined with the domestic currency as the price currency.)

A and B are incorrect. An increase in the expected correlation between movements in the foreign-currency asset returns and movements in the spot rates from 0.50 to 0.80 would increase the domestic-currency return risk but would not impact the expected domestic-currency return.

12. A is correct. Guten believes that, due to efficient currency markets, there should not be any long-run gains for speculating (or active management) in currencies, especially after netting out management and transaction costs. Therefore, both currency hedging and actively trading currencies represent a cost to the portfolio with little prospect of consistently positive active returns. Given a long investment horizon and few immediate liquidity needs, Guten is most likely to choose to forgo currency hedging and its associated costs.

B and C are incorrect because given a long investment horizon and little immediate liquidity needs, Guten is most likely to choose to forgo currency hedging and its associated costs. Guten believes that due to efficient currency markets there should not be any long-run gains when speculating in currencies, especially after netting out management and transaction costs.

13. B is correct. Umlauf develops a market view based on underlying fundamentals in exchange rates (an economic fundamental approach). When directed by clients, Umlauf uses options and a variety of trading strategies to *unbundle* all of the various risk factors and trades them separately (a volatility trading approach). A market technical approach would entail forming a market view based on technical analysis (i.e., a belief that

historical prices incorporate all relevant information on future price movements and that such movements have a tendency to repeat).

A is incorrect because, in using options and a variety of trading strategies to *unbundle* all of the various risk factors and trade them separately, Umlauf is likely to periodically employ volatility trading-based currency strategies.

C is incorrect because, in developing a market view based on underlying fundamentals in exchange rates, Umlauf does utilize an economic fundamentals approach.

14. B is correct. Braunt Pensionskasse provides the manager with limited discretion in managing the portfolio's currency risk exposures. This would be most consistent with allowing the currency overlay manager to take directional views on future currency movements (within predefined bounds) where the currency overlay is limited to the currency exposures already in the foreign asset portfolio. It would not be appropriate to use a fully-passive hedging approach since it would eliminate any alpha from currency movements. Further, a currency overlay program, which considers "foreign exchange as an asset class," would likely expose Braunt's portfolio to more currency risk than desired given the given primary performance objectives.

A is incorrect because a directional view currency overlay program is most appropriate given the limited discretion Braunt Pensionskasse has given the manager. A fully passive currency overlay program is more likely to be used when a client seeks to hedge all the currency risk.

C is incorrect because a directional view currency overlay program is most appropriate given the limited discretion Braunt Pensionskasse has given the manager. In contrast, the concept of "foreign exchange as an asset class" allows the currency overlay manager to take currency exposure positions in any currency pair where there is value-added to be harvested.

15. C is correct. The primary performance objective of Franz Trading GmbH is to add alpha to the portfolio, and thus has given the manager discretion in trading currencies. This is essentially a "foreign exchange as an asset class" approach. Braunt Pensionskasse and Kastner have more conservative currency strategies, and thus are less likely to benefit from the different strategies that a new overlay manager might employ.

A is incorrect because Franz Trading GmbH is more likely to benefit from the introduction of an additional overlay manager. Kastner is more likely to have a fully passive currency overlay program.

B is incorrect because Franz Trading GmbH is more likely to benefit from the introduction of an additional overlay manager. Braunt is more likely to have a currency overlay program where the manager takes a directional view on future currency movements.

16. A is correct. Exchange-traded futures contracts not only have initial margin requirements, they also have daily mark-to-market and, as a result, can be subject to daily margin calls. Market participants must have sufficient liquidity to meet margin calls, or have their positions involuntarily liquidated by their brokers. Note that the risk of daily margin calls is not a feature of most forwards contracts; nor is initial margin. (However, this is changing among the largest institutional players in FX markets as many forward contracts now come with what are known as Collateral Support Annexes—CSAs—in which margin can be posted. Posting additional margin would typically not be a daily event, however, except in the case of extreme market moves.)

B is incorrect because futures contracts have low transactions costs. C is incorrect because whether the EUR is the price or the base currency in the quote will not affect the hedging process. In fact, on the CME the quote would be the market-standard USD/ EUR quote, with the EUR as the base currency.

17. C is correct. Based on predicted export trends, Subscriber 2 most likely expects the KRW/ USD rate to increase (i.e., the won—the price currency—to depreciate relative to the USD). This would require a long forward position in a forward contract, but as a country with capital controls, a NDF would be used instead. (Note: While forward contracts offered by banks are generally an institutional product, not retail, the retail version of a non-deliverable forward contract is known as a "contract for differences" (CFD) and is available at several retail FX brokers.)

    A is incorrect because Subscriber 2 expects the KRW/USD rate to increase. A short straddle position would be used when the direction of exchange rate movement is unknown and volatility is expected to remain low.

    B is incorrect because a put option would profit from a decrease of the KRW/USD rate, not an increase (as expected). Higher volatility would also make buying a put option more expensive.

18. B is correct. Subscriber 3's carry trade strategy is equivalent to trading the forward rate bias, based on the historical evidence that the forward rate is not the center of the distribution for the spot rate. Applying this bias involves buying currencies selling at a forward discount and selling currencies trading at a forward premium. So a higher forward premium on the lower yielding currency—the USD, the base currency in the INR/USD quote—would effectively reflect a more profitable trading opportunity. That is, a higher premium for buying or selling the USD forward is associated with a lower US interest rate compared to India. This would mean a wider interest rate differential in favor of Indian instruments, and hence potentially more carry trade profits.

    A is incorrect because Subscriber 3's carry trade strategy depends on a wide interest rate differential between the high-yield country (India) and the low-yield country (the United States). The differential should be wide enough to compensate for the unhedged currency risk exposure.

    C is incorrect because a guide to the carry trade's riskiness is the volatility of spot rates on the involved currencies, with rapid movements in exchange rates often associated with a panicked unwinding of carry trades. All things being equal, higher volatility is worse for carry trades.

19. C is correct. Emerging market currencies are often the investment currencies in the carry trade. This reflects the higher yields often available in their money markets compared to Developed Market economies (funding currencies are typically low-yield currencies such as the JPY). This can lead to higher holding returns, but these higher returns can also come with higher risks: carry trades are occasionally subject to panicked unwinds in stressed market conditions. When this occurs, position exit can be made more difficult by market illiquidity and higher trading costs (wider bid/offer spreads). The leverage involved in the carry trade can magnify trading losses under these circumstances.

    A is incorrect because return distributions are often *negatively* skewed, reflecting the higher event risk (panicked carry trade unwinds, currency pegs being re-set, etc.) associated with the carry trade.

    B is incorrect because although FX markets are typically efficient (or very close thereto) this does not mean that higher returns are not available. The key question is whether these are abnormally high *risk-adjusted* returns. Higher return in an efficient market comes with higher risk. The higher (short-term) return in the carry trade reflects the risk premia for holding unhedged currency risk, in the context of a favorable interest rate differential.

20. B is correct. The GBP value of the assets has declined, and hence the hedge needs to be *reduced* by GBP 7,000,000. This would require buying the GBP forward to net the outstanding (short) forward contract to an amount less than GBP 100,000,000.

   A is incorrect because to rebalance the hedge (reduce the net size of the short forward position) the GBP must be bought *forward*, not with a spot transaction.

   C is incorrect because the GBP must be bought, not sold. Buying SEK against the GBP is equivalent to selling GBP. Moreover, the amount of SEK that would be sold forward (to buy GBP 7,000,000 forward) would be determined by the *forward* rate, not the spot rate (7,000,000 × 10.6875 = 74,812,500).

21. C is correct. The fund holds CHF-denominated assets and hence Björk wants to protect against a depreciation of the CHF against the SEK, which would be a down-move in the SEK/CHF cross rate. An OTM put option provides some downside protection against such a move, while writing an OTM call option helps reduce the cost of this option structure. Note that Björk does not expect that the SEK/CHF rate will increase, so this option (in her view) will likely expire OTM and allow her to keep the premia. This hedging structure is known as a short risk reversal (or a collar) and is a popular hedging strategy.

   A is incorrect because the ATM call option will not protect against a decrease in the SEK/CHF rate. An ATM option is also expensive (compared to an OTM option). Note that Björk does not expect the SEK/CHF rate to increase, so would not want a long call option position for this rate.

   B is incorrect because this structure is expensive (via the long ITM call option) and does not protect against a decrease in the SEK/CHF rate.

22. B is correct. To hedge the EUR-denominated assets Björk will be selling forward contracts on the SEK/EUR cross rate. A higher forward premium will result in higher roll return as Björk is selling the EUR forward at a higher all-in forward rate, and closing out the contract at a lower rate (all else equal), given that the forward curve is in contango.

   A is incorrect because Björk is hedging EUR-denominated assets with a EUR-denominated forward contract. While it is true that the gap between spot and forward rates will be higher the higher the interest rate differential between countries, this gap (basis) converges to zero near maturity date, when the forward contracts would be rolled.

   C is incorrect because forward contracts do not generate premia income; writing options does.

23. C is correct. A cross hedge exposes the fund to basis risk; that is, the risk that the hedge fails to protect against adverse currency movements because the correlations between the value of the assets being hedged and the hedging instrument change.

   A is incorrect because movements in forward points (and hence roll yield) would be of secondary importance compared to the basis risk of a cross hedge.

   B is incorrect because exchange rate volatility would not necessarily affect a hedge based on forward contracts, as long as the correlations between the underlying assets and the hedge remained stable. Although relevant, volatility in itself is not the "most" important risk to consider for a cross-hedge. (However, movements in volatility would affect hedges based on currency options.)

24. A is correct. The fund has a long-term perspective, few immediate liquidity needs, and a lower weight in fixed income than in equities (bond portfolios are typically associated with hedge ratios closer to 100% than equity portfolios). The emerging market exposure would also support active management, given these countries' typically higher yields (carry trade) and often volatile exchange rates.

B is incorrect because the characteristics of the fund and the beneficial investor (in this case, the royal family) do not argue for a conservative currency strategy.

C is incorrect because a more active currency management strategy would be more suitable for this fund.

25. Currency movements contributed 1.5% to the account's 7.0% total (US dollar) return, calculated as follows:

The domestic-currency return (R_{DC}) on a portfolio of multiple foreign assets is

$$R_{DC} = \sum_{i=1}^{n} \omega_i (1 + R_{FC,i})(1 + R_{FX,i}) - 1$$

Where $R_{FC,i}$ is the foreign-currency return on the ith foreign asset, $R_{FX,i}$ is the appreciation of the ith foreign currency against the domestic currency, and ω_i is the weight of the asset as a percentage of the aggregate domestic-currency value of the portfolio. This equation can be rearranged as

$$R_{DC} = \sum_{i=1}^{n} \omega_i [R_{FC,i} + R_{FX,i} + (R_{FC,i} \times R_{FX,i})]$$

Therefore, the domestic-currency return is equal to the sum of the weighted asset return, the weighted currency return, and the weighted cross-product of the asset return and the currency return. The latter two terms explain the effects of foreign-currency movements on the Bhatt account's total (US dollar) return of 7.0%.

The weighted asset return is equal to 5.5%, calculated as follows:

$$(0.50 \times 10.0\%) + (0.25 \times 5.0\%) + [0.25 \times (-3.0\%)] = 5.5\%.$$

The weighted currency return is equal to 1.5% calculated as follows:

$$(0.50 \times 0.0\%) + (0.25 \times 2.0\%) + (0.25 \times 4.0\%) = 1.5\%.$$

The weighted cross-product is equal to −0.005%, calculated as follows:

$$[0.50 \times (10.0\% \times 0.0\%)] + [0.25 \times (5.0\% \times 2.0\%)] + [0.25 \times (-3.0\% \times 4.0\%)] = -0.005\%.$$

Therefore, the contribution of foreign currency equals 1.5%, calculated as the 7.0% total (US dollar) return less the 5.5% weighted asset return. Alternatively, the contribution of foreign currency to the total return can be calculated as the sum of the weighted currency return of 1.5% and the weighted cross-product of −0.005%:

$$1.5\% + (-0.005\%) = 1.495\%, \text{ which rounds to } 1.5\%.$$

26.

Determine the *most appropriate* currency management strategy for Bhatt. (Circle one.)		
Passive hedging	Discretionary hedging	Active currency management

Justify your response.

Active currency management is the most appropriate currency management strategy because with this approach, the portfolio manager is supposed to take currency risks and manage them for profit with the primary goal of adding alpha to the portfolio through successful trading. This primary goal differs from the discretionary hedging approach in which the manager's primary duty is to protect the portfolio from currency risk and secondarily seek alpha within limited bounds. While the difference between active currency management and discretionary hedging is one of emphasis more than degree, the bounded discretion that Bhatt has granted Darden (plus or minus 25% from the neutral position) strongly suggests that Darden is expected to take currency risk and seek alpha with priority over portfolio protection from currency risk.

Passive hedging is not appropriate because with this approach, the goal is to keep the portfolio's currency exposures close, if not equal to, those of a benchmark portfolio used to evaluate performance. Passive hedging is a rules-based approach that removes all discretion from the portfolio manager, regardless of the manager's market opinion on future movements in exchange rates. In this case, Bhatt has granted Darden the discretion to manage currency exposures within a range of plus or minus 25% from the neutral benchmark position.

A discretionary hedging approach is not appropriate because Bhatt has granted Darden more than limited discretion (plus or minus 25% from the neutral position), indicative of an active currency management approach. The discretion granted suggests that Darden's primary goal is to take currency risks and manage them for profit with a secondary goal of protecting the portfolio from currency risk. The primary goal of a discretionary hedging approach is to protect the portfolio from currency risk while secondarily seeking alpha within limited bounds.

27. Given C&M's research conclusion and the IPS constraints, the currency team should under-hedge Bhatt's portfolio by selling the US dollar forward against the Indian rupee in a forward contract (or contracts) at no less than a 75% hedge ratio of the portfolio's USD10,000,000 market value. By under-hedging the portfolio relative to the "neutral" (100% hedge ratio) benchmark, the team seeks to add incremental value on the basis of its view that the US dollar will appreciate against the Indian rupee while maintaining compliance with the IPS.

Since the Indian rupee is assumed to depreciate against the US dollar, a 100% hedge ratio would largely eliminate any alpha opportunity. However, a hedge ratio greater than 75% but less than 100% (as dictated by the plus or minus 25% versus neutral IPS constraint) provides the opportunity to capture currency return in the expected US dollar appreciation against the Indian rupee.

28. In currency markets, volatility is not constant, nor are its movements completely random. Instead, volatility is determined by a wide variety of underlying factors, both fundamental and technical, for which a trader can express an opinion. Movements in volatility are cyclical and typically subject to long periods of relative stability punctuated by sharp upward spikes in volatility as markets come under stress. Speculative volatility traders among overlay managers often want to be net short volatility because most options expire out of the money and the option writer then gets to keep the premium without delivery of the underlying currency pair. Ideally these traders would want to flip their position and be long volatility ahead of the volatility spikes, but these episodes can be notoriously difficult to time. Most hedgers, in contrast, typically run option positions that are net long volatility because they are buying protection from the unanticipated price volatility.

In this case, Konev would most likely be interested in speculative gains on US dollar weakness, while the other institutional clients would be hedgers seeking to minimize trading risks. The concept of foreign exchange as an asset class for Konev will most likely permit Murimi to take foreign exchange exposure in any currency pair where there is additional value to capture. A volatility-based strategy for Konev would typically be net short, as opposed to net long, volatility to earn the related risk premium for absorbing volatility risk. In contrast, the institutional investors, as hedgers in managing net long volatility positions, would be exposed to the time decay of an option's time value.

29. In forming a market view on such turning points in future exchange rate movements (e.g., peaking in the US dollar) or timing-related position entry and exit points, market technicians follow three principles: (1) Historical price data can be helpful in projecting future movements, (2) historical price patterns have a tendency to repeat and identify profitable trade opportunities, and (3) technical analysis attempts to determine not where market prices *should* trade but where they *will* trade.

    Thus, when devising a volatility strategy, Murimi can use her technical skills to time entry and exit points of positions. She can identify patterns in the historical price data on the US dollar, such as when it was overbought or oversold, meaning it has trended too far in one direction and is vulnerable to a trend reversal. She would appropriately position US dollar trades to maximize potential returns from volatility shifts that could be associated with US dollar exchange rate movements.

30. Emerging market currency trades are subject to relatively frequent extreme events and market stresses. Thus, return probability distributions for emerging market investments exhibit fatter tails than the normal distributions that are customarily used to evaluate developed market investment performance. Additionally, emerging market return probability distributions also have a pronounced negative skew when compared with developed market (normal) distributions.

    Given these differences, risk management and control tools (such as VAR) that depend on normal distributions can be misleading under extreme market conditions and greatly understate the risks to which the portfolio is exposed. Likewise, many investment performance measures used to evaluate performance are also based on the normal distribution. As a result, historical performance evaluated by such measures as the Sharpe ratio can look very attractive when market conditions are stable, but this apparent outperformance can disappear into deep losses faster than most investors can react.

    Short-term stability in emerging markets can give investors a false sense of overconfidence and thereby encourage over-positioning based on the illusion of normally distributed returns. Thus, CCM should not assume a normal distribution for its "model" emerging market portfolio. CCM should assume a fatter-tailed, negatively skewed return probability distribution better reflecting the risk exposure to extreme events.

31.

Identify the *most likely* approach for Lee to optimally locate Wilson's portfolio on the currency risk spectrum, consistent with IPS. (Circle one.)

Passive Hedging	Discretionary Hedging	Active Currency Management	Currency Overlay

Justify your response with *two* reasons supporting the approach.

1. The portfolio is said to be in its flat natural neutral position because Lee does not have market conviction, which is consistent with a discretionary hedging approach.	2. The currency hedge ratio requirement reflects some discretion with actual portfolio currency risk exposures allowed to vary from the neutral position within a 3% band.

Passive hedging is not likely because the IPS allows the 3% band around the neutral position. In addition, passive hedging is a rules-based approach, which is contrary to Wilson's preference.

Active currency management is not likely because the 3% band around the neutral position is too limited for that approach. In many cases, the difference between discretionary hedging and active currency management is more of emphasis than degree. The primary duty of the discretionary hedger is to protect the portfolio from currency risk. Active currency management is supposed to take currency risks and manage them for profit. Leaving actual portfolio exposures near zero for extended periods is typically not a viable option.

Currency overlay is not likely because the 3% band is too small to indicate active currency management in a currency overlay program. In addition, currency overlay programs are often conducted by external, FX-specialized sub-advisers to a portfolio, whereas Lee is a generalist managing a variety of portfolios across asset classes. Finally, currency overlay allows for taking directional views on future currency movements, and a lack of market conviction is noted here.

32. The IPS revision allows for a more proactive currency risk approach in the portfolio because it was determined Wilson was too short-term focused and risk averse. Lee should structure the currency overlay so that it is as uncorrelated as possible with other asset or alpha-generation programs in the portfolio. By introducing foreign currencies as a separate asset class, the more currency overlay is expected to generate alpha that is uncorrelated with the other programs in the portfolio, the more likely it is to be allowed in terms of strategic portfolio positioning.

33.

Determine which type of hedge instrument combination is *most* appropriate for Rivera's situation. (Circle one.)

Static Forward	Static Futures	Dynamic Forward	Dynamic Futures

Justify your selection.

Static vs. Dynamic Justifications:
1. Both Rivera and Delgado are risk averse.
2. The portfolio's IPS requires monthly rebalancing.
Forward vs. Futures Justifications:
1. A forward contract is less expensive.
2. A forward contract has greater liquidity.

The hedge instrument combination most appropriate for Rivera's portfolio is a dynamic forward hedge for the reasons noted below.

First, a dynamic hedge is most appropriate here. A static hedge (i.e., unchanging hedge) will avoid transaction costs but will also tend to accumulate unwanted currency exposures as the value of the foreign-currency assets change. This characteristic will cause a mismatch between the market value of the foreign-currency asset portfolio and the nominal size of the forward contract used for the currency hedge; this is pure currency risk. Given this potential mismatch and because both Rivera and Delgado are risk averse, Delgado should implement a dynamic hedge by rebalancing the portfolio at least on a monthly basis.

Delgado must assess the cost–benefit trade-offs of how frequently to dynamically rebalance the hedge. This depends on a variety of factors (manager risk aversion, market view, IPS guidelines). The higher the degree of risk aversion, the more frequently the hedge is likely to be rebalanced back to the "neutral" hedge ratio.

A forward contract is more suitable because in comparison to a futures contract, a forward contract is more flexible in terms of currency pair, settlement date, and transaction amount. Forward contracts are also simpler than futures contracts from an administrative standpoint owing to the absence of margin requirements, reducing portfolio management expense. Finally, forward contracts are more liquid than futures for trading in large sizes because the daily trade volume for OTC currency forward contracts dwarfs those for exchange-traded futures contracts.

34. When hedging one month ago, Delgado would have sold USD2,500,000 one month forward against the euro. Now, with the US dollar-denominated portfolio increasing in value to USD2,650,000, a mismatched FX swap is needed to settle the initial expiring forward contract and establish a new hedge given the higher market value of the US dollar-denominated portfolio.

To calculate the net cash flow (in euros) to maintain the desired hedge, the following steps are necessary:

- Buy USD2,500,000 at the spot rate. Buying US dollars against the euro means selling euros, which is the base currency in the USD/EUR spot rate. Therefore, the bid side of the market must be used to calculate the outflow in euros.

$$USD2,500,000 \times 0.8875 = EUR2,218,750.$$

- Sell USD2,650,000 at the spot rate adjusted for the one-month forward points (all-in forward rate). Selling the US dollar against the euro means buying euros, which is the base currency in the USD/EUR spot rate. Therefore, the offer side of the market must be used to calculate the inflow in euros.

$$\text{All-in forward rate} = 0.8876 + (25/10,000) = 0.8901.$$
$$USD2,650,000 \times 0.8901 = EUR2,358,765.$$

- Therefore, the net cash flow is equal to EUR2,358,765 − EUR2,218,750, which is equal to EUR140,015.

35.

Identify *two* strategies Delgado should use to earn a positive roll yield.	**Describe** the specific steps needed to execute *each* strategy.
1. Implement the carry trade.	Buy (invest in) the high-yield currency and sell (borrow) the low-yield currency.
2. Trade the forward rate bias.	Buy (invest in) the forward discount currency and sell (borrow) the forward premium currency.

Given that the base currency (the US dollar) is trading at a forward premium, the hedge requires the sale of US dollar forward, resulting in a positive roll yield. The concept of roll yield is very similar to forward rate bias and the carry trade. Here, Delgado is suggesting a strategy to pursue when there is a negative roll yield, because a hedger trading against the forward bias would be buying US dollars at a forward premium instead of selling them. The carry trade strategy of borrowing in low-yield currencies and investing in high-yield currencies is equivalent to trading the forward rate bias, not against it.

CHAPTER 8

OPTIONS STRATEGIES

SOLUTIONS

1. C is correct. To construct a synthetic long put position, Nuñes would buy a call option on IZD. Of course, she would also need to sell (short) IZD shares to complete the synthetic long put position.

2. A is correct. Strategy 2 is a covered call, which is a combination of a long position in shares and a short call option. The breakeven point of Strategy 2 is €91.26, which represents the price per share of €93.93 minus the call premium received of €2.67 per share $(S_0 - c_0)$. So, at any share price less than €91.26 at option expiration, Strategy 2 incurs a loss. If the share price of IZD at option expiration is greater than €91.26, Strategy 2 generates a gain.

3. A is correct. Strategy 3 is a covered call strategy, which is a combination of a long position in shares and a short call option. The breakeven share price for a covered call is the share price minus the call premium received, or $S_0 - c_0$. The current share price of IZD is €93.93, and the IZD April €97.50 call premium is €1.68. Thus, the breakeven underlying share price for Strategy 3 is $S_0 - c_0 = $ €93.93 − €1.68 = €92.25.

4. B is correct. Strategy 4 is a protective put position, which is a combination of a long position in shares and a long put option. By purchasing the €25.00 strike put option, Nuñes would be protected from losses at QWY share prices of €25.00 or lower. Thus, the maximum loss per share from Strategy 4 would be the loss of share value from €28.49 to €25.00 (or €3.49) plus the put premium paid for the put option of €0.50: $S_0 - X + p_0 = $ €28.49 − €25.00 + €0.50 = €3.99.

5. A is correct. Strategy 5 describes a collar, which is a combination of a long position in shares, a long put option with an exercise price below the current stock price, and a short call option with an exercise price above the current stock price.

6. B is correct. Strategy 5 describes a collar, which is a combination of a long position in shares, a long put option, and a short call option. Strategy 5 would require Nuñes to buy 100 QWY shares at the current market price of €28.49 per share. In addition, she would purchase a QWY April €24.00 strike put option contract for €0.35 per share and collect €0.32 per share from writing a QWY April €31.00 strike call option. The collar offers protection against losses on the shares below the put strike price of €24.00 per share, but

it also limits upside to the call strike price of €31.00 per share. Thus, the maximum gain on the trade, which occurs at prices of €31.00 per share or higher, is calculated as $(X_2 - S_0) - p_0 + c_0$, or (€31.00 − €28.49) − €0.35 + €0.32 = €2.48 per share.

7. B is correct. Strategy 6 is a bear spread, which is a combination of a long put option and a short put option on the same underlying, where the long put has a higher strike price than the short put. In the case of Strategy 6, the April €31.00 put option would be purchased and the April €25.00 put option would be sold. The long put premium is €3.00 and the short put premium is €0.50, for a net cost of €2.50. The breakeven share price is €28.50, calculated as $X_H - (p_H - p_L)$ = €31.00 − (€3.00 − €0.50) = €28.50.

8. B is correct. Strategy 7 describes a short straddle, which is a combination of a short put option and a short call option, both with the same strike price. The maximum gain is €5.76 per share, which represents the sum of the two option premiums, or $c_0 + p_0$ = €2.54 + €3.22 = €5.76. The maximum gain per share is realized if both options expire worthless, which would happen if the share price of XDF at expiration is €75.00.

9. C is correct. Nuñes would implement Strategy 8, which is a long calendar spread, if she expects the XDF share price to increase between the February and December expiration dates. This strategy provides a benefit from the February short call premium to partially offset the cost of the December long call option. Nuñes likely expects the XDF share price to remain relatively flat between the current price €74.98 and €80 until the February call option expires, after which time she expects the share price to increase above €80. If such expectations come to fruition, the February call would expire worthless and Nuñes would realize gains on the December call option.

10. C is correct. Nuñes should recommend a long straddle, which is a combination of a long call option and a long put option, both with the same strike price. The committee's announcement is expected to cause a significant move in XDF's share price. A long straddle is appropriate because the share price is expected to move sharply up or down depending on the committee's decision. If the merger is approved, the share price will likely increase, leading to a gain in the long call option. If the merger is rejected, then the share price will likely decrease, leading to a gain in the long put option.

11. C is correct. A protective put accomplishes Hopewell's goal of short-term price protection. A protective put provides downside protection while retaining the upside potential. Although Hopewell is concerned about the downside in the short term, he wants to remain invested in Walnut shares because he is positive on the stock in the long term.

12. A is correct. The long straddle strategy is based on expectations of volatility in the underlying stock being higher than the market consensus. The straddle strategy consists of simultaneously buying a call option and a put option at the same strike price. Singh could recommend that French buy a straddle using near at-the-money options ($67.50 strike). This allows French to profit should the Walnut stock price experience a large move in either direction after the earnings release.

13. A is correct. The straddle strategy consists of simultaneously buying a call option and buying a put option at the same strike price. The market price for the $67.50 call option is $1.99, and the market price for the $67.50 put option is $2.26, for an initial net cost of $4.25 per share. Thus, this straddle position requires a move greater than $4.25 in either direction from the strike price of $67.50 to become profitable. So, the straddle becomes profitable at $67.50 − $4.26 = $63.24 or lower, or $67.50 + $4.26 = $71.76 or higher. At $63.00, the profit on the straddle is positive.

14. A is correct. The bull call strategy consists of buying the lower-strike option and selling the higher-strike option. The purchase of the $65 strike call option costs $3.65 per share, and selling the $70 strike call option generates an inflow of $0.91 per share, for an initial net cost of $2.74 per share. At expiration, the maximum profit occurs when the stock price is $70 or higher, which yields a $5.00 per share payoff ($70 – $65) on the long call position. After deduction of the $2.74 per share cost required to initiate the bull call spread, the profit is $2.26 ($5.00 – $2.74).

15. B is correct. The bear put spread consists of buying a put option with a high strike price ($70) and selling another put option with a lower strike price ($65). The market price for the $70 strike put option is $3.70, and the market price for the $65 strike put option is $1.34 per share. Thus, the initial net cost of the bear spread position is $3.70 – $1.34 = $2.36 per share. If Walnut shares are $66 at expiration, the $70 strike put option is in the money by $4.00, and the short position in the $65 strike put expires worthless. After deducting the cost of $2.36 to initiate the bear spread position, the net profit is $1.64 per contract.

16. B is correct. The $67.50 call option is approximately at the money because the Walnut share price is currently $67.79. Gamma measures the sensitivity of an option's delta to a change in the underlying. The largest gamma occurs when options are trading at the money or near expiration, when the deltas of such options move quickly toward 1.0 or 0.0. Under these conditions, the gammas tend to be largest and delta hedges are hardest to maintain.

17. B is correct. Ahlim could mitigate the risk of the Brazilian real weakening against the US dollar over the next six months by (1) purchasing an at-the-money six-month BRL/USD call option (to buy US dollars), (2) purchasing an at-the-money six-month USD/BRL put option (to sell Brazilian reals), or (3) taking a long position in a six-month BRL/USD futures contract (to buy US dollars).

    Purchasing an at-the-money six-month USD/BRL put option (to sell Brazilian reals) would mitigate the risk of a weakening Brazilian real. If the Brazilian real should weaken against the US dollar over the next six months, Ahlim could exercise the put option and sell his Brazilian reals at the contract's strike rate (which would have been the prevailing market exchange rate at the time of purchase, since the option is at the money).

    A is incorrect because purchasing (not selling) an at-the-money six-month BRL/USD call option (to buy US dollars) would mitigate the risk of the Brazilian real weakening against the US dollar over the next six months. The long call position would give Ahlim the right to buy US dollars (and sell Brazilian reals). A call on US dollars is similar to a put on Brazilian reals. So, a put to sell Brazilian reals at a given strike rate can be viewed as a call to buy US dollars.

    C is incorrect because going long (not short) a six-month BRL/USD futures contract (to buy US dollars) would mitigate the risk of the Brazilian real weakening against the US dollar over the next six months. A long futures position would obligate Ahlim to buy US dollars (and sell Brazilian reals) at the futures contract rate.

18. C is correct. Ngoc recommends a protective put position with a strike price of $35 using May options. The maximum loss per share on the protective put is calculated as

    Maximum loss per share of protective put = $S_0 - X + p_0$.

    Maximum loss per share of protective put = $37.41 - $35.00 + $1.81 = 4.22.

In summary, with the protective put in place, Ahlim is protected against losses below $35.00. Thus, taking into account the put option purchase price of $1.81, Ahlim's maximum loss occurs at the share price of $33.19, resulting in a maximum loss of $4.22 per share (= $37.41 – $33.19).

A is incorrect because $0.60 reflects incorrectly subtracting (rather than adding) the put premium in the calculation of the maximum loss of protective put (i.e., $37.41 – $35.00 – $1.81 = $0.60).

B is incorrect because $2.41 does not include the put premium in the calculation but only reflects the difference between the current share price ($37.41) and the put exercise price ($35.00).

19. C is correct. Ngoc recommends a protective put position with a strike price of $35 using May options. The breakeven price per share on the protective put is calculated as

$$\text{Breakeven price per share of protective put} = S_0 + p_0.$$

$$\text{Breakeven price per share of protective put} = \$37.41 + \$1.81 = \$39.22.$$

In summary, Ahlim would need PSÔL's share price to rise by the price of the put option ($1.81) from the current price of $37.41 to reach the breakeven share price—the price at which the gain from the increase in the value of the stock offsets the purchase price of the put option.

A is incorrect because $35.60 represents incorrectly subtracting (rather than adding) the put premium in the calculation of the protective put breakeven price: $37.41 – $1.81 = $35.60.

B is incorrect because $36.81 represents incorrectly adding the put premium to the strike price (not the current share price): $35.00 + $1.81 = $36.81.

20. B is correct. Ngoc recommends a $40/$50 bull call spread using December options. To construct this spread, Ahlim would buy the $40 call, paying the $6.50 premium, and simultaneously sell the $50 call, receiving a premium of $4.25. The maximum gain or profit of a bull call spread occurs when the stock price reaches the high exercise price ($50) or higher at expiration. Thus, the maximum profit per share of a bull call spread is the spread difference between the strike prices less the net premium paid, calculated as

$$\text{Maximum profit per share of bull call spread} = (X_H - X_L) - (c_L - c_H).$$

$$\text{Maximum profit per share of bull call spread} = (\$50 - \$40) - (\$6.50 - \$4.25).$$

$$\text{Maximum profit per share of bull call spread} = \$7.75.$$

A is incorrect because $2.25 represents only the net premium and does not include the spread difference.

C is incorrect because $12.25 represents the net premium being incorrectly added (rather than subtracted) from the spread difference.

21. A is correct. Ngoc recommends a $40/$50 bull call spread using December options. To construct this spread, Ahlim would buy the $40 call, paying a $6.50 premium, and simultaneously sell the $50 call, receiving a $4.25 premium. The breakeven price per share of a bull call spread is calculated as

$$\text{Breakeven price per share of bull call spread} = X_L + (c_L - c_H).$$

$$\text{Breakeven price per share of bull call spread} = \$40 + (\$6.50 - \$4.25).$$

$$\text{Breakeven price per share of bull call spread} = \$42.25.$$

In summary, in order to break even, the PSÔL stock price must rise above $40 by the amount of the net premium paid of $2.25 to enter into the bull call spread. At the price of $42.25, the lower $40 call option would have an exercise value of $2.25, exactly offsetting the $2.25 cost of entering the trade.

B is incorrect because $47.75 represents the net premium being incorrectly subtracted from the high exercise price (rather than being added to the low exercise price): $50 − ($6.50 − $4.25) = $47.75.

C is incorrect because $52.25 represents the net premium being added to the high exercise price (rather than the low exercise price): $50 + ($6.50 − $4.25) = $52.25.

22. B is correct. When the implied volatility decreases for OTM (out-of-the-money) calls relative to ATM (at-the-money) calls and increases for OTM puts relative to ATM puts, a volatility skew exists. Put volatility is higher, rising from 16.44 ATM to 17.72 OTM, likely because of the higher demand for puts to hedge positions in the index against downside risk. Call volatility decreases from 12.26 for ATM calls to 11.98 for OTM calls since calls do not offer this valuable portfolio insurance.

A is incorrect because a risk reversal is a delta-hedged trading strategy seeking to profit from a change in the relative volatility of calls and puts.

C is incorrect because a volatility smile exists when both call and put volatilities, not just put volatilities, are higher OTM than ATM.

23. A is correct. The research report concludes that the consensus forecast of the implied volatility of index options is too low and anticipates greater-than-expected volatility over the next month. Given the neutral market direction forecast, Ngoc should recommend a long straddle, which entails buying a one-month 11,600 call and buying a one-month put with the same exercise price. If the future NIFTY 50 Index level rises above its current level plus the combined cost of the call and put premiums, Ahlim would exercise the call option and realize a profit. Similarly, if the index level falls below the current index level minus the combined cost of the call and put premiums, Ahlim would exercise the put option and realize a profit. Thus, Ahlim profits if the index moves either up or down enough to pay for the call and put premiums.

B is incorrect because the strategy to buy a call option would be reasonable given an increase in expected implied volatility with a bullish NIFTY 50 Index forecast, not a neutral trading range.

C is incorrect because a long calendar spread is based on the expectation that implied volatility will remain unchanged, not increase, until the expiry of the shorter-term option.

CHAPTER 9

SWAPS, FORWARDS, AND FUTURES STRATEGIES

SOLUTIONS

1. A is correct. The portfolio manager would *most likely* use a longer-dated fixed-income (bond) futures contract to hedge his interest rate risk exposure. The choice of the hedging instrument, in fact, will depend on the maturity of the bond being hedged. Interest rate futures, like 90-day Eurodollar futures, have a limited number of maturities and can be used to hedge short-term bonds. The mark-to-market value of a receive-fixed 10-year interest rate swap will become negative if interest rates rise, and thus the swap cannot be used as a hedge in this case.

2. B is correct. The portfolio manager's goal is to use the receive-fixed, pay-floating swap such that the €30 million of bonds, with modified duration of 3, and the €20 million swap will combine to make up a portfolio with a market value of €30 million and modified duration of 5. This relationship can be expressed as follows:

$$€30,000,000(3) + (N_S \times MDUR_S) = €30,000,000(5).$$

Given the swap's notional (N_S) of €20,000,000, its required modified duration can be obtained as:

$$MDUR_S = [(5 - 3)€30,000,000]/€20,000,000 = 3.$$

3. B is correct. The CIO sells the relevant interest rate futures contracts at 98.05. After six months, the CIO initiates the bridge loan at a rate of 2.70%, but he unwinds the hedge at the lower futures price of 97.30, thus gaining 75 bps (= 98.05 − 97.30). The effective interest rate on the loan is 1.95% (= 2.70% − 0.75%).

4. C is correct. In a cross-currency basis swap, the goals of the transaction are to achieve favorable funding and exchange rates and to swap the foreign currency amounts back to the currency of choice—in this case, the US dollar—at maturity. There is one exchange rate specified in the swap that is used to determine the notional principals in the two currencies, exchanged at inception and at maturity.

5. B is correct. By hedging the position in Italian government bonds with the cross-currency basis swap, the US investor will most likely increase the periodic net interest she receives in US dollars. The reason is that the periodic net interest payments made by the swap counterparty to the investor will include the positive basis resulting from the relatively strong demand for US dollars versus euros.

6. B is correct. To reduce the current allocation by 20%, to 80%, in US large-cap stocks, the portfolio manager will sell S&P 500 futures. At the same time, to allocate this 20% to US small caps, he will purchase Russell 2000 futures for the same notional amount.

7. C is correct. VIX futures converge to the spot VIX as expiration approaches, and the two must be equal at expiration. When the VIX futures curve is in contango and assuming volatility remains stable, the VIX futures will get "pulled" closer to the spot VIX, and they will decrease in price as they approach expiration. Traders calculate the difference between the front-month VIX futures price and the VIX as 0.60, and the spread between the front-month and the second-month futures is 1.30. Assuming that the spread declines linearly until settlement, the trader would realize roll-down gains as the spread decreases from 1.30 to 0.60 as the front-month futures approaches its expiration. At expiration, VIX futures are equal to the VIX, and the spread with the old second-month (and now the front-month) futures contract will be 0.60. Finally, since one cannot directly invest in the VIX, trades focusing on the VIX term structure must be implemented using either VIX futures or VIX options, so Answers A and B are not feasible.

8. The swap is structured such that the executive pays the return on 10 million shares of the company's stock, which is 10% of his holdings, and he receives the return based on a floating interest rate, such as the market reference rate, on a notional principal of €300 million (= €30/share × 10 million shares).

9. Currently the allocation is $10 million in stocks and $20 million in bonds. Within the stock category, the current allocation is $7 million domestic and $3 million foreign. The desired allocation is $15 million in stocks and $15 million in bonds. Thus, the allocation must change by moving $5 million into stocks and out of bonds. The desired stock allocation is $9 million domestic and $6 million foreign. The desired bond allocation is $15 million, all domestic corporate.

   To make the changes with swaps, the manager must enter into swaps against the market reference rate, which is assumed to be flat for all swaps in this example. Using the swaps, the bank trust fund portfolio manager needs to (1) receive the returns on $2 million based on a domestic equity index and on $3 million based on a foreign equity index and (2) pay the return on $5 million based on a domestic corporate bond index. The market reference rate outflows from the swaps in (1) and the inflows from the swap in (2) will cancel out through summation.

10. First, Ko knows that the FFE rate implied by the futures contract price of 97.175 is 2.825% (= 100 − 97.175). This is the rate that market participants expect to be the average federal funds rate for that month.

    Second, Ko should determine the probability of a rate change. She knows the 2.825% FFE rate implied by the futures signals a fairly high chance that the FOMC will increase rates by 25 bps from its current target range of 2.50% − 2.75% to the new target range of 2.75% − 3.00%. She calculates the probability of a rate hike as follows:

    $$\frac{2.825\% - 2.625\%}{2.875\% - 2.625\%} = 0.80, \text{ or } 80\%$$

Ko can now incorporate this probability of a Fed rate hike into her forecast of short-term US interest rates.

11. B is correct. The basis point value of Portfolio A (BPV_P) is $130,342.94, and the basis point value of the cheapest-to-deliver bond (BPV_{CTD}) is $127.05 with a conversion factor of 0.72382. The basis point value hedge ratio ($BPVHR$), in the special case of complete hedging, provides the number of futures contracts needed, calculated as follows:

$$BPVHR = \frac{-BPV_P}{BPV_{CTD}} \times CF = \frac{-\$130,342.94}{\$127.05} \times 0.72382 = -742.58$$

Therefore, Whitacre should sell 743 Treasury bond futures to fully hedge Portfolio A.

A is incorrect because it incorrectly uses the price of the cheapest-to-deliver bond (rather than its basis point value, BPV_{CTD}) in the denominator of the $BPVHR$ calculation:

$$BPVHR = \frac{-BPV_P}{CTD \ Bond \ Price} \times CF = \frac{-\$130,342.94}{\$145.20} \times 0.72382 = -649.76$$

C is incorrect because it does not include the conversion factor for the cheapest-to-deliver bond when calculating $BPVHR$:

$$BPVHR = \frac{-BPV_P}{BPV_{CTD}} = \frac{-\$130,342.94}{\$127.05} = -1,025.92$$

12. A is correct. Monatize wants to reduce Portfolio A's modified duration to a target of 3.10. BPV_T is calculated as follows:

$$BPV_T = MDUR_T \times 0.01\% \times MV_P$$
$$BPV_T = (3.10) \times 0.0001 \times \$143,234,000 = \$44,402.54$$

The basis point value of Portfolio A (BPV_P) is $130,342.94, and the basis point value of the cheapest-to-deliver bond (BPV_{CTD}) is $127.05 with a conversion factor of 0.72382. The basis point value hedge ratio ($BPVHR$), which provides the number of futures contracts needed, is then calculated as follows:

$$BPVHR = \frac{BPV_T - BPV_P}{BPV_{CTD}} \times CF$$
$$BPVHR = \frac{\$44,402.54 - \$130,342.94}{\$127.05} \times 0.72382 = -489.6134$$

Thus, to decrease the modified duration of Portfolio A to 3.10, Whitacre should sell 490 Treasury bond futures contracts.

B is incorrect because it incorrectly subtracts 6.00 from the modified duration (equal to 9.10 − 3.10, or the change in the modified duration for Portfolio A) of the cheapest-to-deliver bond, rather than from the modified duration of the bond portfolio, in computing BPV_T:

$$BPV_T = (8.75 - 6.00) \times 0.0001 \times \$143,234,000 = \$39,389.35$$

This error results in an incorrect calculation of $BPVHR$:

$$BPVHR = \frac{\$39,389.35 - \$130,342.94}{\$127.05} \times 0.72382 = -518.1741$$

C is incorrect because it does not include the conversion factor for the cheapest-to-deliver bond when calculating *BPVHR*:

$$BPVHR = \frac{\$44,402.54 - \$130,342.94}{\$127.05} = -676.4298$$

13. A is correct. The number of equity index futures contracts to purchase in order to equitize Monatize's excess cash position is calculated as follows:

$$N_f = \left(\frac{\beta_T}{\beta_f}\right)\left(\frac{S}{F}\right) = \left(\frac{1.00}{1.00}\right)\left(\frac{\$4,800,000}{\$825,000}\right) = 5.82, \text{ or 6 contracts}$$

The actual futures contract purchase value of $825,000 is the product of the quoted S&P 500 futures price of 3,300 and the designated multiplier of $250 per index point.

B is incorrect because $100,000,000, the total value of Portfolio B, is incorrectly used as the market value of the stock portfolio to equitize (*S*), instead of Portfolio B's excess cash position:

$$N_f = \left(\frac{\beta_T}{\beta_f}\right)\left(\frac{S}{F}\right) = \left(\frac{1.00}{1.00}\right)\left(\frac{\$100,000,000}{\$825,000}\right) = 121.21, \text{ or 121 contracts}$$

C is incorrect because 3,300, the quoted S&P 500 futures price, is incorrectly used as the actual futures contract price, instead of calculating the actual futures contract price of $825,000:

$$N_f = \left(\frac{\beta_T}{\beta_f}\right)\left(\frac{S}{F}\right) = \left(\frac{1.00}{1.00}\right)\left(\frac{\$4,800,000}{\$3,300}\right) = 1,454.54, \text{ or 1,455 contracts}$$

14. C is correct. The first hedging strategy suggested by Regan is entering into a total return equity swap in exchange for a fee. Equity swaps, which are relatively illiquid contracts and are OTC derivative instruments in which each party bears counterparty risk, do not confer voting rights to the counterparty receiving the performance of the underlying. Under the terms of the total return equity swap, at pre-specified dates, the counterparties will net the index total return (increase/decrease plus dividends) against the fixed interest payment. If the index total return exceeds the fixed interest payment, Monatize will pay the counterparty the net payment. If the index total return is less than the fixed interest payment, then Monatize will receive the net payment from the counterparty.

A is incorrect because equity swaps are relatively illiquid contracts.

B is incorrect because equity swaps are OTC derivative instruments, and each counterparty in the equity swap bears the risk exposure to the other counterparty. For this reason, equity swaps are usually collateralized in order to reduce credit risk exposure.

15. A is correct. The gain on the variance swap is calculated as:

$$VarSwap_t = Variance\ Notional \times PV_t(T) \times \left\{\frac{t}{T} \times [RealizedVol(0,\ t)]^2 + \frac{T-t}{T}\right.$$
$$\left. \times [ImpliedVol(t,\ T)]^2 - Strike^2\right\}$$

Values for the inputs are as follows:
Volatility strike on existing swap = 15
Variance strike on existing swap = 15^2 = 225

$$Variance\ Notional = \frac{Vega\ Notional}{2 \times Strike} = \frac{\$1,000,000}{2 \times 15} = \$33,333.33$$

$$\text{RealizedVol}(0, t)^2 = 20^2 = 400$$
$$\text{ImpliedVol}(t, T)^2 = 18^2 = 324$$
$$t = 5$$
$$T = 12$$

$$PV_t(T) = \cfrac{1}{1 + \left[1.50\%\left(\frac{7}{12}\right)\right]} = 0.991326, \text{ which is the present value interest factor}$$

after five months (i.e., discounting for seven remaining months, from t to T), where the annual interest rate is 1.50%.

Thus, the value of the swap in five months is calculated as follows:

$$VarSwap_t = \$33,333.33 \times 0.991326 \times \left\{\frac{5}{12} \times 400 + \frac{12-5}{12} \times 324 - 225\right\}$$
$$= \$4,317,774.59$$

Given that Monatize would be long the swap, the mark-to-market value would be positive (i.e., a gain) for Monatize, equal to $4,317,775.

B is incorrect because the value of the variance swap in five months incorrectly omits the present value interest factor of 0.991326.

The value of the swap in five months, incorrectly omitting the present value interest factor, is calculated as follows:

$$VarSwap_t = \$33,333.33 \times \left\{\frac{5}{12} \times 400 + \frac{12-5}{12} \times 324 - 225\right\} = \$4,355,555.56$$

C is incorrect because the values of $[RealizedVol(0, t)]^2$ and $[ImpliedVol(t, T)]^2$ are incorrectly switched.

The value of the swap in five months, incorrectly switching the values of $[RealizedVol(0, t)]^2$ and $[ImpliedVol(t, T)]^2$, is calculated as follows:

$$VarSwap_t = \$33,333.33 \times 0.991326 \times \left(\frac{5}{12} \times 324 + \frac{12-5}{12} \times 400 - 225\right)$$
$$= \$4,736,334.37$$

16. A is correct. Typical end-of-month (EOM) activity by large financial and banking institutions often induces "dips" in the effective federal funds (FFE) rate that create bias issues when using the rate as the basis for probability calculations of potential Federal Open Market Committee rate moves. If EOM activity increases the price for the relevant fed funds contract, the FFE rate would decline. A decline in the FFE rate would decrease the probability of a change in the fed funds rate. To overcome this EOM bias, data providers have implemented various methods of "smoothing" EOM dips.

Statement 2 is incorrect because the probabilities inferred from the pricing of fed funds futures usually do not have strong predictive power, especially for the longer-term horizon.

Statement 3 is incorrect because, to derive probabilities of Fed interest rate actions, market participants look at the pricing of fed funds futures, which are tied to the FFE rate—that is, the rate used in actual transactions between depository institutions, not the Fed's target fed funds rate.

B is incorrect because the probabilities inferred from the pricing of fed funds futures usually do not have strong predictive power, especially for the longer-term horizon.

C is incorrect because, to derive probabilities of Fed interest rate actions, market participants look at the pricing of fed funds futures, which are tied to the FFE rate—that is, the rate that depository institutions actually use for lending to each other, not the Fed's target federal funds rate. The underlying assumption is that the implied futures market rates are predicting the value of the monthly average FFE rate.

17. A is correct. If the basis is positive, a trader would make a profit by "selling the basis"—that is, selling the bond and buying the futures. In contrast, when the basis is negative, the trader would make a profit by "buying the basis," in which the trader would purchase the bond and short the futures.

B is incorrect because Statement 5 is incorrect. If the basis is negative, a trader would make a profit by "buying the basis"—that is, purchasing (not selling) the bond and shorting (not buying) the futures.

C is incorrect because Statement 5 is incorrect. If the basis is negative, a trader would make a profit by "buying the basis"—that is, purchasing (not selling) the bond and shorting (not buying) the futures.

18. The number of equity index futures contracts required to achieve the target portfolio beta of 1.2 is calculated as follows:

$$N_f = \left(\frac{\beta_T - \beta_S}{\beta_f} \right) \left(\frac{S}{F} \right)$$

$$N_f = \left(\frac{1.2 - 0.9}{1.0} \right) \left(\frac{€168,300,000}{€45,000} \right)$$

$$N_f = 1,122$$

Because the number of futures contracts (N_f) is positive, Uff should buy 1,122 equity index futures contracts.

19. The swap notional principal required to achieve the target portfolio modified duration is calculated as follows:

$$N_S = \left(\frac{MDUR_T - MDUR_P}{MDUR_S} \right) (MV_P)$$

$$N_S = \left(\frac{5.0000 - 7.8000}{-2.4848} \right) (€90,100,000)$$

$$N_S = €101,529,298.13$$

Therefore, Uff should enter into the selected three-year par pay-fixed, receive-floating interest rate swap with a notional principal of approximately €101,529,298.

20. Uff needs to reduce the equity allocation by €13,202,500 (= €201,384,000 − €188,181,500).

The number of equity index futures contracts required to rebalance the Fund's portfolio to the target allocation is calculated as follows:

$$N_f = \left(\frac{\beta_T - \beta_S}{\beta_f} \right) \left(\frac{S}{F} \right)$$

Uff needs to move to a notional "cash" position ($\beta_T = 0$) to reduce equity exposure, and the portfolio beta is $\beta_S = 1.28$. The beta of the equity index futures contract (β_f) is 1.00, so the number of equity index futures contracts required is calculated as follows:

$$N_f = \left(\frac{0.00 - 1.28}{1.00}\right)\left(\frac{€13,202,500}{€35,000}\right)$$

$$N_f = -482.83$$

Because the number of futures contracts (N_f) is negative, Uff should sell 483 equity index futures contracts (after rounding).

Uff needs to increase the bond allocation by €13,202,500 (= €101,328,500 − €88,126,000).

The number of bond futures contracts required to rebalance the Fund's portfolio to the target allocation is calculated as follows:

$$BPVHR = \left(\frac{BPV_T - BPV_P}{BPV_{CTD}}\right) \times CF,$$

where

$$BPV_T = MDUR_T \times 0.01\% \times MV_P$$
$$BPV_T = 4.59 \times 0.0001 \times €13,202,500$$
$$BPV_T = €6,059.95$$

Now, starting with a notional "cash" position ($BPV_P = 0$) provided by the reduction in equity exposure above, and noting that BPV_{CTD} = €91.26 and CF = 0.733194, the number of bond futures contracts is calculated as follows:

$$BPVHR = \left(\frac{€6,059.95 - €0.00}{€91.26}\right) \times 0.733194$$

$$BPVHR = 48.69$$

Because the BPVHR is positive, Uff should buy 49 bond futures contracts (after rounding).

21. Explain how to construct the swap that Tioga wants to use with regard to the swap:
    i. The swap tenor will be three years, consistent with the length of time for which Tioga expects interest rates to remain low.
    ii. Tioga will establish an interest rate swap in which Wyalusing will make payments based on a floating reference rate and will receive payments based on a fixed rate. The source of the reference rate and the value of the fixed rate will be set at the time of the swap's inception. The net effect for Wyalusing of the combination of making fixed payments on its coupon bond, receiving fixed payments on the swap, and making floating payments on the swap is to convert the fixed obligations of its bond coupon payments into floating-rate-based obligations. This scenario will allow Wyalusing to benefit if Tioga's expectation of low interest rates is realized.
    iii. The notional value of the swap should be set such that the fixed payments that Wyalusing receives will equal the fixed coupon payments that Wyalusing must make on its fixed-rate bond obligations.
    iv. Swap settlement dates should be set on the same days as the fixed-rate bond's coupon payment dates.
22. Describe how the swap will function, from the perspective of Wyalusing, in terms of the:
    i. At inception, Wyalusing will pay the notional principal of CAD and will receive an amount of USD according to the USD/CAD exchange rate, agreed to at inception.

ii. At each swap payment date, Wyalusing will receive interest in CAD and will pay interest in USD. Both payments are based on floating reference rates for their respective currencies. The CAD rate will also include a basis rate that is quoted separately. On each settlement date, Wyalusing will receive an amount of CAD based on the CAD floating rate minus the basis rate applied to the swap notional value, and it will pay an amount of USD based on the USD floating rate and the USD/CAD exchange rate that was set at inception.

iii. At maturity, Wyalusing will receive the notional principal of CAD and will pay an amount of USD according to the USD/CAD exchange rate that was set at inception, applied to the CAD notional principal. The cash flows at maturity are the inverses of the cash flows at inception.

23. The Lushland 100 Index futures contract value is calculated as the quoted futures price multiplied by the designated contract multiplier:

$$F = 1{,}247 \times LLD200$$
$$F = LLD249{,}400$$

The target beta is the index beta, which equals 1.00. The number of Lushland 100 Index futures contracts that the Sanctuary must buy to equitize its excess cash position is calculated as follows:

$$N_f = \left(\frac{\beta_T}{\beta_f}\right)\left(\frac{S}{F}\right)$$

$$N_f = \left(\frac{1}{1}\right)\left(\frac{LLD1{,}000{,}000}{LLD249{,}400}\right)$$

$$N_f = 4.01 \text{ (rounded to 4)}$$

Therefore, the CFO should buy four Lushland 100 Index futures contracts to equitize the excess cash position.

24. The Sanctuary's CFO can use currency futures contracts to lock in the current LLD/JPY exchange rate. The CFO can hedge the Sanctuary's exchange rate risk by selling JPY futures contracts with the closest expiry to the expected future JPY inflow. When the futures contracts expire, the Sanctuary will receive (pay) any depreciation (appreciation) in JPY relative to LLD (when compared with the original LLD/JPY futures contract price). The CFO can determine the number of contracts needed by dividing the property's sale price of JPY500,000,000 by the JPY futures contract value. Because the hedge ratio is assumed to equal 1, the changes in futures and spot prices will be equal during the life of the futures contract, and so the hedge will be fully effective.

CHAPTER 10

INTRODUCTION TO RISK MANAGEMENT

SOLUTIONS

1. B is correct. For individuals, risk management concerns maximizing utility while taking risk consistent with individual's level of risk tolerance.

2. A is correct. Many decision makers focus on return, which is not something that is easily controlled, as opposed to risk, or exposure to risk, which may actually be managed or controlled.

3. C is correct. Risks need to be defined and measured so as to be consistent with the organization's chosen level of risk tolerance and target for returns or other outcomes.

4. A is correct. Risk governance is the top-down process that defines risk tolerance and provides risk oversight and guidance to align risk with enterprise goals.

5. C is correct. While risk infrastructure, which a risk management framework must address, refers to the people and systems required to track risk exposures, there is no requirement to actually name the responsible individuals.

6. A is correct. In establishing a risk management system, determining risk tolerance must happen before specific risks can be accepted or reduced. Risk tolerance defines the appetite for risk. Risk budgeting determines how or where the risk is taken and quantifies the tolerable risk by specific metrics. Risk exposures can then be measured and compared against the acceptable risk.

7. C is correct. *Risk infrastructure* refers to the people and systems required to track risk exposures and perform most of the quantitative risk analysis to allow an assessment of the organization's risk profile. The risk management infrastructure identifies, measures, and monitors risk (among other things).

8. C is correct. Risk governance is not about specifying methods to mitigate risk at the business line level. Rather, it is about establishing an appropriate level of risk for the entire enterprise. Specifics of dealing with risk fall under risk management and the risk infrastructure framework.

9. A is correct. The risk management committee is a part of the risk governance structure at the operational level—as such, it does not approve the governing body's policies.

10. B is correct. When risk tolerance has been determined, the risk framework should be geared toward measuring, managing, and complying with the risk tolerance, or aligning risk exposure with risk tolerance. The risk tolerance decision begins by looking at what shortfalls within an organization would cause it to fail to achieve some critical goals and what are the organization's risk drivers.

11. C is correct. A company's ability to adapt quickly to adverse events may allow for a higher risk tolerance. There are other factors, such as beliefs of board members and a stable market environment, which may but should not affect risk tolerance.

12. A is correct. Risk budgeting does not include determining the target return. Risk budgeting quantifies and allocates the tolerable risk by specific metrics.

13. A is correct. The process of risk budgeting forces the firm to consider risk tradeoffs. As a result, the firm should choose to invest where the return per unit of risk is the highest.

14. A is correct. A financial risk originates from the financial markets. Credit risk is one of three financial risks identified in the reading: Credit risk is the chance of loss due to an outside party defaulting on an obligation. Solvency risk depends at least in part on factors internal to the organization, and operational risk is an *internal* risk arising from the people and processes within the organization.

15. B is correct. Liquidity risk is also called transaction cost risk. When the bid–ask spread widens, purchase and sale transactions become increasingly costly. The risk arises from the uncertainty of the spread.

16. C is correct. Settlement risk is related to default risk, but deals with the timing of payments rather than the risk of default.

17. A is correct. The VaR measure indicates the probability of a loss of at least a certain level in a time period.

18. C is correct. Risk acceptance is similar to self-insurance. An organization choosing to self-insure may set up a reserve fund to cover losses. Buying insurance is a form of risk transfer and using derivatives is a form of risk-shifting, not risk acceptance.

19. C is correct. Among the risk-modification methods of risk avoidance, risk acceptance, risk transfer, and risk shifting, none has a clear advantage. One must weigh benefits and costs in light of the firm's risk tolerance when choosing the method to use.

CHAPTER 11

MEASURING AND MANAGING MARKET RISK

SOLUTIONS

1. B is correct. Duration is a measure of interest rate risk. To reduce risk in anticipation of an increase in interest rates, Montes would seek to shorten the portfolio's duration. He is limited, however, in the amount he can shift from P_2 to P_1. Selling $15 million of P_2 reduces that portfolio to the lower end of the permitted 40% to 60% range. By reinvesting the proceeds at the shortest maturities allowed, Montes substantially reduces the portfolio duration.

2. B is correct. An index-tracking portfolio without options has a delta of 1. To achieve a delta of 0.9, the delta of the options position must be negative. Of the three choices, only short calls have a negative delta. Long call options have deltas ranging from 0 to 1. Short calls, therefore, have deltas ranging from 0 to −1. The short call position lowers the portfolio's overall delta as desired.

3. B is correct. VaR measures the frequency of losses of a given minimum magnitude. Here the VaR indicates that on 5% of trading days, the portfolio will experience a loss of at least $6.5 million. (Although C may appear to say the same thing as B, it actually implies that the portfolio will experience a loss on 95% of trading days.) The correct interpretation is that returns will be equal to or greater than −$6.5 million on 95% of trading days; those returns include gains as well as losses.

4. A is correct. The bank policy requires the addition of forward-looking risk assessments, and management is focused on tail risk. Conditional VaR measures tail risk, and stress tests and scenario analysis subject current portfolio holdings to historical or hypothetical stress events.

5. A is correct. VaR measures do *not* capture liquidity risk. "If some assets in a portfolio are relatively illiquid, VaR could be understated, even under normal market conditions. Additionally, liquidity squeezes are frequently associated with tail events and major market downturns, thereby exacerbating the risk."

6. C is correct. The Monte Carlo simulation method can accommodate virtually any distribution, an important factor given the increased frequency of large daily losses. This method can also more easily accommodate the large number of portfolio holdings. The Monte

Carlo method allows the user to develop her own forward-looking assumptions about the portfolio's risk and return characteristics, unlike the historical simulation method, which uses the current portfolio and re-prices it using the actual historical changes in the key factors experienced during the lookback period. Given the limited return history for infrastructure investments and Hamilton's expectations for higher-than-normal volatility, the historical simulation method would be a suboptimal choice.

7. C is correct. Conditional VaR is a measure of tail risk that provides an estimate of the average loss that would be incurred if the VaR cutoff is exceeded.

8. C is correct. A hypothetical scenario analysis allows the risk manager to estimate the likely effect of the scenario on a range of portfolio risk factors. A sovereign ratings downgrade would affect Hiram's India equity and corporate bond exposures as well as the government bond exposure. In addition, the assumptions used in constructing the scenario analysis can specifically address the effect of a need to sell large position sizes under decreased liquidity conditions resulting from a ratings downgrade. VaR alone does not accurately reflect the risk of large position sizes, which may be difficult to trade.

9. C is correct. A hypothetical scenario analysis allows Hamilton to estimate the direct effect of a ratings downgrade on the portfolio's government bond holdings and the resulting need to sell a number of the portfolio's holdings because they no longer meet the ratings guidelines. VaR alone does not accurately reflect the risk of large position sizes, which may be difficult to trade. The hypothetical scenario analysis will also highlight the effect of increased economic turmoil on all of the portfolio's exposures, not only the government bond exposures.

10. B is correct. The VaR is derived as follows:

$$\text{VaR} = \{[E(Rp) - 2.33\sigma_p](-1)\}(\text{Portfolio value}),$$

where

$$E(R_p) = \text{Annualized daily return} = (0.00026 \times 250) = 0.065$$

$$250 = \text{Number of trading days annually}$$

$$2.33 = \text{Number of standard deviations to attain 1\% VaR}$$

$$\sigma_p = \text{Annualized standard deviation} = (0.00501 \times \sqrt{250}) = 0.079215$$

$$\text{Portfolio value} = \text{CAD260,000,000}$$

$$\text{VaR} = -(0.065 - 0.184571) \times \text{CAD260,000,000}$$

$$= \text{CAD31,088,460}.$$

11. B is correct. Given the large fixed-income exposure in the LICIA portfolio, examining the portfolio duration more closely would be prudent. Duration is the primary sensitivity exposure measure for fixed-income investments.

12. B is correct. VaR is the minimum loss that would be expected a certain percentage of the time over a specified period of time given the assumed market conditions. A 5% VaR is often expressed as its complement—a 95% level of confidence. Therefore, the monthly VaR in Exhibit 5 indicates that $5.37 million is the minimum loss that would be expected to occur over one month 5% of the time. Alternatively, 95% of the time, a loss of more than $5.37 million would not be expected.

13. C is correct. Flusk experienced zero daily VaR breaches over the last year yet incurred a substantial loss. A limitation of VaR is its vulnerability to different volatility regimes. A portfolio might remain under its VaR limit every day but lose an amount approaching this limit each day. If market volatility during the last year is lower than in the lookback period, the portfolio could accumulate a substantial loss without technically breaching the VaR constraint.

    A is incorrect because VaR was calculated using historical simulation, so the distribution used was based on actual historical changes in the key risk factors experienced during the lookback period. Thus, the distribution is not characterized using estimates of the mean return, the standard deviation, or the correlations among the risk factors in the portfolio. In contrast, the parametric method of estimating VaR generally assumes that the distribution of returns for the risk factors is normal.

    B is incorrect because a specification with a higher confidence level will produce a higher VaR. If a 99% confidence interval was used to calculate historical VaR, the VaR would be larger (larger expected minimum loss). During the last year, none of Flusk's losses were substantial enough to breach the 5% VaR number (95% confidence interval); therefore, if McKee used a 1% VaR (99% confidence interval), the number of VaR breaches would not change.

14. B is correct. In order to simulate the impact of the latest financial crisis on the current bond portfolio holdings, McKee's valuation model for bonds should use the historical yields of bonds with similar maturity. Historical yields drive the pricing of bonds more than the price history or the current duration. Historical prices for the fixed-income positions currently held in the portfolio may not exist, and even when historical prices do exist, they may not be relevant to the current characteristics (e.g., maturity) of the instrument. Even if the same bonds existed at the time of the latest financial crisis, their durations would change because of the passage of time.

    A is incorrect because using a bond's past price history would mischaracterize the risk of the current portfolio holdings. For this reason, the historical yields are more important in explaining the risks. Historical prices for the fixed-income positions currently held in the portfolio may not exist, and even when historical prices do exist, they may not be relevant to the current characteristics (e.g., maturity) of the instrument.

    C is incorrect because historical bond durations would not capture the current characteristics of the bonds in the portfolio. Duration is a sensitivity measure and is the weighted-average time to maturity of a bond. Even if the same bonds existed at the time of the latest financial crisis, their remaining time to maturity and durations would change because of the passage of time.

15. C is correct. Ming suggested in Analysis 1 to use a historical scenario that measures the hypothetical portfolio return that would result from a repeat of a particular period of financial market history. Historical scenarios are complementary to VaR but are not going to happen in exactly the same way again, and they require additional measures to overcome the shortcomings of the VaR.

16. B is correct. Analysis 2 describes surplus at risk. Surplus at risk is an application of VaR; it estimates how much the assets might underperform the liabilities with a given confidence level, usually over a year.

17. B is correct. Incremental VaR measures the change in a portfolio's VaR as a result of adding or removing a position from the portfolio or if a position size is changed relative to the remaining positions.

18. B is correct. McKee suggests running a stress test using a historical scenario specific to emerging markets that includes an extreme change in credit spreads. Stress tests, which apply extreme negative stress to a particular portfolio exposure, are closely related to scenario risk measures. A scenario risk measure estimates the portfolio return that would result from a hypothetical change in markets (hypothetical scenario) or a repeat of a historical event (historical scenario). When the historical simulation fully revalues securities under rate and price changes that occurred during the scenario period, the results should be highly accurate.

   A is incorrect because marginal VaR measures the change in portfolio VaR given a very small change in a portfolio position (e.g., change in VaR for a $1 or 1% change in the position). Therefore, marginal VaR would not allow McKee to estimate how much the value of the option-embedded bonds would change under an extreme change in credit spreads.

   C is incorrect because sensitivity risk measures use sensitivity exposure measures, such as first-order (delta, duration) and second-order (gamma, convexity) sensitivity, to assess the change in the value of a financial instrument. Although gamma and convexity can be used with delta and duration to estimate the impact of extreme market movements, they are not suited for scenario analysis related to option-embedded bonds.

19. A is correct. VaR has emerged as one of the most popular risk measures because global banking regulators require or encourage the use of it. VaR is also frequently found in annual reports of financial firms and can be used for comparisons.

20. A is correct. VaR is an estimate of the loss that is expected to be exceeded with a given level of probability over a specified time period. The parametric method typically assumes that the return distributions for the risk factors in the portfolio are normal. It then uses the expected return and standard deviation of return for each risk factor and correlations to estimate VaR.

21. B is correct. Value at risk is the minimum loss that would be expected a certain percentage of the time over a certain period of time. Statement 2 implies that there is a 5% chance the portfolio will fall in value by $90,000 (= $6,000,000 × 1.5%) or more in a single day. If VaR is measured on a daily basis and a typical month has 20–22 business days, then 5% of the days equates to about 1 day per month or once in 20 trading days.

22. A is correct. Statement 2 indicates that the Equity Opportunities Fund reported a daily VaR value. One of the limitations of VaR is that it focuses so heavily on left-tail events (the losses) that right-tail events (potential gains) are often ignored.

   B is incorrect because VaR is viewed as forward looking in that it uses the current portfolio holdings and measures its potential loss. The Sharpe ratio represents a backward-looking, return-based measure and is used to assess the skill of the manager.

   C is incorrect because VaR does not provide an accurate risk estimate in either trending or volatile regimes. A portfolio might remain under its VaR limit every day but lose an amount approaching this limit each day. Under such circumstances, the portfolio could accumulate substantial losses without technically breaching the VaR constraint. Also, during periods of low volatility, VaR will appear quite low, underestimating the losses that could occur when the environment returns to a normal level of volatility.

23. C is correct. Measuring VaR at a 5% threshold produces an estimated value at risk of 2.69%.

   From Exhibit 6, the expected annual portfolio return is 14.1% and the standard deviation is 26.3%. Annual values need to be adjusted to get their daily counterparts.

Assuming 250 trading days in a year, the expected annual return is adjusted by dividing by 250 and the standard deviation is adjusted by dividing by the square root of 250.

Thus, the daily expected return is $0.141/250 = 0.000564$, and volatility is $0.263/\sqrt{250} = 0.016634$.

5% daily VaR = $E(R_p) - 1.65\sigma_p = 0.000564 - 1.65(0.016634) = -0.026882$. The portfolio is expected to experience a potential minimum loss in percentage terms of 2.69% on 5% of trading days.

24. C is correct. The change in value of a bond is inversely related to a change in yield. Given a bond priced at B with duration D and yield change of Δy, the rate of return or percentage price change for the bond is approximately given as follows: $\Delta B/B \approx -D\Delta y/(1 + y)$. Under Scenario 3, interest rates decrease by 20 bps. In an environment of decreasing interest rates, the bond with the highest duration will have the greatest positive return. Bond 3 has a duration of 10.2, which is greater than that of both Bond 1 (duration = 1.3) and Bond 2 (duration = 3.7).

25. C is correct. A traditional asset manager uses *ex post* tracking error when analyzing backward-looking returns. The Diversified Fixed-Income Fund prospectus stipulates a target benchmark deviation of no more than 5 bps. Tracking error is a measure of the degree to which the performance of a given investment deviates from its benchmark.

26. B is correct. Position limits are limits on the market value of any given investment; they are excellent controls on overconcentration. Position limits can be expressed in currency units or as a percentage of net assets. The Alpha Core Equity Fund restricts the exposure of individual securities to 1.75% of the total portfolio.

CHAPTER 12

RISK MANAGEMENT FOR INDIVIDUALS

SOLUTIONS

1. C is correct. Gregory is in the early career stage of life, and human capital represents a large proportion of his total wealth. Gregory is relatively young; therefore, the present value of his expected earnings implies positive human capital. Furthermore, Gregory's savings are rather low, so his financial capital is small. Consequently, his human capital is greater than his financial capital.

2. A is correct. The present value of expected future earnings is reflected on an economic balance sheet but not on a traditional balance sheet.

3. C is correct. A health maintenance organization plan is a type of medical insurance that allows office visits at no, or very little, cost. Gregory would like to avoid paying for office visits related to minor medical problems; hence this alternative is the most appropriate.

4. A is correct. The income volatility adjustment reflects the fact that income from different professions can vary significantly. Molly works in an industry that has low correlation with the capital markets; she also earns income from an additional source. Kirk works in an industry that has high correlation with capital markets, and so he might experience higher income variability than Molly. Consequently, in estimating Molly's human capital, the income volatility adjustment for Molly should be lower than Kirk's.

5. B is correct. The policy would be on Kirk's life; his death would trigger the insurance payment. Therefore, Kirk would be the insured.

6. A is correct. The whole life insurance policy feature described is a non-forfeiture clause, whereby there is the option to receive some portion of the benefits if premium payments are missed (i.e., before the policy lapses).

7. B is correct. Statement 2 is correct because, all else equal, the income yield is higher when expected longevity is shorter; therefore, the income yield will be higher for an older person.

8. C is correct. Molly is concerned about a potential late-life medical condition that may require extended home care for Gabriel. Long-term care insurance is designed to cover a portion of the cost of home care, assisted living facilities, and/or nursing home expense. Gabriel has enough resources to cover her living expenditures, but her medical insurance might be insufficient to cover the costs of extended home care, medicine, or hospital stays. Consequently, long-term care insurance is the most appropriate insurance choice given Gabriel's situation.

9. A is correct. Unvested pension benefits are typically contingent on future work and are thus considered to be part of human capital. Statement #2 is incorrect: vested pension benefits can be considered components of financial capital.

10. A is correct. Economic net worth is calculated as follows:

    Economic net worth = Net worth from the traditional balance sheet +
    (Present value of future earnings + Present value of unvested pension benefits) −
    (Present value of consumption goals + Present value of bequests)

    Perrin's economic net worth is less than his net worth because the sum of the present values of consumption and bequests is greater than the sum of the present values of future earnings and unvested pensions.

11. C is correct. Human capital, HC_0, is calculated as follows:

$$HC_0 = \sum_{t=1}^{N} \frac{p(s_t)\, w_{t-1}(1 + g_t)}{(1 + r_f + y)^t}$$

    Holding all else equal as Perrin directs, a reduction in the nominal risk-free rate, r_f, would decrease the total discount rate, thus increasing the present value of human capital.

12. C is correct. The projected slowdown in his employer's sales growth may result in Perrin's unemployment, indicating that he may be subject to earnings risk. Human capital would be reduced by the loss of future earnings and halt accrual of pension benefits at Perrin's present employer. Financial capital could also be affected because assets may need to be sold to make up for any loss of income.

13. A is correct. Life insurance best meets Perrin's immediate need for estate liquidity. A life insurance policy can provide liquidity without the delay involved in the legal process of settling the estate. This liquidity can be particularly valuable if the estate contains illiquid assets or assets that are difficult to separate and distribute equitably among heirs. Currently, it would be difficult to separate and equitably distribute Perrin's financial assets to his three children such that the oldest son inherits the vineyard and winery while keeping the other two children uninvolved because the business is worth more than one-third of Perrin's investment assets. The problem of separating and equitably distributing the estate exists presently regardless of the value of Perrin's personal property.

14. B is correct. Perrin's estate distribution plan indicates a need for estate liquidity funded by permanent insurance that can remain in force until his death. Perrin prefers a policy that offers a range of investment options. Universal life is thus most appropriate because it is a form of permanent insurance that can remain in force until Perrin's death and typically has more options for investing the cash value than do whole life policies.

15. C is correct. The net payment cost index assumes that the insured will die at the end of a specified period—in this case, the given life expectancy of 20 years. Calculating the net payment cost index includes the following steps.

Future value of premiums (annuity due, 5%, 20 years)	$416,631.02

Financial calculator operations:

N = 20, I = 5, PV = 0, PMT = –12,000, mode = begin: FV →
416,631.02

Future value of dividends (ordinary annuity, 5%, 20 years)	($66,131.91)

N = 20, I = 5, PV = 0, PMT = 2,000, mode = end: FV → –66,131.91

20-year insurance cost	$350,499.11

Annual payments for insurance cost (annuity due, 5%, 20 years)	($10,095.24)

N = 20, I = 5, PV = 0, FV = 350,499.11, mode = begin: PMT →
–10,095.24

Net payment cost index ($10,095.24/500)	($20.19)

16. B is correct. The most comprehensive policy would define disability as the inability to perform Adrian's regular occupation. For professionals with specialized skills, policies that use regular occupation are generally preferred even though they are more expensive. Mr. Barksdale works in a specialized, high-paying occupation, and the family depends on his income.

17. B is correct. The additional amount of life insurance coverage needed is calculated as the difference between the family's total financial needs and total capital available.

Total financial needs are calculated as follows.

Cash Needs	AUD (A$)
Final expenses and taxes	20,000
Mortgage retirement	400,000
Education fund	300,000
Emergency fund	30,000
Total cash needs	750,000
Capital Needs	Present Value
Olivia's living expenses, 44 years	1,377,175
Children's living expenses, 6 years	84,848
(Olivia's income, 18 years)	–880,756
Total capital needs	581,267
Total financial needs	1,331,267

Capital needs are determined as the present value of an annuity due: growth rate = 3.5%, discount rate = 6.0%. Growth of payments is incorporated by adjusting the discount rate to account for the growth rate of earnings. As long as the discount rate is larger than the growth rate, the adjusted rate i can be calculated as follows: [(1 + Discount rate)/(1 + Growth rate)] – 1, or $i = (1.06/1.035) - 1 = 2.42\%$.

The present value of Olivia's living expenses is calculated as follows:

PMT = –$50,000; i = 2.42%, n = 44. Set for payments at beginning of year.
PV = $1,377,175.

The present value of the children's living expenses is calculated as follows:

PMT = –15,000; i = 2.42%, n = 6. Set for payments at beginning of
year. PV = $84,848.

The present value of Olivia's income is calculated as follows:

PMT = –$85,000 × (1 – Tax rate); PMT = $85,000 × 0.70 = 59,500; i = 2.42%,
n = 18. Set for payments at beginning of year. PV = –$880,756.

Total capital needs are calculated as follows:

$1,377,175 + $84,848 – $880,756 = $581,267. Adding this amount to total
cash needs of $750,000 results in total financial needs of $1,331,267.

The total capital available is calculated as follows.

Capital Available	AUD (A$)
Cash and investments	900,000
Current life insurance	100,000
Total capital available	1,000,000

The additional life insurance need is calculated as follows.

Total financial needs	1,331,267
Total capital available	1,000,000
Life insurance shortfall (excess)	331,267

18. B is correct. The Barksdales want an annuity with a deferred payout (beginning at retirement) and an ability to invest in a diversified mix of securities. Most deferred variable annuities offer a diversified menu of potential investment options, whereas a fixed annuity locks the annuitant into a portfolio of bond-like assets at whatever rate of return exists at the time of purchase.

19. A is correct. A joint life annuity best addresses the Barksdales' goal of receiving a payout as long as either of them is alive. Under a joint life annuity, two or more individuals, such as a husband and a wife, receive payments until all beneficiaries die.

20. B is correct. With immediate fixed annuities, Brown will trade a sum of money today for a promised income benefit for as long as she is alive. Brown is already age 75 and is concerned about longevity risk; she wants a known income stream currently and in the future. Therefore, an immediate fixed annuity is the most appropriate choice.

21. C is correct. In contrast to an immediate payout annuity, an advanced life deferred annuity's (ALDA's) payments begin later in life—for example, when the individual turns 80 or 85. An ALDA would provide the greatest supplemental level income relative to the

cost because the payments are made far in the future, life expectancy is shorter when the payments begin, and some policyholders will die without receiving payments.

22. C is correct. The equity allocation of the Barksdale's financial capital is calculated as follows:

Total economic wealth = Human capital + Financial capital = $2,900,000 + $900,000 = $3,800,000.

Target equity allocation of total economic wealth = $3,800,000 × 40% = $1,520,000

Human capital equity allocation = $2,900,000 × 35% = $1,015,000

Financial capital equity allocation = $1,520,000 – $1,015,000 = $505,000

% Financial capital equity allocation = Financial equity allocation/Total financial capital

= $505,000/$900,000

= 0.5611, or 56.1%

23. C is correct. People with higher risk and potential volatility in income (human capital) should take on lower risk in their investment portfolios. Adrian's income is more than two-thirds of the household total and is somewhat volatile because of cyclical demand for his employer's product. Additionally, because income is tied to a particular industry or sector, the Barksdales should underweight securities having a high correlation with bauxite demand.

CHAPTER 13

CASE STUDY IN RISK MANAGEMENT: PRIVATE WEALTH

SOLUTIONS

1. Human capital, which is the present value of the expected stream of income from employment using a wage-risk adjusted discount rate, is an important and large component of the Josephs' total wealth given that they have combined savings of only $50,000 with no other financial assets.

   The Josephs are richly endowed in human capital because they are both highly educated, trained in a high-demand field of computer science, and are in their career development stage. Further, both have been employed for a few years, accruing valuable working experience.

   The value of human capital is a function of several factors:

   - survival probabilities (usually proxied by mortality tables)
   - current employment income
   - expected annual wage growth
   - the risk-free rate
   - a risk adjustment based on occupational income volatility
   - the expected number of working years

   Both Ron and Jennifer are young and in good health, so their survival probabilities are likely to be in line with mortality tables. Their young age also suggests that the expected number of working years for both Ron and Jennifer is probably in the range of 35–40 years. From a financial point of view, the Josephs' marriage results in human capital diversification. As a civil servant, Jennifer's salary income can be described as being bond-like (excellent job security, modest salary increases, limited earnings risk), whereas Ron's salary income can be best described as being equity-like (significant uncertainties in future employment income with significant potential upside). Therefore, the risk adjustment based on occupational income volatility is likely to be low for Jennifer and high for Ron.

2. The needs analysis method determines the amount of life insurance required by estimating the amount needed to cover the surviving spouse's annual living expenses. It is calculated as the difference between the family's total financial needs (total cash needs plus total capital needs) and total capital available.

The amount of life insurance coverage that the Josephs require is calculated as follows:

Cash needs	Ron	Jennifer
Funeral and burial costs plus taxes	$20,000	$20,000
Emergency fund	$15,000	$15,000
Debts to be repaid	$0	$0
Total cash needs	**$35,000**	**$35,000**
Capital needs		
PV of surviving spouse's $35,000 annual living expenses until death at age 85	$1,798,197	$1,745,354
Less PV of surviving spouse's income until retirement at age 65	$748,837	$1,304,662
Total capital needs	**$1,049,360**	**$440,692**
Total financial needs	**$1,084,360**	**$475,692**
Capital available:		
Cash and investments	$50,000	$50,000
Total capital available	**$50,000**	**$50,000**
Life insurance needs	**$1,034,360**	**$425,692**

The present value of the surviving spouse's annual living expenses of $35,000 until death at age 85 is determined as the present value of an annuity due. Growth in expenses is incorporated into the calculations by adjusting the discount rate to account for the growth in expenses. The adjusted discount rate is calculated as $[(1 + \text{Discount Rate})/(1 + \text{Growth Rate in Expenses})] - 1$.

The present value of the surviving spouse's annual living expenses of $35,000 until death at age 85 for Jennifer ($n = 59$) in the case of Ron's death is calculated as follows:

First, adjust the discount rate to account for the growth rate:

Adjusted Discount Rate $= (1.025/1.02) - 1 = 0.4902\%$ (rounded up)

Now, setting the calculator for beginning-of-period payments, compute the PV:

$n = 59$
$I/Y = 0.4902$
$PMT = \$35,000$
$CPT\ PV = \$1,798,197$

Similarly, the present value of the surviving spouse's annual living expenses of $35,000 until death at age 85 for Ron ($n = 57$) in the case of Jennifer's death is calculated as follows:

Again, setting the calculator for beginning-of-period payments, compute the PV:

$n = 57$
$I/Y = 0.4902$
$PMT = \$35,000$
$CPT\ PV = \$1,745,354$

The Josephs' additional life insurance needs are summarized in the following table:

	Ron	Jennifer
Total financial needs	$1,084,360	$475,692
Less: total capital available	$50,000	$50,000
Additional life insurance needs	**$1,034,360**	**$425,692**

Based on the needs analysis method, the Josephs should purchase life insurance policies in the amounts of $1,034,360 and $425,692 on Ron and Jennifer, respectively.

3. **Part i:** Premature death risk is high because the Hunters have two young children, ages 10 and 12, who need to be cared for. The death of a parent would mean that the family's household living expenses, now covered jointly, would fall solely to the surviving spouse. The surviving spouse would potentially suffer a reduction in income because all of the family responsibilities would fall to this individual. Alternatively, the surviving spouse could hire outside help, at a cost. Life insurance would provide support for the children and enable the surviving spouse to better cope with unexpected events.

   Part ii: Risk in the retirement portfolio is high. Hunter's investment portfolio lacks diversification because it is concentrated in the energy industry and is represented by small, microcap stocks. Further, the investment in the energy stocks is correlated with Susan's human capital. If prospects in the energy industry deteriorate, both Susan's human capital and the stock portfolio value would likely decline at the same time. Finally, their investment portfolio is also rather modest compared with their spending and income.

   Part iii: The key risk here is that the Hunters' retirement income is insufficient to meet the standard of living they desire. This risk arises for two reasons. First, the couple's annual contribution to their pension or private saving plans may be insufficient to generate the required fund balance at retirement. Second, the pension plans might perform poorly, generating returns below those expected. This risk can be somewhat offset by the government Social Security benefits the Hunters can elect to receive when they retire at age 67.

   Part iv: Earnings risk resulting from potential loss of employment is significant for the Hunters and particularly relevant for Susan given the nature of his employer's business. Susan has a relatively high salary and works for a small oil company in a highly cyclical and risky industry.

   Robert's earnings risk is relatively low, because his salary is lower than Susan's. In addition, he works in a highly stable occupation and would lose employment only under extreme circumstances. A job loss for Robert would be less significant for the family because Susan's annual after-tax income of $90,000 would cover all of the family's yearly expenditures of $90,000.

4. The human life value method is based on the value of human capital and estimates the amount of future earnings that must be replaced. The calculations involve adjusting

after-tax income for the amount of annual expenses and value of the person's employee benefits. The amount of pretax income needed to replace the lost income is then estimated and assumed to grow until retirement, reflecting career advancement. For both Susan and Robert, the amount of life insurance required is the PV of an annuity due of their respective future pretax incomes, less any existing life insurance policy amounts. The amount of life insurance coverage required by the Hunters is calculated as follows:

	Susan	Robert
Present value of annuity due of pretax income	$1,700,000	$394,000
Less existing life insurance	$200,000	$300,000
Less existing life insurance at Susan's employer (calculated as $135,000 × 2)	$270,000	
Recommended additional life insurance	$1,230,000	$94,000

In conclusion, the Hunters should increase their life insurance coverage by $1,230,000 for Susan and $94,000 for Robert.

5. Chapman suggests that the Hunters increase their contributions to their DC pension plans. The Hunters are able to do so because they have considerable savings with their combined annual after-tax income of $126,000 being well above their current annual household living expenses of $90,000. The additional contributions total only $9,500 (5% of their combined pretax salaries of $190,000), and the after-tax effect would be only $6,650 (70% of $9,500). Even after increasing their DC contributions, the Hunters would still be able to save about $30,000 each year.

By increasing the contribution to the DC plans, the Hunters would gain the tax advantage of the DC plans because income and capital gain distributions within the plan are tax free. In addition, Susan Hunter could take advantage of the additional 5% contribution match offered as a benefit by her employer. The expected return on the DC plans would likely be significantly higher than in the highly liquid and low-interest bank account preferred by the Hunters. The increased contribution would build up their investment portfolio and boost retirement savings. Thus, the tax and return advantages of making additional contributions to the DC plans reduces the risk of a shortfall in projected retirement income while also leaving a significant amount of current income available for savings.

6. **Part i:** The Changs are in a good position to maintain their current lifestyle in retirement. Their total annual pretax retirement income of $194,500 will leave them with after-tax income of about $145,875 (given the assumption of a 25% tax rate). This expected after-tax income exceeds the expected nominal level of spending in their retirement year of $130,477 (given the assumption of a 3% inflation rate and nine years until retirement). One particular risk that could affect the Changs' projected retirement income, however, is that inflation may reduce the purchasing power of their after-tax income over time. This risk is of particular concern given the expectation that the retirement plan balances are expected to be used to purchase an annuity with no inflation adjustment. Thus, purchasing the fixed annuity with no inflation adjustment should be reconsidered.

Part ii: Another risk factor that could adversely affect the Changs' projected retirement income is the potential loss of employment. If James were to lose his job or Wendy's freelance work were to decrease unexpectedly, and they were unable to obtain comparable levels of compensation, their projected retirement income would likely be lower.

Part iii: A third risk factor that could affect the Changs' projected retirement income is poor investment returns. Lower returns resulting from poor market conditions in the equity and bond markets would adversely impact the Changs' pension fund balances at retirement and likely result in lower retirement income.